SUCCESSFUL GARDENING

A-Z of
HOUSE PLANTS

Published by The Reader's Digest Association Limited.

First Edition Copyright © 1995
The Reader's Digest Association Limited,
Berkeley Square House, Berkeley Square, London W1X 6AB

Copyright © 1995
The Reader's Digest Association Far East Limited
Philippines Copyright 1995
The Reader's Digest Association Far East Limited

Originally published as a partwork.
Successful Gardening
Copyright © 1990
Eaglemoss Publications Ltd.

Consultant editor: Lizzie Boyd

Typeset in Century Schoolbook

PRINTED IN SPAIN

ISBN 0 276 42099 3

Opposite: Foliage plants range in size from the diminutive, tiny-leaved
mind-your-own-business (*Soleirolia*) to impressively tall shrubs such as
glossy-leaved radermachera. Young bamboos thrive in cool rooms and
can be moved into the garden when they outgrow their space.

Overleaf: Crab and Christmas cacti (*Schlumbergera*) flower from an early age,
brightening year after year the dark days of winter with a myriad of
pink, purple or rose-coloured blooms.

Pages 6-7: Highly coloured foliage is found especially among *Codiaeum* and
Coleus species. They require higher light levels than all-green house plants.

Reader's
Digest

PUBLISHED BY THE READER'S DIGEST ASSOCIATION LIMITED
LONDON NEW YORK MONTREAL SYDNEY CAPE TOWN

Originally published in partwork form
by Eaglemoss Publications Limited

SUCCESSFUL GARDENING

A-Z of
HOUSE PLANTS

CONTENTS

SPECIAL FEATURES

A-Z OF HOUSE PLANTS

House plants

Pot plants for the home, conservatory or greenhouse embrace a multitude of different types, ranging from desert cacti to jungle orchids, from delicate ferns to large-leaved shrubs and from those which boast colourful foliage to exotic flowering plants. The one factor common to them all is their need for the kind of sheltered growing conditions that, in temperate climates, can only be provided indoors.

Some house plants, notably those from tropical rainforests, demand a high degree of warmth, air moisture and filtered light. Others, such as desert cacti, revel in bright sun and dry air and put up with near freezing temperatures. Between these extremes are plenty of easy-to-grow plants to fill the home with year-round greenery and brilliant flowers.

CONSERVATORY GARDENING

**A conservatory can combine the best of two
worlds – the beauty of a garden filled with exotic plants
and flowers, and the comforts of the home.**

Conservatories are the most popular form of house extension today. They are an economical way to increase living space, and provide both a bright multi-purpose room and an ideal environment in which to grow plants.

A conservatory visually and physically links house and garden and has the potential for indoor gardening all year round whatever the weather. The range of plants that can be grown extends from temperate-climate types to semi-tropical jungle exotics, such as orchids, clivias, Chilean bellflowers, tender jasmines, hoyas and lantanas. And because temperature, humidity, feeding, watering and growing compost can be controlled, success is almost assured.

Choosing and siting

Conservatories come in a wide range of sizes, shapes and styles. Choice depends largely on the size and layout of garden and house, and on costs – not only the structure and its foundation, but also on-going heating and maintenance costs. Least expensive are kit form DIY conservatories; those fitted by specialists are more expensive, and purpose-built extensions are the most costly.

Aspect affects when and how much light and solar heat will reach a conservatory. A south- or southwest-facing site is pleasant from autumn until spring, but is often too hot in summer, for people and plants.

A west-facing conservatory gets afternoon sun and summer evening light, and is less fiercely hot at mid-day. In an east-facing site, the light has gone by afternoon. And unless a north-facing conservatory extends some way out from the house wall, it is unlikely to suit plants or people.

Roofing and glazing

The roof of a conservatory may be flat, lean-to, ridged, hipped or

▼ **Conservatory shading** In the summer, a conservatory, especially one which faces south, is likely to become too hot for comfort. Shades or blinds are essential to prevent scorching of plant foliage. Fabric roller blinds look attractive, and double as heat insulators at night, but they are less satisfactory than reeded or slatted types that can be adjusted as the need dictates.

vaulted. It can be constructed from glass, rigid plastic or tiles. Glass is long-lasting, allows excellent light penetration and does not discolour; toughened roof glass is available, flat or in curved sections. Opaque roofing tiles cut down on solar gain in summer, and also considerably reduce the amount of light let through. Rigid plastic retains less heat than glass and tends to become brittle and discoloured with age.

Some conservatories are fitted with thin, single-glazed horticultural glass – this is cheap, but provides poor insulation and is also subject to condensation. Double glazing, though expensive, is vital if the conservatory is to be

▶ **Cool conservatories** A grape vine trained up the wall and under the roof of an unheated conservatory provides natural shade in summer for foliage plants at floor level. In winter, the leafless branches let in maximum light through the glass roof.

▼ **Summer colour** The annual half-hardy butterfly flower (*Schizanthus pinnatus*) flourishes in an enclosed sun-room. Other flowering pot plants for cool conservatories include begonias, Cape primroses (*Streptocarpus*), calceolarias, Italian bellflower and flowering Katy (*Kalanchoë blossfeldiana*).

heated. As well as conserving heat, double glazing helps to reduce condensation and also keeps out external noise.

Heating and lighting

Where a conservatory is built against a house wall, it will retain some heat from the sun, and mild spells in spring and autumn can often be spent comfortably in an unheated conservatory. Plants, however, will be limited to forced bulbs and hardy species grown out of season.

A cool conservatory kept at 5°C (41°F) is fine for many popular hardy and half-hardy garden plants. Hyacinths and narcissi, fuchsias and hydrangeas, pelargoniums and chrysanthemums

▶ **Conservatory furniture** Ideally choose furnishings to reflect the character of a conservatory. Here, wicker furniture, with green and floral cushions, perfectly complements the jungle-like effect of lush foliage and exotic lilies.

will start to flower earlier and finish later than in the open garden.

Semi-tropical plants, such as plumbagos, cymbidiums and many bromeliads, will thrive in a steady temperature of 10°C (50°F); normal living room temperatures (15-21°C/59-70°F) suit tropical plants such as crotons, anthuriums and African violets.

By installing extra radiators from the domestic central-heating system, or some other form of

independent heating, the choice of plants is much larger, and the conservatory can become an all-year live-in extension of the home. Seek expert advice before spurring off central-heating pipes which should have a separate thermostatic control unit for the conservatory.

If the conservatory is used chiefly as a living-room extension, plan areas of strong light for reading and dining, with softer background illumination. Specimen plants, group arrangements and other decorative features can be spotlit. Ordinary tungsten light bulbs are suitable, but they give off strong heat which can scorch nearby foliage. Fluorescent tubes and bulbs give off little heat

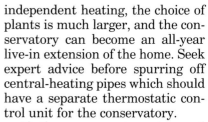

◀ **Bistro setting** A couple of white marble-topped washstands make an unusual dining table surrounded by cool greenery. White-painted wicker armchairs in the far corner are tailor-made for a post-prandial slumber.

▲ **Victorian conservatory** Less ornate than the traditional Victorian conservatory with its cast-iron furniture and potted palms and ferns, this modern structure is nevertheless reminiscent of the era. An ornamental bird cage, suspended from the ceiling, and old-fashioned wicker furniture blend well with the modern design.

and are more economical to run. They come in warm and cool whites; warm whites are better for plants.

Special growth-promoting plant lamps, which mimic natural daylight, are available, but they are expensive.

Ventilation and humidity

Most conservatories tend to get too hot in summer and too cold in winter. These factors also influence the amount of moisture held in the air – the humidity level and the condensation rate. Ensure that the conservatory has adequate opening windows or ventilators, ideally automatically operated, so that excessively hot air can be continually replaced by cooler outside air in summer.

In winter, ventilation is just as important, as a means of eliminating stagnant, humid air – a common cause of fungal rot disease, and excessive condensation.

The level of humidity required in a conservatory depends on the type of plants being grown. In general, high humidity is beneficial when the air temperature is high – hot, dry air is invariably fatal and encourages serious pests such as red spider mites. Tropical plants like the highest humidity, while plants from arid regions prefer drier air.

The frequency and quantity of watering is one of the main regulators of humidity. You can also provide localized humidity by standing each plant pot in a saucer or tray filled with clay pebbles or gravel kept permanently moist without waterlogging the roots. Groups of plants which demand higher humidity than is desirable for the rest of the conservatory can be catered for by installing a mist-irrigation system, perhaps with automatic regulation.

Conservatory plants

Permanent plant residents should be attractive throughout the year and include mainly evergreen types. Tall-growing shrubs, such as several *Ficus* and *Philodendron*

species, *Fatsia japonica* and palms make perfect specimen plants. Climbers are almost obligatory, and such rapid growers as *Hoya carnosa*, variegated ivies, scented jasmines, *Stephanotis floribunda* and bougainvillea will quickly romp upwards and along the roof.

Grow shrubs and climbers in large tubs or containers on the floor; they can be underplanted with smaller foliage or temporary flowering plants. Alternatively, display these on fixed shelving or tiered plant stands. Hanging baskets suspended from the roof or the walls can hold trailing plants, such as ferns, fuchsias, spider plants, Christmas cacti and orchids. Small-growing bromeliads, notably tillandsias and earth stars (*Cryptanthus*), can be wired on to bark slabs or tree branches.

Plant window Hibiscus, Christmas cactus and cyclamens, along with red-berried winter cheer, add colour to chilly winter days.

A-Z of house plants

The home and the conservatory provide an environment in which plants from all over the world can flourish. As pot plants they never assume the proportions they reach in the wild, but part of their charm lies in the mini-jungle or desert effect they can create in an ordinary living room.

The choice of plants is as wide as for outdoor gardening and ranges from short-term annuals to long-lived evergreen shrubs and succulents. Most homes are centrally heated, and near-constant temperatures have allowed the introduction of many exotic foliage and flowering plants previously restricted to hot houses in botanical gardens. Tropical climbers, epiphytic orchids and bromeliads adapt well to indoor conditions provided there is a tolerable level of air moisture. The air in most centrally-heated homes is excessively dry, and it is sensible to install humidifiers, for the health of humans and plants. Small humid micro-climates can be created by arranging plants in groups and by spraying them with a fine mist of tepid water – avoid spraying buds and opening flowers.

Light – or lack of it – is probably the most critical factor for healthy growth. Many house plants need as bright light as possible, but few, with the exception of desert cacti, can tolerate mid-day sun reflected through glass; they should be shielded by net curtains or blinds to avoid scorching. In general, flowering house plants and those with variegated and colourful foliage need brighter light than green types.

All house plants should be grown in sterilized potting compost rather than garden soil. Proprietary potting composts, soil- or peat-based, are suitable for most pot plants. There are also specially formulated composts for particular plant groups, such as ericaceous (lime-hating) plants, cacti, orchids, bromeliads and even African violets. It is a fallacy that all house plants should be potted on every spring into fresh compost and a larger pot size; most house plants perform and flower better when slightly pot-bound. Repot when roots fill the pot, when water drains through immediately or when leaf tips turn brown and shrivel.

Abutilon

abutilon, flowering or parlour maple

Abutilon striatum 'Thompsonii'

Abutilon megapotamicum 'Variegatum'

□ Height 60cm-1.2m (2-4ft)
□ Temperature minimum 10°C (50°F)
□ Bright light
□ Soil-based compost
□ Flowering and foliage shrub

Abutilons, grown for their drooping bell-shaped flowers and attractive foliage, originate from South America though most of the popular types are of hybrid origin.

The flowers are in shades of red, yellow and orange and often have ornamental calyces in a contrasting colour. The evergreen leaves are lobed like maple foliage or heart-shaped, and usually mottled or variegated.

Popular species and varieties

Abutilon x *hybridum*, 60cm-1.2m (2-4ft) high and as much across, has mid green leaves with three to five lobes, and orange and red flowers from late summer to autumn. Varieties include 'Ashford Red' (salmon-red); 'Boule de Neige' (white); 'Canary Bird' (yellow); and 'Golden Fleece' (rich yellow).

Abutilon megapotamicum, 90cm-1.2m (3-4ft) high, is a slender-stemmed species suitable for trailing in hanging baskets or training up canes. The toothed, heart-shaped leaves are bright green, and the flowers, which appear from late spring to mid autumn, are yellow with red calyces. 'Variegatum' has yellow mottled leaves. *Abutilon striatum* 'Thompsonii',

syn. *A. thompsonii*, up to 60cm-1.2m (2-4ft) high, has three to five lobed leaves heavily mottled with yellow. The flowers are salmon-orange with red veins.

Cultivation

Abutilons thrive in the house or conservatory at normal room temperatures. Bright light is best. Water moderately and feed fortnightly during the growing season. During the rest period, when the temperature should not fall below 10°C (50°F), water just enough to keep the plants from drying out.

Discard plants when they grow leggy, or pot on every two years in soil-based compost.

Propagation Take 7.5-10cm (3-4in) long tip cuttings in late spring or summer.

Pests and diseases Scale insects, aphids, glasshouse whitefly and mealy bugs may infest stems and foliage.

Abutilon x *hybridum 'Canary Bird'*

Acacia

acacia, wattle

Acacia dealbata

☐ Height 3m (10ft)
☐ Temperature minimum 5-7°C (41-45°F)
☐ Bright light
☐ Soil-based compost
☐ Flowering shrub

The evergreen acacias, from Australia, thrive outdoors in mild frost-free regions where they reach tree proportions. As pot plants in a cool greenhouse or conservatory, their growth is much restricted. They are prized for their tiny yellow flowers clustered in fluffy balls or long sprays. Some species are almost leafless, others have ferny foliage.

Popular species

Acacia dealbata (mimosa), a tree-like shrub up to 7.5m (25ft) high in the open but 3m (10ft) as a pot plant, has ferny grey-green leaves. The 15-23cm (6-9in) long pendent sprays of fragrant flowers appear from early winter to early spring.

Acacia longifolia has willow-like grey-green leaf stalks instead of leaves. The fragrant golden yellow flowers appear in upright sprays in early spring.

Cultivation

Acacias need bright light and cool to warm temperatures not exceeding 5-10°C (41-50°F) in winter. Water well in spring and summer, sparingly in autumn and winter. Ventilate as freely as possible.

Repot established plants every other year in spring. Feed fortnightly from early spring to late summer. Large specimens can be pruned hard after flowering.

Propagation Grow from seed or heel cuttings of lateral shoots.

Pests and diseases Root mealy bugs may cause foliage to wilt.

Acalypha

copperleaf

Acalypha wilkesiana 'Obovata'

☐ Height up to 1.8m (6ft)
☐ Temperature minimum 15°C (59°F)
☐ Bright but filtered light
☐ Soil-based compost
☐ Foliage and flowering shrub

Some species of copperleaf are grown for their tassel-like flower spikes, others for their attractive coppery foliage. They are fast-growing, eventually reaching a height of 1.8m (6ft) or more, and are usually raised annually from cuttings, when they will be considerably smaller.

Popular species

Acalypha hispida (red-hot cattail, chenille plant) has conspicuous

Acalypha wilkesiana

Acalypha hispida, flowers

Achimenes
hot water plant

Achimenes grandiflora 'Rose Red' and 'India'

tassel-like spikes of bright red flowers in late summer. It bears broadly oval, slightly hairy, bright green leaves. 'Alba' has white flowers.

Acalypha wilkesiana (Jacob's coat, beefsteak plant, match-me-if-you-can, fire dragon plant) is an outstanding foliage plant. The pointed oval leaves are coppery green mottled copper, red and purple. Varieties include: 'Godseffiana' (shiny green, white edged leaves); 'Macrophylla' (russet brown leaves, marked pale brown, almost heart-shaped); 'Marginata' (heart-shaped, olive-green leaves tinged bronze, edged carmine-red); 'Musaica' (heart-shaped, bronze-green leaves, orange and red markings); and 'Obovata' (pink-edged leaves).

Cultivation
Acalyphas need bright but indirect light and high humidity in normal to warm room temperatures from 15-27°C (59-81°F). Liquid feed every two weeks and water plentifully during the growing season. If overwintered, keep plants just moist. They are best grown from cuttings every year. Mist-spray the foliage of *A. hispida* daily from early spring until flowering starts.
Propagation Take 7.5-10cm (3-4in) long tip cuttings or short side-shoots in spring.
Pests and diseases Mealy bugs and red spider mites may be troublesome.

☐ Height 15-45cm (6-18in)
☐ Temperature minimum 13°C (55°F)
☐ Bright light
☐ Soil- or peat-based compost
☐ Flowering perennial

Hot water plants are valued for their long-lasting show of satiny tubular or trumpet-shaped flowers in shades of purple, red and pink in summer. The plants are bushy, with toothed, mid green leaves. The trailing species are ideal for hanging baskets; upright species sometimes need support. The plants die back in autumn and the scaly rhizomes should be stored until the following spring.

Popular species and hybrids
Achimenes grandiflora, up to 45cm (1½ft) high, is an upright plant with tubular red-purple flowers opening out flat. Varieties include 'Rose Red' (pink-red flowers) and 'India' (violet).

Achimenes hybrids include: 'Little Beauty' (upright, bright pink); 'Peach Blossom' (trailing, magenta-pink); and 'Yellow Beauty' (upright, yellow).
Achimenes longiflora, a trailing plant with stems up to 30cm (1ft) long, has pale red to lavender or deep purple-blue flowers.

Cultivation
Achimenes need bright light, filtered from midday sun. Grow at temperatures from 13-27°C (55-81°F). Start the tubers into growth in spring and keep them moist until early autumn; feed fortnightly. Dry off and store at 15°C (59°F).
Propagation Divide and replant dormant rhizomes. Start rhizomes into growth by soaking them with hot water.
Pests and diseases Trouble free.

Acorus
sweet flag

Acorus gramineus 'Variegatus'

☐ Height 15-45cm (6-18in)
☐ Temperature minimum 5°C (41°F)
☐ Medium light or filtered direct sunlight
☐ Soil-based compost
☐ Foliage plant

Grown for its narrow, elegant foliage, sweet flag (*Acorus gramineus*) provides attractive leaf contrast throughout the year in cooler parts of the house or conservatory.

The sedge-like leaves grow in clumps up to 45cm (1½ft) high. In spring the plant produces a rather inconspicuous flower spathe which is hidden among the leaves.

Varieties include 'Albovariegatus' (rarely more than 15cm/6in high, white striped leaves) and 'Variegatus' (up to 45cm/18in high, white striped leaves).

Cultivation
Sweet flag should never be allowed to dry out at the roots. Water plentifully as often as necessary to keep the potting mixture thoroughly moist. Alternatively, stand the pot in a shallow container of water.

Keep in a cool to warm position, at a minimum temperature of 5°C (41°F), in medium or filtered light. Feed fortnightly in spring and summer and maintain high humidity.
Propagation Divide crowded clumps in spring or summer; pot the divisions separately.
Pests and diseases Generally trouble free.

Adiantum
maidenhair fern

Adiantum hispidulum

☐ Height 25-90cm (10-36in)
☐ Temperature minimum 10-13°C (50-55°F)
☐ Bright filtered light
☐ Peat-based, open compost
☐ Fern

The popular and well-known maidenhair ferns are valued for their delicate foliage. They are easy to grow in bright but filtered light and make fine contrast with other foliage plants.

The leaf fronds are divided into numerous leaflets and often have black stalks.

Popular species
Adiantum capillus-veneris (Venus hair), 25-30cm (10-12in) high, has light green triangular fronds with fan-shaped leaflets.
Adiantum hispidulum, up to 30cm (1ft) high, has fine fronds divided into finger-like sections, and leaflets which are coppery when young, then mid green.
Adiantum raddianum, syn. *A. cuneatum*, up to 45cm (1½ft) high and 60cm (2ft) across, is suitable for hanging baskets. The leaves are divided into numerous leaflets which are less delicate than those of *A. capillus-veneris*. Several varieties include 'Fragrantissimum' (fragrant) and 'Fritz Luthii' (longer, narrower fronds).
Adiantum tenerum (fan maidenhair fern), up to 90cm (3ft) high, has rounded to fan-shaped

Adiantum capillus-veneris

leaflets. Varieties include: 'Farleyense' (lobed and ruffled fan-shaped leaflets).

Cultivation
Maidenhair ferns tolerate normal room temperatures above 10°C (50°F), provided the air is not too dry. Bright light is suitable but not direct sunlight. Keep slightly moist at all times. Feed occasionally during the growing season.
Propagation Divide rhizomes and pot up in early spring.
Pests and diseases Root mealy bugs may infest the roots.

Aechmea

urn plant

Aechmea fasciata

Aechmea fulgens, berries

Aechmea chantinii

☐ Height 23-90cm (9-36in)
☐ Temperature minimum 15°C (59°F)
☐ Bright, indirect light
☐ Bromeliad compost
☐ Bromeliad

Urn plant is a bromeliad and belongs to a fascinating group of plants which absorb much of their food and moisture through their leaves rather than their roots. In the wild, many are epiphytic, growing on the branches of trees; they make exotic house plants.

The thick arching leaves form a rosette, with a water-holding reservoir at the centre. The foliage is often dusted with silvery scales in crosswise bands. A colourful, single flower head appears on mature plants after which the main rosette dies after several months. New plants can be grown from offshoots.

Popular species

Aechmea chantinii (vase plant), up to 90cm (3ft) high, has tough greyish leaves coated with silvery crossbands. The flower head consists of pointed orange-red bracts and yellow and red flowers.

Aechmea fasciata, syn. *Billbergia rhodocyanea*, up to 60cm (2ft) high, has spiny green or grey-green leaves with silvery crossbands. The tubular flowers, first blue and then pink, are crowded into a conical head.

Aechmea fulgens, up to 38cm (15in) high, has green leaves and waxy blue flowers followed by vermilion berries. The variety *discolor* has green leaves with purple undersides, and is more common than the species.

Cultivation

Urn plants need bright but fil-tered light and thrive in warm temperatures from 15°C (59°F) upwards. Water the potting compost moderately and keep the rosette filled with fresh water, preferably rainwater. Mist-spray regularly to maintain humidity.

Propagation Remove offsets when they are half the size of the parent plant. Allow the cut edge to dry out for a day or two before rooting in potting compost mixed with perlite, or a specially formulated bromeliad compost.

Pests and diseases Trouble free.

Aeonium

aeonium

Aeonium arboreum 'Schwarzkopf'

Aeonium arboreum

☐ Height 30-90cm (1-3ft)
☐ Temperature minimum 10-13°C
  (50-55°F)
☐ Full sun
☐ Cactus compost
☐ Succulent

Grown for their rosettes of plump, often spoon-shaped leaves, aeoniums are fascinating, quick growing succulents from the Southern Hemisphere.

The rosettes, sometimes measuring up to 30cm (1ft) across, are carried at the tips of thick stems, which are usually marked with old leaf scars. Some species produce only one rosette, while others, including *A. arboreum*, have several branching stems, each with a rosette at its tip.

Aeoniums flower only when mature, which may be in the fourth or fifth year. A spray or cluster of star-shaped yellow to cream flowers appears in spring on a long stalk rising from the centre of the rosette, which dies when flowering has finished.

Popular species

Aeonium arboreum is a tree-like shrub up to 90cm (3ft) high, with shiny green spoon-shaped leaves on branching stems. The flowers are yellow. Varieties include 'Atropurpureum' (deep purple) and 'Schwarzkopf' (almost black).
Aeonium canariense (giant velvet rose), up to 60cm (2ft) high, has pale green spoon-shaped leaves 10-30cm (4-12in) long. The plant often produces only one rosette on a thick trunk-like stem. Pale yellow flowers appear on stalks up to 45cm (1½ft) high.
Aeonium haworthii (pin wheel), up to 60cm (2ft) high, bears rosettes of blue-grey leaves edged with reddish brown hairs on the tips of woody, branching stems. The white to creamy yellow flowers are sometimes tinged pink.
Aeonium tabuliforme, up to 30cm (1ft) high, produces a flat, plate-like rosette up to 50cm (20in) across, with a very short stem. The tightly packed, spoon-shaped leaves are light green. The dull

yellow flowers appear on a stem up to 45cm (1½ft) high.
Aeonium undulatum (saucer plant), up to 90cm (3ft) high, produces rosettes up to 30cm (1ft) wide. The dark green, wavy-edged leaves are slightly glossy and up to 15cm (6in) long. Many plants produce only one rosette, though others may have a few side-shoots, each topped by a rosette. The flowers are mustard-yellow.

Cultivation
Aeoniums need full sunlight. During the growing period keep in temperatures above 18°C (64°F). Moisten the compost throughout when watering; allow the top 12mm (½in) to dry out before watering again. Feed fortnightly.

During the winter resting period move to a cooler position with a temperature of 10°C (50°F) and water just enough to prevent shrivelling.

Repot taller species annually, in cactus compost or a proprietary potting compost with added sand or perlite.
Propagation All species except *A. tabuliforme* can be propagated from tip cuttings in spring. *A. tabuliforme* can only be raised from seed.
Pests and diseases Trouble free.

Aeschynanthus
basket plant

Aeschynanthus speciosus

☐ Height 30-60cm (1-2ft)
☐ Temperature minimum 10°C (50°F)
☐ Bright light
☐ Lime-free potting compost
☐ Flowering perennial

Basket plants are ideal for hanging baskets, where they provide a spectacular summer display with their trailing stems and showy flowers in shades of red, orange and green. The fleshy leaves are lance-shaped to oval. The species are sometimes listed in the genus *Trichosporum*.

Popular species
Aeschynanthus lobbianus (lipstick vine) has 45-60cm (1½-2ft) long trailing stems set with deep green, glossy leaves. The crimson hooded flowers are 4cm (1½in) long with a purple-brown calyx.
Aeschynanthus marmoratus trails 60cm (2ft) stems. The leaves are red-purple beneath and pale green above with a lacy network of yellow veins. The green, brown-blotched flowers appear throughout summer.
Aeschynanthus pulcher climbs or trails to 60cm (2ft). It has mid green leaves and scarlet tubular flowers with yellow throats.
Aeschynanthus speciosus has lax arching stems 60cm (2ft) long. It has pale green leaves and bears spectacular clusters of tubular, bright orange flowers with darker lips in late winter and spring.

Cultivation
Basket plants thrive in ordinary

Aeschynanthus pulcher

room temperature if humidity is kept high. Bright light is best, but do not expose them to more than 2-3 hours of direct sunlight a day. Keep moist during the growing season; water sparingly in winter. After flowering, cut stems back to 15cm (6in). Repot in spring, in acid, free-draining compost.
Propagation Take tip cuttings in late spring or early summer.
Pests and diseases Leaf spot shows as white spots.

AFRICAN HEMP – see *Sparmannia*
AFRICAN LILY – see *Agapanthus*
AFRICAN VIOLET – see *Saintpaulia*

Agapanthus
African lily

Agapanthus africanus

☐ Height 30-75cm (1-2½ft)
☐ Temperature minimum 4°C (39°F)
☐ Full sun
☐ Soil-based compost
☐ Flowering perennial

Grown for its rounded flower heads, African lily (*Agapanthus africanus*) is a spectacular near-hardy perennial usually grown in large pots or tubs outdoors or in a cool conservatory.

The blooms are a lovely shade of bluish purple and are borne in dense clusters in late summer and early autumn. The leaves are strap-shaped. The species grows up to 60cm (2ft) high and 30cm (1ft) across.

The popular 'Headbourne Hybrids', which are hardier than the species, are generally 60-75cm (2-2½ft) high. The bright to pale blue flowers appear in dense clusters from late summer.

Cultivation
African lilies need cool temperatures indoors and full sunlight. Water well during the growing season.

In winter, when the plants die down, store the fleshy roots in a frost-free site.
Propagation Divide and replant the roots in mid to late spring.
Pests and diseases Trouble free.

Agave

agave, century plant

Agave americana 'Medio-picta'

Agave filifera

- ☐ Height 20cm-1.2m (8in-4ft)
- ☐ Temperature minimum 10°C (50°F)
- ☐ Full sun
- ☐ Cactus compost
- ☐ Succulent

Agaves belong to a large genus of dramatic succulents from Mexico. They form rosettes of tough, sword-shaped leaves in shades of green to grey, sometimes with distinctive striped edges.

They are slow-growing plants, flowering in the wild when they are mature. As house plants they rarely flower and are grown for their handsome foliage.

Popular species

Agave americana eventually grows up to 1.2m (4ft) high and across. It flourishes outdoors in frost-free regions and is suitable as a house plant only while young. It has narrow, grey-green, spine-edged leaves. Variegated forms include 'Marginata' (yellow margins) and 'Medio-picta' (central silvery yellow stripes).

Agave angustifolia is similar to *A. americana,* but with smaller, denser rosettes.

Agave attenuata has pointed bright mid green, spineless leaves. The rosette may grow up to 30cm (1ft) high and over 90cm (3ft) across.

Agave ferdinandi-regis, up to 25cm (10in) high, has a loose rosette of tapering, dark green, white-edged leaves tipped with spines.

Agave filifera, up to 25cm (10in) high, has narrow, shiny green leaves edged with white threads.

Agave parviflora, up to 20cm (8in) high, is similar to *A. filifera,* with leaves that split into threads at the tips.

Agave victoriae-reginae, up to 25cm (10in) high, has dark green, white marked, fleshy leaves with a tough spine at the tip.

Cultivation

Agaves need a sunny position at normal room temperatures above 10°C (50°F). Water moderately during the growing period; sparingly in winter. Repot annually in spring.

Propagation Detach offsets, allow to dry for a couple of days before potting up. Increase *A. victoriae-reginae* from seed.

Pests and diseases Trouble free.

Agave attenuata

Aglaonema

aglaonema

Aglaonema crispum 'Silver Queen'

☐ Height 30-60cm (1-2ft)
☐ Temperature minimum 10°C (50°F)
☐ Partial shade
☐ Soil-based compost
☐ Foliage plant

Aglaonemas are outstanding house plants with their ornamental foliage splashed in different shades of green and silver. They grow in clumps of stems topped with lance-shaped leaves.

Arum-like flowers appear in mid summer on a short spike (spadix) with a cream to green spathe, but they are inconspicuous compared with the foliage.

Aglaonemas can be grown away from windows, as they thrive in relatively poor light.

Popular species

Aglaonema commutatum, up to 60cm (2ft) high, is a variable plant with lance-shaped, mid green leaves marked with grey. They measure up to 25cm (10in) long. Varieties include 'Pseudobracteatum' (yellow and green mottled leaves, white veins, white marked stems) and 'Treubii' (compact, bluish green, silver marked leaves).

Aglaonema costatum, slow-growing to 60cm (2ft) high, has heart-shaped mid green leaves with ivory mid-ribs.

Aglaonema crispum, syn. *A. roebelinii* (painted drop tongue), up to 60cm (2ft) high, has leathery, thick, grey-green leaves edged with darker green. 'Silver Queen' has silver marbled leaves.

Aglaonema pictum, up to 60cm (2ft) high, has blue-green leaves marked with mid, dark and silvery green.

Cultivation

Grow aglaonemas away from direct light in temperatures above 10°C (50°F). Water moderately in spring and summer, sparingly in autumn and winter.

Propagation Detach and pot up basal shoots or suckers with several leaves.

Pests and diseases Mealy bugs infest the bases of leaf stalks.

AIRPLANE PROPELLER PLANT – see *Crassula*
AIR PLANT – see *Tillandsia*

Allamanda

golden trumpet

Allamanda cathartica 'Hendersonii'

☐ Height 1.8-4.5m (6-15ft)
☐ Temperature minimum 16°C (61°F)
☐ Bright light
☐ Soil-based compost
☐ Evergreen flowering climber

Golden trumpet (*Allamanda cathartica*) is a tropical climber best suited to a well-lit conservatory or large plant window.

Native to South America, golden trumpet grows rapidly to 4.5m (15ft) high and 3m (10ft) across in warm, humid conditions but tolerates pruning.

The flowers, which are borne in summer, are trumpet-shaped, often fragrant and measure up to 10cm (4in) across. The evergreen leaves are lance-shaped.

The variety 'Grandiflora' has pale yellow flowers. 'Hendersonii' has golden yellow flowers.

Cultivation

Golden trumpet needs bright light and full sun for three or four hours a day. Keep the temperature at a minimum of 16°C (61°F) and high humidity. During active growth water well and feed fortnightly.

In winter keep the compost almost dry. Prune plants back by up to two-thirds in late winter.

Propagation Take tip cuttings in early spring.

Pests and diseases Aphids may infest plants and transmit virus diseases and sooty mould.

Aloe

aloe

Aloe arborescens

- ☐ Height 15-30cm (6-12in)
- ☐ Temperature minimum 7-10°C (45-50°F)
- ☐ Bright light
- ☐ Cactus compost
- ☐ Succulent

Aloes belong to a large genus of South African succulent plants. They are easy to grow as house plants, for their ornamental foliage of thick, fleshy leaves growing in rosettes. Flower stems bearing sprays of pink, red or orange flowers may appear from the centre of the rosettes in winter, spring or summer, further improving the ornamental value.

Popular species

Aloe arborescens (candelabra plant) is only suitable as a house plant when young as it can eventually reach up to 4.5m (15ft) high. Loose rosettes of narrow, toothed grey-green leaves are borne at the tips of the branching woody stems. Clusters of red flowers sometimes appear in winter.

Aloe aristata (lace aloe), up to 15cm (6in) high, forms a dense, stemless rosette of grey-green leaves with a white bloom and horny white edges. Orange tubular flowers appear in clusters on 30cm (1ft) high stalks in late spring to early summer.

Aloe barbadensis, syn. *A. vera* (medicine plant), is cultivated medicinally for its sap, which is used in the cosmetic industry and to treat burns. It forms a rosette of toothed grey-green, pink-edged leaves up to 60cm (2ft) long. Yellow flower sprays appear on stems up to 90cm (3ft) high in late spring or summer.

Aloe brevifolia, syn. *A. prolifera*, forms a short-stemmed rosette made up of grey-green, roughly triangular leaves which are up to 15cm (6in) long. Pink to red flowers are borne on stalks up to 30cm (1ft) high in late spring to summer.

Ananas
pineapple

Ananas bracteatus 'Striatus'

Aloe variegata

Aloe ferox is only suitable as a house plant when young as it eventually grows up to 3.5m (12ft) high. The unbranched stem carries a rosette of bronze-green leaves edged with brown spines. Clusters of red flowers appear on stalks up to 90cm (3ft) long in spring; only mature plants bloom. *Aloe variegata* (partridge-breasted aloe), up to 30cm (1ft) high, forms a rosette of overlapping, tiered, almost upright fleshy leaves. They are dark green, marked with irregular bands of white, and have white, very fine toothed edges. Loose sprays of orange flowers appear on 30cm (1ft) high stalks in spring.

Cultivation
Aloes thrive in normal room temperatures above 16°C (61°F), with a minimum night temperature of 7°C (45°F) in winter. They prefer bright light and dry air. During the growing period, water well, keeping the compost thoroughly moist, and feed at fortnightly intervals.

During the resting period water moderately. Repot when plants become crowded; use a cactus compost or a proprietary potting mixture with added sharp sand for drainage.

Propagation Remove and pot up offsets in summer; sow seeds in early spring.

Pests and diseases Mealy bugs may infest the plants.

ALUMINIUM PLANT – see *Pilea*
AMARYLLIS – see *Hippeastrum*

☐ Height 30-90cm (1-3ft)
☐ Temperature minimum 16°C (61°F)
☐ Bright light
☐ Lime-free compost
☐ Bromeliad

The genus *Ananas* includes the edible pineapple, as well as ornamental foliage plants suitable for growing indoors. They have rosettes of rough-edged, strap-shaped leaves and sometimes long-stalked flower heads which eventually ripen to the typical pineapple fruit, complete with a short leaf cluster on top.

Flowering and fruiting rarely occur on indoor plants.

Popular species
Ananas bracteatus, syn. *A. sagenaria* (red pineapple), eventually grows up to 90cm (3ft) high and across. It forms a dense rosette of dark green, strap-shaped leaves with spiny edges. The lavender-coloured flowers with showy red bracts are rarely produced indoors. The variety 'Striatus' has leaves edged creamy white.

Ananas comosus, syn. *A. sativus*, is the commercially grown pineapple. Up to 90cm (3ft) high and across, it has arching, strap-shaped grey-green leaves with serrated edges. Under ideal conditions, an oval head of blue flowers is followed later by the typical pineapple. The variety usually cultivated for indoor decoration is 'Variegatus', which has ivory-edged leaves.

Cultivation
Pineapples thrive in bright light, including direct sunlight and warm rooms with a minimum temperature of 16°C (61°F). Keep the atmosphere humid by standing the pots in trays of damp pebbles. Water freely during periods of active growth, allowing the compost to dry out before watering again. Feed fortnightly. Water moderately during the winter rest period. Repot annually in early spring in a specially formulated bromeliad compost, or in a proprietary lime-free potting mixture.

Propagation Detach and pot up offsets from the base of the plants.

Pests and diseases Trouble free.

ANGEL'S TEARS – see *Billbergia*
ANGEL'S TRUMPET – see *Datura*
ANGEL'S WINGS – see *Caladium*

Angraecum

angraecum

Angraecum sesquipedale

Anthurium

anthurium

Anthurium andreanum 'Aztec'

☐ Height 23-45cm (9-18in)
☐ Temperature minimum 16°C (61°F)
☐ Indirect light
☐ Peat-based compost
☐ Foliage and flowering plant

The magnificent anthuriums make outstanding plants for the home. They originate from the tropical rainforests of South America and offer both lush foliage and dramatic, brilliantly coloured flowers.

The deep green, heart-shaped leaves are thick and glossy and sometimes patterned with a showy network of veins.

The exotic blooms are not true flowers, but consist of spathes (modified leaves) with the true, tiny flowers clustered in a spadix (a short spike). This is up to 7.5cm (3in) long and may be straight or twisted. The spathes of some species are scarlet and yellow or white, the vivid colours enhanced by a brilliant gloss. They persist for several weeks.

Anthuriums are demanding plants, requiring constant warmth and humidity, but their outstanding beauty makes it well worth the extra effort.

Popular species

Anthurium andreanum (painter's palette), 45cm (1½ft) or more high, has long-stalked, dark green, heart-shaped leaves which are up to 20cm (8in) long. From

☐ Height 60cm-1.8m (2-6ft)
☐ Temperature minimum 15°C (59°F)
☐ Partial shade
☐ Orchid compost
☐ Epiphytic orchid

Angraecums are evergreen, tree-dwelling orchids from tropical Africa. They bear starry white or pale green flowers with long narrow spurs in winter and spring.

Popular species

Angraecum eburneum, up to 90cm (3ft) high, has light green, strap-shaped leaves. The pale green flowers appear on long, drooping or arching stems from winter to early spring.

Angraecum sesquipedale, up to 60cm (2ft) high, has short, strap-shaped dark blue-green to grey-green leaves. The waxy, ivory-cream flowers appear from early to late spring.

Cultivation

Angraecums grow best in filtered light, at normal room temperatures that do not fall below 15°C (59°F). Good humidity is essential. Water freely from late spring to mid autumn, and feed occasionally. Reduce the amount of water from late autumn to mid spring. Grow the plants in orchid baskets or wired to slabs of bark.

Propagation Detach and pot up basal shoots in spring.

Pests and diseases Trouble free.

Anthurium scherzerianum

late spring to early autumn it bears glossy, brilliant red flower spathes. They have a corrugated surface and are about 10cm (4in) long and 7.5cm (3in) wide. The spadix is white to yellow. Varieties include: 'Album' (white spathes, stained purple at the base); 'Aztec' (magenta-red, yellow-tipped spadix); 'Giganteum' (larger, salmon-red spathes); and 'Rubrum' (deep red spathes, spadix tipped yellow).

Anthurium crystallinum, up to 45cm (1½ft) high, has dark green heart-shaped leaves. They are marked with a prominent network of white veins and measure up to 60cm (2ft) long and 30cm (1ft) across. The green spathes are insignificant.

Anthurium scherzerianum (flamingo flower), 30cm (1ft) or more high, has dark green lance-shaped leaves about 15cm (6in) long. The glossy, roughly oval spathes are brilliant scarlet and measure 7.5-10cm (3-4in) long. The orange-red spadix is twisted in a spiral. This species flowers from mid spring to mid autumn. Varieties offer spotted, deeper red, white or pink spathes with twisted spadices.

Anthurium crystallinum

Cultivation

Anthuriums require warm, constant temperatures from 16-21°C (61-70°F) throughout the year. Maintain high humidity by placing pots on trays of damp pebbles and mist-spray regularly. *A. crystallinum* needs shade in summer; other species prefer medium light or slight shade.

Water moderately from mid autumn to early spring. Keep thoroughly moist during the growing period and feed fort-

nightly. Repot every third year in mid spring, using a peat-based or similar potting compost.

Propagation Divide and replant in spring. Alternatively, grow *A. andreanum* and *A. crystallinum* from seed.

Pests and diseases Aphids, particularly mottled arum aphid, may extract sap and leave sticky encrustations. Leaf spot appears as dead brown or yellowish spots on the foliage.

Aphelandra

saffron spike

Aphelandra squarrosa 'Dania'

☐ Height 30-45cm (12-18in)
☐ Temperature minimum 18°C (64°F)
☐ Bright, filtered light
☐ Multi-purpose compost
☐ Flowering and foliage plant

Popular plants for both the house and the conservatory, aphelandras bear dark green leaves with a showy pattern of white veins, and spikes of glowing yellow flowers and flower bracts.

Popular species

Aphelandra chamissoniana, up to 45cm (18in) high, flowers in autumn and winter.
Aphelandra squarrosa 'Louisae' (zebra plant), 30cm (12in) high, is the most popular. It flowers from late summer to early winter. The variety 'Dania' is smaller with silvery veins.

Cultivation

Aphelandras need bright but filtered light and warm temperatures over 18°C (64°F). Maintain high humidity by placing the pots in trays of damp pebbles. Water well, never allowing the compost to dry out, and feed weekly from mid spring to early autumn; keep just moist and feed fortnightly at other times.
Propagation Take tip cuttings in late spring.
Pests and diseases Scale insects cause crusty brown marks and aphids make the plants sticky.

Aporocactus

aporocactus, rat's tail cactus

Aporocactus flagelliformis

☐ Height 90cm-1.8m (3-6ft)
☐ Temperature minimum 5°C (41°F)
☐ Full sunlight
☐ Cactus compost
☐ Epiphytic cactus

The fast-growing aporocactus with its long, trailing stems is a fascinating plant for hanging baskets. In spring the stems are studded with a profuse display of magenta or red trumpet-shaped flowers.

Popular species

Aporocactus flagelliformis (rat's tail cactus) has ribbed, mid green stems up to 90cm (3ft) long and dotted with short brown spines. It bears profuse funnel-shaped magenta flowers.
Aporocactus mallisonii is a hybrid correctly known as x *Heliaporus smithii*. The stems are shorter, stiffer and more deeply ribbed than *A. flagelliformis* and it has larger, but fewer, red flowers.

Cultivation

Aporocactus thrives in full sunlight in normal room temperatures during the growing season. Water well and feed fortnightly. Rest at a temperature of about 5°C (41°F) and keep barely moist.
Propagation Take stem cuttings in summer.
Pests and diseases Mealy bugs show as tufts of white waxy wool. Root mealy bugs infest the roots, checking growth.

Araucaria

Norfolk Island pine

Araucaria heterophylla

☐ Height 90cm-1.8m (3-6ft)
☐ Temperature minimum 5°C (41°F)
☐ Bright filtered light
☐ Soil-based compost
☐ Conifer

Norfolk Island pine (*Araucaria heterophylla*, syn. *A. excelsa*) grows up to 60m (200ft) in its native habitat, but as a pot plant it is slow-growing, making a decorative small indoor tree when young.

A member of the same genus as the monkey puzzle (*A. araucana*), Norfolk Island pine is broadly conical. The branches grow in whorls and form regular tiers. The bright green, needle-like leaves are awl-shaped and overlap each other.

Norfolk Island pine tolerates a wide temperature range indoors, and can be moved to an outdoor patio during the summer.

Cultivation

Norfolk Island pine likes bright but filtered light and good ventilation; in winter maintain a minimum night temperature of 5°C (41°F). Keep the compost thoroughly moist and feed fortnightly during active growth in spring and summer; keep just moist at other times. Let the surface of the compost dry out before watering.
Propagation Commercial methods are unsuitable for the home grower.
Pests and diseases Generally trouble free.

Ardisia

coralberry

Ardisia crenata

Arisaema

arisaema

Arisaema candidissimum

☐ Height 15cm (6in)
☐ Frost-hardy
☐ Light shade
☐ Peat-based compost
☐ Flowering perennial

Arisaema (*Arisaema candidissimum*) is a small and hardy plant making an elegant feature for cooler parts of the home or conservatory when it flowers in early summer.

The minute true flowers, which have no petals, are clustered on a spike surrounded by an elegant hooded spathe which curves into a point. The spathe is white with green veins and sometimes tinged pink.

The pale green, glossy leaves are divided into three oval leaflets.

The species, part of a large genus of arum plants with tuberous or rhizomatous roots, originates from China.

Cultivation
Arisaema thrives in cool temperatures and prefers partial shade. Water moderately, allowing the surface of the compost to dry out before watering. Feed fortnightly during active growth. Dry off and store the tubers over winter; start into growth in spring.
Propagation Remove offsets in spring or grow from seed.
Pests and diseases Trouble free.

☐ Height 60-90cm (2-3ft)
☐ Temperature minimum 10°C (50°F)
☐ Bright light
☐ Soil-based compost
☐ Flowering and foliage shrub

Coralberry (*Ardisia crenata*, syn. *A. crispa*) is popular for its brilliant red, long-lasting berries, which are set off to perfection by the glossy dark green foliage.

The wavy-edged leaves are oblong to lance-shaped. Clusters of fragrant, starry white flowers, sometimes red-tinged, appear in early summer.

Cultivation
Coralberry thrives in bright light and benefits from several hours of direct sun daily. It prefers cool temperatures; above 16°C (61°F) extra humidity is essential to prevent the berries from shrivelling; mist-spray frequently.

Keep thoroughly moist and feed weekly from mid spring until the berries turn red; keep just moist at other times.
Propagation Take heel cuttings or grow from seeds in spring.
Pests and diseases Generally trouble free.

Arisarum

mouse plant

Arisarum proboscideum

- ☐ Height 15-30cm (6-12in)
- ☐ Frost-hardy
- ☐ Partial shade
- ☐ Peat-based compost
- ☐ Flowering perennial

Mouse plant (*Arisarum proboscideum*) was given its curious common name because the swollen flower spathes resemble long-tailed mice crouching beneath the leaves.

This interesting plant, which is a hardy outdoor perennial, has deep green glossy, rather spear-shaped leaves.

The minute flowers are borne on a spike almost completely hidden by the swollen, tube-like spadix, which is brownish maroon on top and white at the bottom; it terminates in a long trail.

Cultivation

Mouse plant thrives in cool temperatures and prefers partial shade. Water moderately, allowing the top of the compost to dry out before watering again. Feed fortnightly during active growth. Store the rhizomes cool and dry over winter; start them into growth in spring with renewed watering.

Propagation Divide and repot the rhizomatous roots in spring. Alternatively, take offsets. Arisarum may also be grown from seed in early to mid spring.

Pests and diseases Trouble free.

ARROWHEAD VINE – see
Syngonium
ARTILLERY PLANT – see *Pilea*

Asclepias

blood flower

Asclepias curassavica

- ☐ Height 60-90cm (2-3ft)
- ☐ Temperature minimum 7°C (45°F)
- ☐ Full sun
- ☐ Soil-based compost
- ☐ Flowering perennial

Blood flower (*Asclepias curassavica*) is an attractive house plant which, with proper care, will give years of pleasure.

A bushy perennial growing up to 90cm (3ft) high and 60cm (2ft) across, blood flower has mid green, lance-shaped leaves with a slender point.

The orange-red flowers appear from early summer to mid autumn. They have five downward-pointing petals, topped by a circle of upward-pointing stamens giving the appearance of a tiny crown. The flowers are about 2cm (¾in) wide and are densely clustered in flat heads up to 5cm (2in) across towards the top of the stiff, leafy stems.

This woody-based plant, a member of the same species as the garden plant milkweed, originates from tropical parts of America.

Cultivation

Blood flower enjoys full sunlight and intermediate temperatures above 7°C (45°F) in winter. Water well, allowing the surface of the compost to dry out before watering. Feed fortnightly during active growth. At high summer temperatures, increased humidity is essential; stand the pot on a tray of moist pebbles or spray with a fine mist.

During the winter resting period, blood flower tolerates temperatures as low as 7°C (45°F).

Propagation Grow from seed in late winter or early spring.

Pests and diseases Cucumber mosaic virus mottles the leaves with yellow-green, causing distortion and leaf drop.

Asparagus

asparagus fern

Asparagus plumosus

Asparagus densiflorus 'Myers'

□ Height 30cm-3m (1-10ft)
□ Temperature minimum 10°C (50°F)
□ Bright, filtered light
□ Soil-based compost
□ Foliage plant

Grown for its ferny or plume-like foliage in shades of mid to bright green, asparagus is an attractive, easy-grown house plant. The genus, which includes the edible vegetable, has climbing species which can be trained up narrow poles, as well as upright and trailing types for pots and hanging baskets.

Instead of true foliage, asparagus has small leaf-like structures which are really flattened stems and are known as phylloclades. They measure from 6mm (¼in) to 5cm (2in) long and are sometimes carried in clusters.

The tiny star-shaped or bell-shaped flowers are carried in small sprays and are green or white; they appear in summer, but are insignificant though fragrant. They are sometimes followed by berries.

The species described originate from South Africa and tolerate a wide range of indoor temperatures.

Popular species

Asparagus asparagoides (smilax) is a climbing plant up to 3m (10ft) high and 60cm (2ft) across. It has thin wiry stems with bright green, roughly oval leaf-like phylloclades. The greenish flowers may be followed by round purple berries. It is popular with florists for bouquets and buttonholes.

Asparagus densiflorus, up to 1.2m (4ft) high, has arching plume-like stems of bright green foliage; it sometimes produces red berries. Varieties include 'Myers' (*A. myersii*, arching dense plumes up to 60cm/2ft long) and 'Sprengeri' (*A. sprengeri*, 30cm/1ft high, the most popular asparagus fern, with arching or semi-prostrate, yellow to mid green plumes).

Asparagus falcatus (sicklethorn), a climbing plant up to 3m (10ft) high, bears slightly curved lance-shaped phylloclades up to 5cm (2in) long. The flowers are fragrant.

Asparagus plumosus, syn. *A. setaceus*, up to 3m (10ft) high and 60cm (2ft) across, develops a climbing habit when mature. It bears horizontal, frond-like branches with tiny, bright green phylloclades. It sometimes produces red berries. Dwarf, non-climbing varieties include 'Compactus' and 'Nanus'.

Cultivation

Asparagus ferns thrive in bright, indirect or filtered sunlight in normal room temperatures of 16-24°C (61-75°F). In winter, night temperatures should not fall below 10°C (50°F). Water freely in summer and keep just moist in winter. Feed fortnightly from late spring to early autumn.

Propagation Divide and repot the rhizomatous roots.

Pests and diseases Red spider mites cause light mottling and bleaching of the leaves. Scale insects form brown crusty marks on the stems and make the plants sticky and sooty.

Aspidistra
cast-iron plant

Aspidistra elatior

☐ Height 30-45cm (1-1½ft)
☐ Temperature minimum 7°C (45°F)
☐ Light shade
☐ Soil-based compost
☐ Foliage plant

The cast-iron plant (*Aspidistra elatior*) was a great favourite of the Victorians and with its lush dark green foliage looks just as effective today in the setting of modern homes. It is a long-lived plant, tolerating a wide range of indoor temperatures and withstanding, albeit not flourishing in, heat and cold, draughts, dust and shade, as well as neglect.

The leaves, which form an arching clump, are oblong to lance-shaped, narrowing to the stalk at the base, and measure up to 50cm (20in) long. Insignificant purple cup-shaped flowers appear at soil level in late summer but are usually hidden by the leaves.

The variety 'Variegata' has irregular white to cream stripes on the leaves.

Aspidistra elatior 'Variegata'

Cultivation
The cast-iron plant thrives in light shade such as a north-facing window-sill, and in cool to warm room temperatures ranging from 7-24°C (45-75°F). It dislikes direct sunlight.

When watering, moisten the compost thoroughly in summer, but only slightly in winter. Allow the top of the compost to dry out before watering again. Wash the leaves occasionally.

Repot every second or third year in early to mid spring, in a proprietary potting compost. In years when the plant has not been repotted, feed once a month in summer.

Propagation Divide and replant the roots when new growth starts in early to mid spring.

Pests and diseases Red spider mites infest the undersides of the leaves and cause a fine mottling on the upper surfaces. Scale insects, especially aspidistra scale, form small brown scales on leaves and stems. A physiological disorder due to over-wet and cold soil conditions causes browning of the foliage.

Asplenium
spleenwort

Asplenium bulbiferum

☐ Height 45cm-1.2m (1½-4ft)
☐ Temperature minimum 10°C (50°F)
☐ Light shade
☐ Peat-based compost
☐ Fern

Spleenworts make attractive indoor foliage plants whether grown as solitary specimens or grouped with other plants.

In some species, the fronds are divided into numerous smaller sections (pinnae), giving a pretty, lacy effect; in others they are undivided. They are mid to dark green or glossy bright green.

Popular species
Asplenium bulbiferum, up to 60cm (2ft) high, has finely cut mid green fronds with a lacy appearance. Baby plants grow on the back of the fronds, gradually weighing them down as they increase in size.

Asplenium daucifolium, syn. *A. viviparum*, up to 45cm (1½ft) high, is similar to *A. bulbiferum* but with darker green, arching fronds. It produces fewer plantlets.

Asplenium nidus (bird's nest fern), up to 1.2m (4ft) high, has a shuttlecock-shaped bushy rosette of undivided bright green glossy fronds. On each frond, the lower half of the central vein is black. This species, which is epiphytic in the wild, bears spores on the back of the fronds.

Asplenium scolopendrium, syn. *Phyllitis scolopendrium* (hart's tongue fern), up to 60cm (2ft) high, has glossy green strap-shaped fronds, usually with undulating edges. It bears spores rather than plantlets. 'Undulatum', a dwarf form, has crimped edges.

Asplenium nidus

Astrophytum
astrophytum

Astrophytum ornatum

☐ Height 2.5-30cm (1-12in)
☐ Temperature minimum 7-10°C (45-50°F)
☐ Full sun
☐ Cactus compost
☐ Cactus

Astrophytums are easy plants to cultivate in the home. They have leafless globular stems, which become cylindrical with age; the stunning many-petalled yellow flowers in summer can be up to 7.5cm (3in) wide. The green or grey plant bodies are divided into segments or ribs marked or covered with white scales.

Cultivation

Spleenworts thrive in normal room temperatures; *A. nidus* needs a minimum winter night temperature of 16°C (61°F), other species tolerate a temperature of 10°C (50°F). All prefer light shade: they dislike direct sun or full shade and need a humid atmosphere; stand the pots on trays of moist pebbles and mist-spray frequently at high temperatures.

Keep the compost thoroughly moist during active growth and feed every two weeks. At other times water sparingly.

Propagation Detach and pot up plantlets or sow spores.

Pests and diseases Scale insects may infest the plants.

Popular species

Astrophytum asterias (sea urchin cactus, sand dollar cactus), 2.5-5cm (1-2in) high, grows slowly in the shape of a flattened sphere. The eight shallow ribs are flecked with white and edged with woolly areoles.

Astrophytum capricorne (goat's horn cactus), up to 25cm (10in) high, is light green with raised white scales. It has eight ribs bearing curved black, brown or reddish spines.

Astrophytum myriostigma (bishop's cap, monk's hood), up to 20cm (8in) high, has five or six deeply divided ribbed segments densely covered with white scales; the ribs are edged with areoles carrying stout brownish spines and, on mature plants, bright yellow flowers.

Asplenium scolopendrium 'Undulatum'

Astrophytum myriostigma

Astrophytum ornatum, up to 30cm (1ft) high, is grey with darker markings and bands of silvery scales. Stout yellow spines, becoming black, grow from the ribs. This species flowers spectacularly when it is about ten years old.

Cultivation

Astrophytum likes normal room temperatures of 16-21°C (61-70°F) and full sunlight. In spring, summer and autumn, water sparingly when the soil becomes dry. Do not water in the winter and rest the plants at 7-10°C (45-50°F). Pot on when the containers become full of roots, using a proprietary cactus compost or a potting mixture with added sharp sand or perlite.
Propagation Grow new plants from seed.
Pests and diseases Root mealy bugs may check growth.

AZALEA – see *Rhododendron*
BABY'S TEARS – see *Soleirolia*
BAMBOO PALM – see
Chamaedorea
BANANA – see *Musa*
BANYAN TREE – see *Ficus*
BARREL CACTUS – see
Echinocactus
BASKET GRASS – see
Oplismenus
BASKET PLANT – see
Aeschynanthus
BEAD PLANT – see *Nertera*
BEEFSTEAK PLANT – see
Acalypha and *Iresine*

Begonia
begonia

Begonia Rieger-Elatior hybrid

☐ Height 7.5cm-1.8m (3in-6ft)
☐ Temperature minimum 10-16°C (50-61°F)
☐ Bright light
☐ Multi-purpose compost
☐ Foliage and flowering plants

The genus *Begonia* provides the indoor gardener with a wide choice of plants offering attractive foliage and colourful flowers. The numerous species and varieties are often grouped, according to their rootstocks, as tuberous, rhizomatous or fibrous. Tuberous and fibrous begonias are grown for their flowers, rhizomatous types for their ornamental foliage.

Begonia leaves, which measure from 5-25cm (2-10in) across, are often roughly heart-shaped. Some types have more rounded or lance-shaped leaves. Foliage colour is variable, ranging from the silver, red and purple markings of the *B. rex* hybrids to the metallic green of *B. metallica*.

The flowers, in shades of red, pink, apricot and orange or white, are generally borne in sprays or clusters, individual blooms ranging from 10mm-7.5cm (⅜-3in) in diameter.

Popular species and varieties

Begonia boweri (eyelash begonia), up to 23cm (9in) high and across, is rhizomatous, with emerald green leaves which are edged with hairs and have a broken rim of deep brown. Small pale pink flowers appear from late winter to late spring.

Begonia x *cheimantha* is a group of tuberous hybrids known as the Lorraine or Christmas begonias. They have rounded glossy leaves, and profuse flowers in shades of pink which measure up to 5cm (2in) across and appear in early to mid winter. The most popular variety is 'Gloire de Lorraine' with pale pink flowers and mid green leaves.

Begonia coccinea (angel wing begonia) is a shrubby, fibrous-rooted species up to 1.8m (6ft) high. It has bamboo-like stems with pale to mid green, red-edged leaves which are reddish beneath. They are oblong to lance-shaped, resembling an angel's wing, and are up to 15cm (6in) long. Large drooping sprays of bright coral-red flowers, about 2.5cm (1in) wide, appear from late spring to mid autumn. Named varieties

Begonia sutherlandii

Begonia coccinea 'Comte de Mirabelle', flower buds

include 'Comte de Mirabelle' (salmon-pink flowers) and 'President Carnot' (silver-spotted leaves, paler coral-red flowers).

Begonia corallina, sometimes called *B.* x 'Corallina de Lucerna', is a fibrous-rooted shrubby species, about 1.8m (6ft) high and similar to *B. coccinea*. The lance-shaped mid green leaves, up to 20cm (8in) long, are spotted white on top and flushed red beneath. Bright coral-pink flowers, about 2cm (¾in) wide, appear from late spring to early winter.

Begonia x *erythrophylla*, syn. *B.* x *feastii* (beefsteak begonia), is up to 23cm (9in) high. It bears thick, glossy, kidney-shaped leaves, about 20cm (8in) across, from a rhizomatous rootstock. They are mid green above, red beneath and edged with white hairs. Large clusters of small white flowers appear in winter and spring.

Begonia x *hiemalis* (winter-flowering begonia) is a group of outstanding tuberous hybrids that include the popular Rieger-Elatior types. They are up to 45cm (1½ft) high with rounded mid green leaves. They bear profuse, often semi-double flowers, up to 7.5cm (3in) wide, in shades of red, pink and apricot or white.

Begonia maculata, up to 90cm (3ft) high, is a fibrous-rooted species with bamboo-like stems. They bear lance-shaped dark green leaves, up to 23cm (9in) long, and spotted white on top with red beneath. They produce drooping sprays of pinkish flowers mainly in summer.

Begonia masoniana (iron cross), up to 23cm (9in) high, is an outstanding rhizomatous foliage species with mid green to yellow-green, heavily corrugated leaves. They are about 20cm (8in) across and marked with bold bronze-red bars forming a cross.

Begonia corallina

Begonia metallica, up to 90cm (3ft) high, is grown for its glossy, metallic green leaves which are densely covered with rough white hairs; the leaf veins are purple. Short sprays of white to pink flowers are borne in early autumn. Fibrous-rooted.

Begonia rex (painted leaf or fan begonia), up to 30cm (1ft) high, is the parent of numerous rhizomatous hybrids with ornamental foliage. Leaves may be patterned with silver or have dark centres with marks or zones in shades of green, brown, red, purple and pink. Miniature forms, some just 7.5cm (3in) high, are also available.

Begonia scharffii, syn. *B. haageana* (elephant's ears), is up to 1.2m (4ft) high. It is fibrous-rooted, with hairy leaves that are olive-green above and purple-red below, and up to 25cm (10in) long. Hairy, white pink-tinged flowers appear at any time of year.

Begonia sutherlandii, a tuberous-rooted plant for hanging baskets, has trailing stems up to 60cm (2ft) long. The light green leaves are about 10cm (4in) long with red veins and margins; the flowers are pale rusty orange and borne from spring to early autumn.

Cultivation

Fibrous and rhizomatous begonias need bright but filtered light, with some direct sun for flowering types. They thrive at normal room temperatures, with a winter rest at 16°C (61°F). Water moderately

Beloperone

shrimp plant

Beloperone guttata

□ Height 30-45cm (12-18in)
□ Temperature minimum 13°C (55°F)
□ Bright light
□ Multi-purpose compost
□ Flowering shrub

The shrimp plant (*Beloperone guttata*), originating from Mexico, is popular for its pink flower bracts which almost conceal the small white flowers peeping between them. The bracts are borne in drooping spikes that resemble the curved bodies of shrimps; they appear from mid spring until early winter. The mid green, oval leaves are slightly hairy.

The variety 'Yellow Queen', with yellow bracts, is sometimes available.

Cultivation

Shrimp plant likes normal room temperatures, bright light and good ventilation. Move to a cooler position, at 13°C (55°F), in winter. Mist-spray regularly at warm temperatures to maintain humidity.

Water moderately from early spring to late autumn, sparingly in winter. Feed weekly from late spring to early autumn.

Cut back annually to prevent the plant becoming spindly. Pinch out growing tips to encourage bushiness.

Propagation Take tip or stem cuttings.

Pests and diseases A physiological disorder may cause brown or yellow blotches on the leaves.

Begonia masoniana

Begonia rex

during active growth and feed every fortnight; during the rest period, water sparingly. Pot on fibrous-rooted types annually in spring. Rhizomatous begonias are shallow-rooted and best grown in half-pots; pot on when rhizomes cover the entire surface.

Tuberous begonias need bright light throughout the year, at normal room temperature, and a winter rest at 13°C (55°F). The winter-flowering types are usually discarded after flowering. Water moderately and feed fortnightly during active growth, sparingly in winter; stop watering of begonias that lose top growth in late autumn. Pot on or topdress annually in spring.

All begonias suffer from dry air; increase humidity by standing pots on trays of moist pebbles.

Propagation Take stem cuttings of fibrous begonias between late spring and late summer. Increase rhizomatous types by division in mid spring, large-leaved types also by leaf cuttings. Tuberous begonias are raised by heel cuttings of basal shoots in mid spring or division of tubers when young shoots are visible.

Pests and diseases Powdery mildew shows as white powdery spots on leaves and stems. Grey mould forms black or greyish blotches on leaves and flowers.

BELLFLOWER – see *Campanula* and *Lapageria*

Billbergia

billbergia

Billbergia zebrina

Billbergia nutans

☐ Height 30-90cm (1-3ft)
☐ Temperature minimum 15°C (59°F)
☐ Bright light
☐ Bromeliad compost
☐ Epiphytic bromeliad

Despite their exotic appearance, billbergias, from South America, are easy to grow. With their long, strap-shaped leaves and striking flower heads – which may appear at any time – they make fine specimen plants.

The leaves, which are often attractively cross-banded with grey or white, form a spreading rosette, or a tighter, upright water-holding reservoir at the centre.

Popular species

Billbergia nutans (angel's tears, queen's tears, friendship plant), up to 45cm (1½ft) high, has dark green, narrow strap-shaped leaves with serrated edges. The drooping flower heads, up to 10cm (4in) long, have greenish, blue-edged tubular flowers and pink bracts.

Billbergia pyramidalis, up to 38cm (15in) high, has a vase-shaped rosette of broad apple-green leaves. It bears upright flower heads up to 15cm (6in) long with a cluster of red, blue-tipped flowers and pink bracts.

Billbergia vittata, syn. *B. amabilis* and *B. leopoldii*, forms an upright rosette 90cm (3ft) high. It has scaly deep grey-green leaves with grey crosswise stripes on the undersides, and long red flower bracts and pale green flowers tipped with blue and red.

Billbergia zebrina forms a stiff rosette up to 90cm (3ft) high. The dark green and purple-bronze leaves have grey-white crosswise stripes. The drooping flower stems have pink bracts and greenish yellow flowers.

Cultivation

Billbergias enjoy normal room temperatures from 15-24°C (59-75°F) throughout the year, although *B. nutans* will tolerate temperatures as low as 7°C (45°F) for short spells. They thrive in bright light and three or four hours a day of direct sun. Keep the compost moist and place the pots on moist pebbles to maintain a humid atmosphere. On plants with a central water reservoir, keep this topped up with fresh water, preferably rainwater.

Propagation Detach and pot up well-formed suckers or side-shoots in spring. Use a proprietary bromeliad compost or a lime-free potting mixture.

Pests and diseases Trouble free.

BIRD OF PARADISE FLOWER – see *Strelitzia*
BIRDCATCHER TREE – see *Pisonia*
BIRD'S NEST FERN – see *Asplenium*
BISHOP'S CAP – see *Astrophytum*
BLACK-EYED SUSAN – see *Thunbergia*

Blechnum

blechnum

Blechnum gibbum

☐ Height 90cm (3ft)
☐ Temperature minimum 10°C (50°F)
☐ Bright, filtered light
☐ Peat-based compost
☐ Fern

Blechnum is a genus of attractive tropical ferns suitable for growing in warm rooms. Their broad, sweeping fronds are divided into herringbone patterns and grow in circular rosettes. In some species the fern matures to a tree-shape as the rhizome develops a trunk-like stem with the foliage rosette sitting on top.

Popular species
Blechnum brasiliense, up to 90cm (3ft) high, forms a loose rosette of leathery, lance-shaped mid green fronds growing from a brown central core. When mature, the rosette sits on top of a brown scaly, trunk-like stem. The fronds, which are divided into narrow, toothed pinnae, giving them a feathery appearance, are up to 90cm (3ft) long and 30cm (1ft) wide and are bronze when young. The variety 'Crispum' has smaller, wavy-edged fronds which are red when young.
Blechnum gibbum measures up to 90cm (3ft) high when mature. It has a rosette of shiny green fronds, each up to 90cm (3ft) long and 30cm (1ft) across and divided into narrow pinnae. They eventually crown a black scaly trunk-like stem.
Blechnum occidentale (hammock fern), up to 90cm (3ft) high, forms a rosette of rich green arching fronds with paler midribs. The fronds taper to a point and are up to 45cm (1½ft) long and 13cm (5in) wide.

Cultivation
Blechnums thrive in bright light, but out of direct sunlight, in warm rooms with temperatures from 15-24°C (59-75°F). Maintain humidity, particularly during active growth, by placing pots on moist pebbles, and by mist-spraying. Keep the compost thoroughly moist but never allow the pots to stand in water.

Blechnums benefit from a winter rest at cool temperatures from 10-15°C (50-59°F); water sparingly.
Propagation Grow from spores or the occasional offsets. *B. occidentale* is rhizomatous and easily increased by division in spring.
Pests and diseases Generally trouble free.

BLEEDING HEART VINE – see
Clerodendrum

Bletilla

bletilla

Bletilla striata

☐ Height 30-60cm (1-2ft)
☐ Temperature minimum 5°C (41°F)
☐ Bright light
☐ Orchid compost
☐ Terrestrial orchid

Bletilla (*Bletilla striata*) makes an elegant feature for the home with its pleated, lance-shaped leaves and long-stemmed, rich mauve-pink, purple-lipped flowers. The blooms, which appear in late spring, are up to 5cm (2in) across.

Cultivation
Bletilla is almost hardy and thrives in bright, well-ventilated, cool to warm rooms. Water well and feed fortnightly during active growth. Keep the compost just moist at dormancy. Repot or pot on every other year in spring.
Propagation Divide and repot the tuber-like pseudobulbs when growth is restarted in spring.
Pests and diseases Generally trouble free.

BLOOD FLOWER – see
Asclepias
BLOODLEAF – see *Iresine*
BLOOD LILY – see *Haemanthus*
BLUE DRACAENA – see
Cordyline
BOSTON FERN – see
Nephrolepis

Bougainvillea

bougainvillea, paper flower

Bougainvillea x *buttiana* 'Mrs Butt'

☐ Height 90cm (3ft) or more
☐ Temperature minimum 16°C (61°F)
☐ Direct sun
☐ Soil-based compost
☐ Shrub or climber

Bougainvillea makes a spectacular feature with its large, papery flower bracts in brilliant shades of purple, red and orange. They appear mainly in late summer and early autumn, and surround insignificant cream flowers.

The species are vigorous climbers, up to 2.4m (8ft), but smaller, shrubby hybrid forms are available. Bougainvilleas are temperamental and need a great deal of direct sunlight, even during the winter rest.

Popular species

Bougainvillea x *buttiana* can grow 1.5-2.4m (5-8ft) high or kept shrubby by hard pruning. The best known is the rose-crimson 'Mrs Butt'.
Bougainvillea glabra is similar but flowers when quite small. The bracts are red and purple.

Cultivation

Bougainvilleas need plenty of direct sun. During active growth keep in normal room temperatures. Water thoroughly when the compost is dry at the top, and feed weekly. Pinch out growing tips to encourage bushiness.

After flowering and until early spring, move to a cooler position at 16°C (61°F) and keep the compost just moist.
Propagation Stem cuttings.
Pests and diseases Trouble free.

Bouvardia

bouvardia

Bouvardia x *domestica*
'President Cleveland'

☐ Height 60-90cm (2-3ft)
☐ Temperature minimum 13°C (55°F)
☐ Bright light
☐ Soil-based compost
☐ Evergreen flowering shrub

Bouvardia is valued for its autumn flowers of long-lasting fragrant tubular blooms in pink and red or white.

Popular species

Bouvardia x *domestica*, up to 60cm (2ft) high, bears clusters of pink, white or red flowers from summer to autumn. 'President Cleveland' has bright scarlet flowers.
Bouvardia longiflora, up to 90cm (3ft) high, bears deeply fragrant white flowers from autumn to winter.

Cultivation

Bouvardias need bright light and cool to normal room temperatures. Maintain a humid atmosphere by placing the pots on moist pebbles. During active growth, keep the compost moist and feed weekly. Give the plants a winter rest at 13°C (55°F) keeping them just moist.

To encourage flowering, pinch out growing tips of *B.* x *domestica* twice during spring and *B. longiflora* during summer.
Propagation Take tip cuttings in spring.
Pests and diseases Mealy bugs and scale insects may infest the plants.

Bowiea

climbing onion

Bowiea volubilis

☐ Height 30cm (12in) or more
☐ Temperature minimum 6-10°C (43-50°F)
☐ Bright light
☐ Soil- or peat-based compost
☐ Perennial foliage plant

The climbing onion (*Bowiea volubilis*, syn. *Schizobasopsis volubilis*) belongs to the lily family, but any resemblance stops with the bulb. It is native to South Africa and chiefly grown as a house plant for its curiosity value.

The large yellow-green bulb starts into growth in late winter, producing several thin and branching stems which can be trained to twine over a wire framework or be allowed to trail. The fleshy stems are sparsely clothed with small green leaves which soon drop off, indicating the beginning of dormancy. Other stems bear tiny greenish flowers of little impact in spring.

Cultivation

Climbing onion needs bright light, even during dormancy. It grows well at normal room temperatures; move to a cool position (6-10°C/43-50°F) for the winter rest and keep dry. During the growing season, water moderately and feed monthly. Repot annually as growth starts.
Propagation Pot up offset bulbs when repotting.
Pests and diseases Trouble free.

BOX – see *Buxus*
BRAKE FERN – see *Pteris*

Brassia

spider orchid

Brassia verrucosa

- ☐ Height 38-45cm (15-18in)
- ☐ Temperature minimum 13-16°C (55-61°F)
- ☐ Bright filtered light
- ☐ Orchid compost
- ☐ Epiphytic orchid

The elegant brassias are easy to grow in the home. They bear flowers which have petals so long and narrow that they resemble a spider's legs. Each pseudobulb produces one to three narrow leaves and one to two flower stems.

Popular species

Brassia caudata, up to 45cm (1½ft) high, has a yellowish-green tuber-like pseudobulb and two or three leaves up to 23cm (9in) long and 6cm (2½in) wide. Fragrant, yellowish-green flowers with brown markings and a pale yellow lip spotted with reddish brown appear in late summer.
Brassia verrucosa, up to 38cm (15in) high, has a green pseudobulb with two narrow leaves. The pale green flowers are spotted green or red and have a white lip bearing dark green wart-like spots. They appear in spring and summer.

Cultivation

Brassias thrive in bright filtered light, at normal room temperatures with good humidity. Water thoroughly during active growth, allowing the compost to dry out before watering again. Give a half-strength feed at every third or fourth watering. After flowering, induce a three-week rest by sparse watering.
Propagation Divide and pot up pseudobulbs in spring.
Pests and diseases Trouble free.

x *Brassolaeliocattleya*

brassolaeliocattleya

x *Brassolaeliocattleya* 'Rising Sun' x 'La Tuilerie'

- ☐ Height up to 45cm (1½ft)
- ☐ Temperature minimum 13-16°C (55-61°F)
- ☐ Bright, but filtered light
- ☐ Orchid compost
- ☐ Epiphytic orchid

Brassolaeliocattleyas are noteworthy for their flamboyant flowers in shades of magenta, pink and yellow. Like many hybrid orchids, the parentage is complicated – a cross between three different orchid genera: *Brassavola*, *Laelia* and *Cattleya*.

The flowers, which appear in autumn and winter, have six petals. One enlarged petal forms a frilled lip and is often a different colour from the rest of the petals. The blooms measure 20cm (8in) or more across. The upright pseudobulbs produce one or two long, lance-shaped leaves.

Popular varieties

New varieties and hybrids, including multi-generic ones, are constantly being bred and the naming of them is highly complex. The following is a small selection from the numbers available.
'Chinox Nuggett' x 'Trianae Cinderella' has pale orange flowers with the inside of the lip stained magenta-purple.
'Crusader' has pink flowers up to 23cm (9in) across. They have a purple lip with a yellow patch.
'Norman's Bay Lows' has fragrant rose-magenta flowers. They measure 23cm (9in) across and have a frilled, slightly darker lip and gold veining in the throat.
'Norman's Bay' x 'Triumphans' has fragrant flowers with white petals stained rose-pink and a frilled magenta lip. They measure 13cm (5in) across.
'Nugget' has yellow petals and sepals; and 'Rising Sun' x 'La Tuilerie' has yellow flowers.

Cultivation

Brassolaeliocattleyas need bright light but out of direct sun; they should be kept at constant temperatures above 18°C (64°F) in summer and 13°C (55°F) in winter. Maintain a humid atmosphere by placing the pots on moist pebbles and mist-spray with tepid water daily. Give plenty of water during active growth, allowing the compost to dry out before watering. Feed fortnightly.

After flowering, allow the plants to rest for six weeks in a cooler place with a minimum temperature of 13°C (55°F); water sparingly.

Repot every two or three years when a new bud or growing point begins to develop roots.
Propagation In spring, divide mature pseudobulbs, with three or four bulbs in each division.
Pests and diseases Scale insects and aphids may infest leaves and stem bases, causing yellow blotching and making the plants sticky and sooty. Virus diseases may cause brown or black leaf patterns or breaking of the flower colour.

Browallia

browallia

Browallia speciosa 'Blue Troll'

☐ Height 30-60cm (1-2ft)
☐ Temperature minimum 13°C (55°F)
☐ Direct sun
☐ Soil-based compost
☐ Flowering annual

Browallias are attractive plants for pots or hanging baskets with their oval leaves and violet-like flowers in shades of blue or white. They are usually raised from seed annually and discarded after flowering.

Popular species

Browallia speciosa (bush violet), up to 60cm (2ft) high, has bright green, pointed leaves and 5cm (2in) wide violet-blue flowers from early summer to early autumn. Varieties include: 'Blue Troll' (dwarf); 'Major' (larger flowers than the species); and 'Silver Bells' (dwarf, white).

Browallia viscosa, up to 30cm (1ft) high, has sticky mid green leaves. The 2.5cm (1in) wide bright blue flowers have white eyes. Varieties include 'Alba' (white) and 'Sapphire' (compact, deep blue).

Cultivation

Browallias need bright light and plenty of direct sun, with a minimum winter temperature of 13°C (55°F). Water moderately and feed fortnightly.

Pinch out growing tips to encourage bushiness.

Propagation Sow seed in spring for summer-flowering, in summer for winter-flowering.

Pests and diseases Trouble free.

Brunfelsia

brunfelsia

Brunfelsia pauciflora calycina 'Macrantha'

☐ Height 60cm-1.2m (2-4ft)
☐ Temperature minimum 10°C (50°F)
☐ Bright light
☐ Soil- or peat-based compost
☐ Evergreen flowering shrub

Under ideal conditions, brunfelsias flower profusely for most of the year, with a brief rest in late spring. Attractive evergreen shrubs suitable for large pots or containers, they have lance-shaped leaves and flowers consisting of a long tube spreading into five wide petals shading from violet-purple to white.

Popular species

Brunfelsia pauciflora calycina, syn. *B. calycina*, is up to 60cm (2ft) high, with shiny mid green leaves. From mid spring it bears fragrant flowers, up to 5cm (2in) wide, which are violet-purple when they open and fade to near white. The colour change takes about three days, giving the plant its common name of yesterday-today-and-tomorrow. The variety 'Macrantha' has larger flowers.

Brunfelsia undulata (white rain tree), up to 1.2m (4ft) high, has mid to deep green leaves and bears clusters of fragrant white or cream flowers with tubes up to 7.5cm (3in) long. They appear mainly from early summer to mid autumn, though they may open at any time of year.

Cultivation

Brunfelsias need plenty of bright light, with direct sun in winter. They give their best display of flowers at temperatures of 15-18°C (59-64°F). Maintain a moist atmosphere by placing the pots on moist pebbles. Keep well watered during active growth, watering when the top of the compost is dry. Give a weak feed once a month. A winter rest at cooler temperatures is beneficial but not essential.

Pinch out growing tips to encourage bushiness. Repot in early to mid spring when plants are pot-bound.

Propagation Take tip cuttings in spring.

Pests and diseases Generally trouble free.

Buddleia

buddleia

Buddleia colvillei

☐ Height 1.2m (4ft) or more
☐ Temperature minimum 5°C (41°F)
☐ Bright light
☐ Soil-based compost
☐ Shrub

Buddleias are hardy deciduous garden shrubs, though some species are tender while young. These make fine specimen plants for sunny conservatories and enclosed porches.

Popular species
Buddleia colvillei, up to 1.2m (4ft) or more high and across, bears lance-shaped, dark green leaves, and drooping clusters of tubular, rose-pink flowers in summer.
Buddleia salviifolia, the South African sagewood, is 1.2m (4ft) high and across. It bears wrinkled dark green hairy leaves, and pale lavender flowers in summer.

Cultivation
Buddleias like plenty of bright light, including direct sunlight, in temperatures above 5°C (41°F). Water thoroughly during the growing season.
Propagation Take heel cuttings in late summer.
Pests and diseases Trouble free.

BUNNY-EARS – see *Opuntia*
BUSH VIOLET – see *Browallia*
BUSY LIZZIE – see *Impatiens*
BUTTERFLY ORCHID – see *Oncidium*
BUTTERFLY PALM – see *Chrysalidocarpus*
BUTTON FERN – see *Pellaea*
BUTTONS-ON-A-STRING – see *Crassula*

Buxus

box

Buxus microphylla 'Variegata'

☐ Height 23-45cm (9-18in)
☐ Temperature minimum 2°C (35°F)
☐ Bright light
☐ Soil- or peat-based compost
☐ Evergreen foliage shrub

Box is a popular garden shrub, but it is also suitable as an indoor plant, tolerant of low temperatures and draughty places.
The shrubs are slow-growing, and can be pruned into miniature trees, standards or ball shapes.

Popular species
Buxus microphylla (small-leaved box) is a rounded shrub up to 30cm (1ft) high. It has glossy dark green oval leaves. The variety 'Variegata' has yellow variegated leaves.
Buxus sempervirens is a dense, spreading shrub up to 45cm (1½ft) high when kept in a pot, though it grows much larger in a conservatory border and in the open garden. The glossy dark green leaves, up to 3cm (1¼in) long, are larger than those of *B. microphylla*.

Cultivation
Box thrives in bright light in normal room temperatures of 10-21°C (50-70°F), in winter just above freezing. It tolerates direct sunlight. Maintain humidity by placing the pots on trays of moist pebbles. Water moderately and feed monthly during spring and summer. Prune to shape with secateurs at any time during the growing season.
Propagation Take stem cuttings in late summer or autumn.
Pests and diseases Leaf spot shows as pale brown spots.

CABBAGE PALM – see *Cordyline*

Caladium

angel's wings

Caladium x *hortulanum* hybrids

☐ Height 23-38cm (9-15in)
☐ Temperature minimum 13°C (55°F)
☐ Bright, filtered light
☐ Peat-based compost
☐ Foliage perennial

The exquisite colouring and delicate texture of angel's wings (*Caladium* x *hortulanum*) have made it one of the most popular of all foliage house plants.

Caladiums bear arrowhead-shaped, thin leaves which range in length from 15cm (6in) to 38cm (15in). The numerous varieties offer a wide range of leaf colour from dark green to white with pink, red and lilac markings and a network of veins picked out in contrasting colours. A single plant may display a number of leaves of different sizes, with slight variations in pattern and colour distribution.

Also known as elephant's ears, caladiums need more attention than most other plants: they require high humidity and will not tolerate draughts.

Cultivation

Caladiums need bright light but out of direct sunlight in temperatures of 18-24°C (64-75°F). Keep the compost moist during active growth and maintain a humid atmosphere by placing pots on moist pebbles and mist-spraying daily. Feed weekly from mid summer until early autumn.

As the leaves start to fade in autumn, give less water. Overwinter the tubers in the dark at a temperature of 13-16°C (55-61°F). Keep the compost barely moist. Start tubers into growth in early spring at 21-24°C (70-75°F).

Propagation Detach offsets when growth is restarted in spring; pot them up individually in a peat-based compost.

Pests and diseases Trouble free.

CALAMONDIN ORANGE – see *Citrus*

Calathea

peacock plant

Calathea makoyana

☐ Height 15-75cm (6-30in)
☐ Temperature minimum 18°C (64°F)
☐ Filtered light
☐ Soil- or peat-based compost
☐ Foliage plant

The popular and widely available calatheas or peacock plants provide decorative foliage throughout the year, the beautiful leaves rivalling the attractions of many flowering plants.

The foliage varies widely in shape and size, and in colour from silvery green to dark green, patterned with different shades of green, the markings appearing on the undersides in shades of purple or maroon.

Popular species

Calathea bachemiana, up to 38cm (15in) high, has lance-shaped leaves up to 25cm (10in) long. The silvery green upper surface is edged with green and has a pattern of diagonal green patches on each side of the midrib; the patches are greenish purple beneath.

Calathea lancifolia, syn. *C. insignis* (rattlesnake plant), is up to 60cm (2ft) high, with wavy-edged, lance-shaped leaves up to 30cm (1ft) long. They are marked with diagonal dark green blotches on each side of the midrib on the upper surface, with maroon marks beneath.

Calathea lindeniana, up to 60cm (2ft) high, has oblong to oval leaves which are 15-30cm (6-12in) long. They are dark green on top with a feathery emerald-green pattern around the midrib; they are maroon with a darker pattern on the underside.

Calathea makoyana (cathedral windows), up to 60cm (2ft) high,

Calathea ornata

has oblong leaves about 15cm (6in) long. They are silvery green on top, edged with mid green, and the main veins are marked with oval irregular patches of dark green; the pattern is red or purple beneath.

Calathea ornata, up to 45cm (1½ft) high, has dark green, oblong to lance-shaped leaves about 20cm (8in) long. Young leaves have thin rose-pink stripes later fading to ivory. The undersides are dark purple.

Calathea picturata 'Argentea', up to 30cm (1ft) high, has oval leaves about 15cm (6in) long. They are silvery on top with a dark green margin and are maroon beneath.

Calathea zebrina (zebra plant), up to 75cm (2½ft) high, has narrow, oblong leaves about 15cm (6in) long. They are a soft emerald-green with darker green horizontal bands which are purple beneath.

Cultivation

Calatheas need good but filtered light, in normal room temperatures of 18-24°C (64-75°F). Maintain humidity, especially at high temperatures, by placing pots on moist pebbles and mist-spraying daily with tepid water. During active growth, keep the compost moist at all times and feed weekly. Keep just moist in winter.

Propagation Divide the rhizomatous roots in early to mid summer, potting them in a proprietary peat or soil-based compost.

Pests and diseases Trouble free.

Calceolaria
slipper flower

Calceolaria integrifolia

☐ Height 20-60cm (8-24in)
☐ Temperature minimum 7°C (45°F)
☐ Bright, filtered light
☐ Peat or soil-based compost
☐ Temporary flowering plants

Grown for their curious pouch-like blooms, slipper flowers provide a colourful display for a cool, light position. They are short-lived plants, usually discarded after the long flowering season, from late spring until autumn.

The profuse flower clusters come in a wide range of brilliant colours, and are often spotted or blotched with a contrasting colour. The leaves are mid green.

Popular species

Calceolaria x herbeohybrida, up to 45cm (1½ft) high, has hairy, roughly heart-shaped leaves. The flowers come in shades of red, orange, yellow or reddish brown, often spotted or blotched with a contrasting colour.

Calceolaria integrifolia (bush calceolaria) is a shrubby perennial up to 60cm (2ft) high, usually grown as an annual. It has finely wrinkled oblong to lance-shaped leaves and yellow flowers.

Cultivation

Set the potted plants on a bed of moist pebbles or peat substitute and keep in a cool position at temperatures preferably not above

Calceolaria x herbeohybrida

16°C (61°F). Bright light, but not direct sunlight, is best. Keep the potting compost thoroughly moist at all times. Discard when flowering ceases.

Propagation Sow seeds in late spring or early summer. Alternatively, grow *C. integrifolia* from stem cuttings in autumn.

Pests and diseases Aphids make plants sticky and sooty.

Callisia

Callisia

Callisia repens

☐ Trailing to 90cm (3ft)
☐ Temperature minimum 10°C (50°F)
☐ Bright light, some direct sunlight
☐ Soil- or peat-based compost
☐ Foliage plant

An ideal foliage plant for year-round display in hanging baskets, callisia is easy to care for and propagate. The species are closely related to tradescantias.

Popular species
Callisia elegans, syn. *Setcreasea striata*, has trailing stems up to 60cm (2ft) long. The pointed oval leaves clasp the stems. They are purple beneath and olive-green with white stripes on top.
Callisia fragrans trails its fleshy stems to 90cm (3ft); they are set with narrow glossy green to reddish-brown leaves up to 25cm (10in) long.
Callisia repens has trailing stems up to 60cm (2ft) long and glossy bright green leaves.

Cultivation
Callisias do best in bright light with three or four hours a day of direct sunlight in normal room temperatures of 18-24°C (64-75°F). During active growth, keep the compost thoroughly moist and feed fortnightly. Give a short winter rest at 10-16°C (50-61°F), keeping the compost just moist.
Propagation Take tip cuttings in spring or summer.
Pests and diseases Generally trouble free.

Campanula

Italian bellflower

Campanula isophylla

☐ Height 15cm (6in)
☐ Temperature minimum 4°C (40°F)
☐ Bright light
☐ Soil-based compost
☐ Flowering perennial

With its mass of starry blue flowers over a tangle of heart-shaped leaves, Italian bellflower (*Campanula isophylla*) makes a fine display in cool rooms. It flowers from summer to autumn.

Varieties of Italian bellflower include: 'Alba' (white flowers) and 'Mayi' (variegated slightly hairy leaves, larger blue flowers).

Cultivation
Keep bellflowers in bright light with some full sunlight, in cool temperatures. Maintain humidity by placing pots on moist pebbles and mist-spray regularly. Keep the compost thoroughly moist and feed fortnightly. Give a winter rest at maximum 7°C (45°F), with the compost kept barely moist.
Propagation Grow from seed. Or take tip cuttings in spring; alternatively, divide the roots.
Pests and diseases Grey mould, caused by too high humidity, appears as a fluffy grey fungus on leaves and stems.

CANDELABRA PLANT – see *Aloe*
CANDLE PLANT – see *Plectranthus and Senecio*
CAPE COWSLIP – see *Lachenalia*
CAPE GRAPE – see *Rhoicissus*
CAPE LEADWORT – see *Plumbago*
CAPE PRIMROSE – see *Streptocarpus*

Capsicum

ornamental pepper

Capsicum annuum

☐ Height 30-45cm (1-1½ft)
☐ Temperature minimum 13°C (55°F)
☐ Bright light
☐ Soil- or peat-based compost
☐ Temporary fruiting plant

Grown for its colourful fruits, ornamental pepper (*Capsicum annuum*) makes an interesting feature for winter display in cooler parts of the home.

This bushy annual has mid green oblong to lance-shaped leaves. The fruits, which follow small white flowers, may be upright or drooping. They all start off green, turning through creamy white to red or yellow. Different forms have globular, cone-shaped or cylindrical fruits.

Plants may be bought as they come into fruit in autumn, but they are easy to grow from seed. They are usually discarded when the fruits are past their best.

Cultivation
To maintain fruits in a good condition for as long as possible, keep plants in cool temperatures of 15-18°C (59-64°F) in bright light, with three to four hours a day direct sunlight. Keep the compost thoroughly moist and feed fortnightly. Maintain humidity by placing the pots on moist pebbles.
Propagation Sow seeds or buy new plants.
Pests and diseases Red spider mites stunt growth, causing leaf mottling and fine webbing.

CARDINAL FLOWER – see *Sinningia*
CARRION FLOWER – *see Stapelia*

Caryota
fishtail palm

Caryota urens

☐ Height up to 2.4m (8ft)
☐ Temperature minimum 13°C (55°F)
☐ Bright but filtered light
☐ Soil-based compost
☐ Palm

The popular fishtail palm – so called because its leaflets resemble tattered fishtails – is an elegant and slow-growing plant with year-round foliage interest.

Popular species
Caryota mitis, also known as Burmese, crested or tufted fishtail palm, is the most popular species. It eventually grows to 2.4m (8ft) high as a pot plant, though it can grow taller in a conservatory border. The arching leaf fronds are divided into closely packed groups of up to 30 ragged-edged light green leaflets, each measuring about 15cm (6in) long and 13cm (5in) wide. The leaflets are a lopsided, wedge shape. If the plant is grown in a large enough container, it may produce offshoots. *Caryota urens*, also known as sago, wine or jaggery palm, also grows 2.4m (8ft) high in a pot. The dark green leaflets are more triangular and less ragged than those of *C. mitis* and they are less closely grouped.

Cultivation
Fishtail palms thrive in full sunlight filtered through a translucent blind or curtain in warm temperatures over 13°C (55°F). In very warm rooms where the temperature exceeds 22°C (72°F), increase humidity by standing the pots on moist pebbles. Mist-spray frequently. Keep the compost thoroughly moist and feed monthly from spring to autumn.

Give a short winter rest at cool temperatures when growth appears to slow down – usually in autumn and/or winter. During this time allow the top of the compost to dry out before watering.

These palms prefer to have their roots constricted; use pots which seem one size too small; repot only every two or three years.

Propagation Grow from seed in spring. Alternatively, detach suckers or offsets from *C. mitis*.

Pests and diseases Red spider mites cause mottling of the foliage when the air is too dry.

CAST-IRON PLANT – see
Aspidistra

Catharanthus
Madagascar periwinkle

Catharanthus roseus

☐ Height 20-38cm (8-15in)
☐ Temperature minimum 10°C (50°F)
☐ Bright light
☐ Soil-based compost
☐ Flowering perennial

Madagascar periwinkle (*Catharanthus roseus*, syn. *Vinca rosea*) provides a bright display of rose-pink, tubular flowers from spring to autumn.

Also known as rose periwinkle or old maid, it has glossy mid green leaves which are oblong or oval. The flowers have a darker eye and measure up to 4cm (1½in) across. Dwarf varieties, growing about 20cm (8in) high, are sometimes available.

Although a true perennial, Madagascar periwinkle is usually grown as an annual and discarded after flowering has finished.

Cultivation
Madagascar periwinkle thrives in bright light, including three to four hours direct sunlight daily, in normal room temperatures over 15°C (59°F). Keep the compost moist and feed fortnightly.

Propagation Grow from seed sown in early spring or from tip cuttings taken in summer.

Pests and diseases Trouble free.

CATHEDRAL WINDOWS – see
Calathea

Cattleya

cattleya

Cattleya trianae

☐ Height up to 90cm (3ft)
☐ Temperature minimum 10°C (50°F)
☐ Bright, but filtered light
☐ Proprietary orchid compost
☐ Epiphytic orchid

Cattleya skinneri 'Alba'

Cattleya is an important genus of epiphytic orchids, with several species that are suitable for growing as house plants. They produce their large beautiful flowers in sunny sites.

Cattleyas have a single or two narrow, rather leathery leaves rising from each pseudobulb (a swollen stem). Single-leaved types rarely grow more than 30cm (1ft) high; they produce a single arching stem carrying large and full flowers. Double-leaved cattleyas grow taller and carry smaller but more profuse blooms. The flowers have a broad, tongue-shaped lip which is often frilled, and they come in shades of pink, purple, yellow and white.

Popular species

Cattleya aurantiaca, a double-leaved species up to 50cm (20in) high, bears clusters of orange-red flowers on short stalks in summer and autumn.

Cattleya bowringiana, another double-leaved species, grows up to 90cm (3ft) high. It produces sprays of up to 15 flowers in autumn, each about 7.5cm (3in) wide. They are light rose-purple with dark purple lips and yellow-white throats.

Cattleya forbesii 'Aurea', double-leaved and up to 45cm (1½ft) high, has greenish-yellow flowers with a white, frilled lip marked inside with yellow and orange speckles.

Cattleya intermedia, double-leaved and up to 45cm (1½ft) high, bears sprays of 13cm (5in) wide flowers in late spring to early summer. They are pale lilac-pink with a three-lobed lip blotched rose-purple.

Cattleya labiata, up to 38cm (15in) high, is single-leaved, with pink-mauve flowers up to 18cm (7in) across in autumn. The frilled lip has a purple blotch and yellow throat.

Cattleya skinneri, up to 38cm (15in) high and double-leaved, produces 7.5cm (3in) wide flowers from early spring to early summer. They are pale pink-purple with a darker lip and a white throat. 'Alba' has white flowers with a rose-purple throat.

Cattleya trianae, syn. *C. labiata trianae*, up to 45cm (1½ft) high and single-leaved, has pale pink flowers about 18cm (7in) across in winter. The lip is deep purple and the throat orange-yellow.

Cultivation

Cattleyas need bright light but not direct sunlight, and constant temperatures above 18°C (64°F) in summer. Place the pots on moist pebbles and mist-spray daily. Water well when the compost is dry and feed fortnightly.

After flowering, allow the plants to rest for six weeks in a cooler place with a minimum night temperature of 10°C (50°F); give less water.

Propagation Divide pseudobulbs as new growth starts; pot in orchid compost.

Pests and diseases Scale insects and aphids may cause yellow blotches and make the plants sticky and sooty. A physiological disorder disfigures leaves.

Celosia

celosia

Celosia argentea plumosa

☐ Height up to 60cm (2ft)
☐ Temperature minimum 16°C (61°F)
☐ Bright light
☐ Soil-based compost
☐ Flowering annual

Celosia is a colourful plant for a sunny window with its dense flower heads in brilliant shades of red, yellow and pink. The flowers are borne in summer and early autumn, and are shaped like plumes or cockscombs. The oval leaves are mid green and heavily veined.

Celosia argentea cristata

Celosias are easily grown annuals which are discarded after flowering.

Popular species
Celosia argentea cristata (cockscomb), up to 30cm (1ft) high, has flattened and crested cockscomb-like flower heads in shades of red, orange and yellow. *Celosia argentea plumosa* (Prince of Wales feathers), up to 60cm (2ft) high, has feathery flower plumes up to 15 cm (6in) high in shades of red, yellow and pink. Dwarf varieties are especially suitable as pot plants.

Cultivation
Celosias thrive in constant good light in normal room temperatures over 16°C (61°F). Keep the compost moist and feed fortnightly.
Propagation Grow from seed sown in late winter.
Pests and diseases Trouble free.

CENTURY PLANT – see *Agave*

Cephalocereus

old man cactus

Cephalocereus senilis

☐ Height up to 30cm (1ft)
☐ Temperature minimum 7-10°C (45-50°F)
☐ Bright light
☐ Cactus compost
☐ Non-flowering cactus

Old man cactus (*Cephalocereus senilis*) has a curious cylindrical plant body divided into numerous shallow ribs thickly covered with long silvery white hairs. They protect the plant from the desert sun in the wild, while concealing 4cm (1½in) long fierce spines. The plant originates from Mexico.

Old man cactus is slow-growing and unlikely to reach more than 30cm (1ft) in a pot. It never flowers indoors.

Cultivation
Old man cactus thrives in constant bright light and normal room temperatures over 16°C (61°F). Water moderately when the top half of the compost is dry.

In autumn and winter keep in a cooler position at temperatures of 7-18°C (45-64°F) and give only enough water to prevent the compost from drying out completely.

The cactus may be washed down with a mild detergent.
Propagation Grow from seed.
Pests and diseases Mealy bugs may infest the plant.

Cereus

cereus

Cereus forbesii

Cereus jamacaru

Ceropegia

rosary vine, hearts-on-a-string

Ceropegia woodii

☐ Height up to 90cm (3ft)
☐ Temperature minimum 10°C (50°F)
☐ Bright light
☐ Cactus compost
☐ Cactus

Cereus cacti are vigorous plants which make impressive features in the home with their tall, narrow cylindrical plant bodies.

The columnar stem, bluish green when young and later turning green, is divided into ribbed, wing-like sections. The ribs carry clusters of spines arranged in circles around the areoles (cushion-like pads). Mature specimens may produce funnel or trumpet-shaped blooms up to 30cm (1ft) long; they appear in summer and bloom at night.

The species described grow to a much greater height in a greenhouse border. They all come from South America.

Popular species
Cereus forbesii, up to 45cm (1½ft) high, has up to seven wing-like segments. The ribs on the wing edges have clusters of spines up to 12mm (½in) long. The flowers are green and purple-brown with white insides and measure about 25cm (10in) long.
Cereus jamacaru, up to 90cm (3ft) high, grows as a single blue-green column with five to eight ribs. These have clusters of eight yel-

low, 2.5cm (1in) long spines. The white, green-tinged flowers are 20-30cm (8-12in) long.
Cereus peruvianus (Peruvian apple cactus), up to 90cm (3ft) high, is similar to *C. jamacaru* but has thicker ribs and brown spines. The brown-green flowers are smaller. The variety 'Monstrosa' is up to 45cm (1½ft) high, with branched, contorted stems.

Cultivation
Cereus cacti need constant bright light and normal room temperatures over 16°C (61°F). Water moderately when the top half of the compost is dry and feed fortnightly.

A winter rest prevents poor, weak growth. When growth slows down in autumn move to a cooler position with a minimum night temperature of 5°C (41°F) and give only enough water to prevent the compost from drying out completely.
Propagation Grow from seed in mid spring. Alternatively, take stem sections in spring or summer. Leave to dry for a few days before potting up.

Repot annually in early spring.
Pests and diseases Mealy bugs cause conspicuous tufts of white waxy wool. Root mealy bugs may infest the root system.

☐ Height up to 90cm (3ft)
☐ Temperature minimum 10°C (50°F)
☐ Bright light
☐ Soil-based compost
☐ Foliage plant

Rosary vine (*Ceropegia woodii*) is grown for its small marbled, heart-shaped leaves borne in pairs on the trailing, thread-like purple stems.

The leaves are green and silver on top and purple beneath. Small, lantern-shaped, purple flowers sometimes appear in autumn. Tuberous growths on the stems can be used to propagate new plants.

Cultivation
Rosary vine likes bright light with at least three to four hours a day direct sunlight in normal room temperatures. During active growth water moderately when the top two-thirds of the compost are dry and feed plants monthly. In winter, give less water, resting the plants at 10°C (50F).
Propagation Take cuttings or detach and root tuberous growths.
Pests and diseases Mealy bugs may infest the leaves.

Chamaecereus

peanut cactus

Chamaecereus silvestrii

☐ Height 10cm (4in) or more
☐ Temperature minimum 7°C (45°F)
☐ Bright light
☐ Cactus compost
☐ Flowering cactus

The peanut cactus (*Chamaecereus silvestrii*) flowers at an early age, bearing large, bright scarlet blooms in summer. The flowers last only a day or two, but they are produced in succession over several weeks.

Growing 10cm (4in) or more high, the peanut cactus has numerous stems which in the young stages resemble peanut shells but which later lengthen and become cylindrical. They branch freely from the base and quickly creep over the pot rim. Each stem has six to nine ribs studded with short white spines.

Cultivation

Peanut cactus needs bright light throughout the year, and normal room temperatures during the growing season. It requires a cool winter rest to induce flowering; keep it at 7-13°C (45-55°F).

During active growth, water thoroughly when the top half of the compost feels dry, and feed once a month. In winter water just enough to prevent shrivelling. Repot carefully in spring – the branches are brittle and break easily.

Propagation Detach and root small stem cuttings, using a proprietary cactus compost.

Pests and diseases Red spider mites may attack in poorly lit sites.

Chamaedorea

chamaedorea

Chamaedorea elegans

☐ Height 90cm-2.4m (3-8ft)
☐ Temperature minimum 12°C (53°F)
☐ Bright, but filtered light
☐ Soil- or peat-based compost
☐ Palm

The genus *Chamaedorea* includes some of the most popular palms for growing indoors. They have large divided leaves rising from a bamboo-like stem or a short green trunk, and make graceful solitary specimen plants for sunny rooms.

Popular species

Chamaedorea elegans (parlour palm or good luck palm), up to 90cm (3ft) high, is slow-growing with a short green trunk and mid green, arching leaves. These are 45-60cm (1½-2ft) long and divided into up to 30 leaflets. The variety 'Bella' is more compact.

Chamaedorea erumpens (bamboo palm), up to 2.4m (8ft) high, forms clumps of green, bamboo-like stems carrying arching deep green leaves. These are up to 50cm (20in) long and divided into 20 leaflets which are narrowly oval in shape.

Chamaedorea graminifolia (reed palm), up to 1.2m (4ft) high, has cane-like stems topped with delicate looking lacy leaves. They are up to 90cm (3ft) long and divided into up to 30 narrow, dark bluish green leaflets.

Cultivation

Chamaedoreas thrive in bright filtered light in normal room temperatures of 16-24°C (61-75°F). Stand pots on moist pebbles to maintain humidity and mist-spray regularly. Keep the compost thoroughly moist during active growth and feed monthly. During the winter rest at 12°C (53°F), give only enough water barely to moisten the compost when the top two-thirds have dried out.

Propagation Impracticable.

Pests and diseases Red spider mites may infest leaves.

Chamaerops

European fan palm

Chamaerops humilis

- ☐ Height 60-90cm (2-3ft)
- ☐ Temperature minimum 10-13°C (50-55°F)
- ☐ Bright light
- ☐ Soil-based compost
- ☐ Palm

European fan palm (*Chamaerops humilis*) is an exotic, rather tree-like plant for cooler parts of the home or conservatory. Its huge stiff leaves are divided like fans and carried on stems up to 30cm (1ft) long; the thick, rough bark is marked with the scars of old leaf scales.

Cultivation

European fan palm thrives in bright light with three or four hours a day of direct sunlight, and in normal room temperatures. During active growth keep the compost thoroughly moist and feed fortnightly.

During the winter rest period, move the plant to a cooler position, at a temperature of about 13°C (55°F); water sparingly when the top of the compost is dry.

Propagation Grow from seed or detach and root suckers in a proprietary potting compost.

Pests and diseases Trouble free.

CHENILLE PLANT – see
Acalypha
CHILEAN BELLFLOWER – see
Lapageria
CHIN CACTUS – see
Gymnocalycium
CHINESE JADE – see *Crassula*
CHINESE LANTERN – see
Hibiscus

Chlorophytum

spider plant

Chlorophytum comosum 'Vittatum'

- ☐ Height 30cm (1ft)
- ☐ Temperature minimum 7°C (45°F)
- ☐ Bright light
- ☐ Soil-based compost
- ☐ Foliage plant

The graceful spider plant (*Chlorophytum comosum* 'Vittatum') with its long, narrow arching variegated leaves ensures a lush, year-round foliage display.

Remarkably easy to care for, it is at its best growing in hanging baskets on a west- or east-facing window-sill. When mature, spider plant produces long-stalked, pendent stems bearing clusters of baby plants which are easy to detach and root at any time during the growing season.

Cultivation

Spider plant thrives in room temperatures over 7°C (45°F) and requires bright light and some direct sunlight, but not midday sun. Water freely during active growth, sparingly in winter; feed fortnightly throughout the year.

Propagation Root plantlets.

Pests and diseases A physiological disorder or bruising causes the leaf tips to turn brown.

CHRISTMAS CACTUS – see
Schlumbergera
CHRISTMAS CHEER – see
Sedum
CHRISTMAS FERN – see
Polystichum

Chrysalidocarpus
yellow butterfly palm

Chrysalidocarpus lutescens

☐ Height up to 1.5m (5ft)
☐ Temperature minimum 13°C (55°F)
☐ Filtered light
☐ Soil-based compost
☐ Palm

Yellow butterfly palm (*Chrysalidocarpus lutescens*), also known as golden feather palm, makes a striking feature in a sunny room with its gracefully arching fronds.

The fronds, which are up to 1.2m (4ft) long, are borne on deeply furrowed, yellow-orange stalks and are divided into rather stiff glossy light green segments up to 60cm (2ft) long. Older stems resemble bamboo canes, with scars from former fronds.

Though this palm may eventually grow to 1.5m (5ft) it takes several years to reach this height.

Cultivation
Butterfly palm likes filtered sunlight in room temperatures over 13°C (55°F). Keep the compost thoroughly moist and feed actively growing plants fortnightly. If the temperature drops below 13°C (55°F), give only enough water to prevent the compost from drying out completely.

Propagation Detach and root suckers from the base of the plant. Alternatively, grow from seed.

Pests and diseases Red spider mites, mealy bugs, scale insects and whiteflies may infest the foliage.

Chrysanthemum
chrysanthemum

Chrysanthemum morifolium hybrid

☐ Height 30-45cm (1-1½ft)
☐ Temperature minimum 7°C (45°F)
☐ Bright light
☐ Peat or soil-based compost
☐ Temporary flowering plant

Ideal for cheering up a dull room with a splash of instant colour, chrysanthemums are popular plants for growing indoors and can be in flower at any time of the year. Chrysanthemums grown indoors produce a mass of flowers which may last for weeks in ideal conditions. They come in a range of autumnal shades of yellow, bronze, red and orange, but may also be pink, white, pale yellow or purplish.

Indoor chrysanthemums are temporary plants, discarded after flowering; although perennial, they cannot be induced to flower again indoors. Nurserymen use rigid control of light and hormone spray to keep the plants small and sturdy. When buying, choose plants with buds which are just beginning to open – tightly closed buds may fail to bloom.

Popular species
Chrysanthemum frutescens (marguerite), 30-45cm (1-1½ft) high, comes from the Canary Islands. It is a sub-shrubby perennial with pale green to grey-green leaves which are deeply divided and ferny. The white or pale yellow flowers have a single circle of petals around a central disc. They measure about 5cm (2in) across and generally appear from early spring to mid autumn, though the plant may bloom at other times.

Chrysanthemum morifolium, syn. *C. vestitum* (florist's chrysanthemums, pot mums), is a large group of hybrids which are generally up to 30cm (1ft) high and

51

Cissus

cissus

Cissus discolor

Chrysanthemum morifolium hybrid

Cissus antarctica

across. These sub-shrubby autumn- and winter-flowering perennials have deep green or greyish lobed leaves; they have been specially treated to bloom at any time of year. The flowers, measuring 2.5-7.5cm (1-3in) across, are single or double and come in shades of bronze, orange, yellow, red, pink, purple and cream or white. Charm types have single, more profuse and smaller flowers. Cascade types are similar but trailing.

Cultivation

To continue flowering for as long as possible, *C. frutescens* needs bright light with three to four hours daily direct sunlight. Florist's chrysanthemums prefer bright filtered light. Keep in cool to normal room temperatures, ideally around 13°C (55°F); at higher temperatures, increase humidity by standing pots on moist pebbles. Keep the compost thoroughly moist; feeding is unnecessary.

Propagation Buy new plants.

Pests and diseases Greenfly, whitefly, leaf miners, red spider mites and thrips may infest foliage and flower buds.

CIGAR FLOWER – see *Cuphea*
CINDERELLA SLIPPERS – see *Sinningea*
CINERARIA – see *Senecio*
CINNAMON CACTUS – see *Opuntia*

☐ Height 1.8-2.4m (6-8ft)
☐ Temperature minimum 13-18°C (55-64°F)
☐ Bright indirect light
☐ Soil-based compost
☐ Foliage climber or trailer

The genus *Cissus* provides several long-lived plants which provide excellent year-round foliage for training up poles or screens. They may also be allowed to trail from hanging baskets.

The leaves are generally a pointed oval shape or heart-shaped. They range in colour from deep glossy green to pale green; the beautiful *C. discolor* has a fine pattern of silver marbling.

Most species are easy to look after, tolerating a wide range of conditions, but *C. discolor* needs a little more care. The genus originates from tropical and sub-tropical parts of the world.

Popular species

Cissus antarctica (kangaroo vine), up to 1.8m (6ft) high, has shiny dark green, pointed oval leaves with sharply toothed edges. They measure about 10cm (4in) long.

Cissus discolor (rex-begonia vine), up to 1.8m (6ft) high, has pointed, heart-shaped leaves which are about 15cm (6in) long and wide. They are vivid green, marbled with white and purple on top, and are crimson beneath. The stems, too, are red.

Cissus striata (miniature grape

ivy), up to 90cm (3ft) high, is seen only occasionally. It has thin reddish stems clothed with glossy bronze-green leaves divided into five toothed leaflets.

Cultivation

Cissus prefers bright light but out of direct sunlight, in normal room temperatures of 18-24°C (64-75°F). However most species, except *C. discolor*, will tolerate poor light. Water moderately when the top half of the compost is dry and feed fortnightly from late spring to early autumn.

Move to a cooler position at temperatures of 13°C (55°F) in winter and water more sparingly. *C. discolor* needs a minimum winter temperature of 18°C (64°F) to prevent the foliage from dropping.

Propagation Take tip cuttings in spring.

Pests and diseases Red spider mites, aphids or mealy bugs may infest the leaves. A physiological disorder, due to too much sun or too high temperatures, causes wilting and brown patches on the foliage.

Citrus

orange, lemon

Citrus mitis, fruits

☐ Height up to 1.2m (4ft)
☐ Temperature minimum 10-13°C (50-55°F)
☐ Bright light
☐ Soil-based compost
☐ Flowering and fruiting shrub

The genus *Citrus* includes a range of delightful indoor shrubs with deliciously fragrant flowers and colourful fruits.

The glossy oval leaves are dark green, and the white flowers are borne singly or in small clusters. The fruits, which sometimes appear on plants only 30cm (1ft) high, start green, slowly ripening to yellow or orange. Flowers and developing fruits may appear at the same time.

Citrus plants are slow-growing indoors, reaching up to 1.2m (4ft) high. In the wild they develop into small trees. They are unlikely to produce edible fruit indoors.

Popular species

Citrus limon (lemon) bears white, red-flushed flowers in mid spring to early summer. They are followed later by dark green fruits which take many months to ripen to yellow. Varieties and hybrids which fruit when small include 'Meyeri' and 'Ponderosa' (American wonder lemon, spiny stems, orange-yellow fruit up to 13cm/5in long).

Citrus mitis, syn. *C. microcarpa* (calamondin orange), produces fruit when it is still very small. The clusters of white flowers

Citrus sinensis, flowers

appear at any time and fruits are freely produced throughout the year on even young plants. They are round, up to 4cm (1½in) across, and ripen to bright orange. *Citrus sinensis* (sweet orange) is spiny with white flowers up to 5cm (2in) across. They appear in mid spring to early summer and are followed by smooth orange fruits over 5cm (2in) across. This species produces edible fruit.

Cultivation

Citrus trees thrive in bright light, with several hours of direct sun daily, in normal room temperatures. Mist-spray daily in warm weather and stand pots on moist pebbles; water moderately when the top of the compost is dry. Feed fortnightly.

The plants enjoy a well-ventilated position but should be protected from draughts. Move them outside on sunny summer days. Pinch out new growing tips to control shape and size.

During the winter rest period, move to a cooler position with a minimum temperature of 10°C (50°F) and give only enough water to prevent the compost from drying out.

Propagation Take cuttings in summer or grow from the seed.

Pests and diseases Mealy bugs cause conspicuous tufts of white waxy wool on leaves and stems. Scale insects may infest the undersides of the leaves.

CLAW CACTUS – see
Schlumbergera

Cleistocactus

silver torch cactus

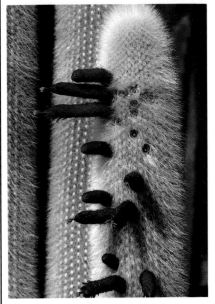

Cleistocactus strausii

☐ Height 1m (3ft) or more
☐ Temperature minimum 10°C (50°F)
☐ Bright light
☐ Cactus compost
☐ Cactus

Silver torch cactus (*Cleistocactus strausii*) is an eye-catching plant with tall, upright, narrow cylindrical stems.

Each stem is up to 1m (3ft) or more high and just 7.5cm (3in) across. Plants generally branch from the base. The stems are light green and densely covered with bristly white spines, giving the plant a silvery appearance. Mature plants may produce red tubular flowers in summer; they never open fully.

Cultivation

Silver torch cactus needs bright light, preferably full sun, and temperatures of 16-24°C (61-75°F). Turn the pot regularly to prevent the stems bending towards the light. Water moderately when the top of the compost is dry and feed fortnightly during active growth. In winter move to a cooler position with a minimum temperature of 10°C (50°F) and give only enough water to prevent the compost from drying out completely.

Propagation Grow from seed in early spring or take stem cuttings in summer.

Pests and diseases Trouble free.

Clerodendrum

clerodendrum

Clerodendrum thomsoniae

☐ Height up to 3m (10ft)
☐ Temperature minimum 10-13°C (50-55°F)
☐ Bright but filtered light
☐ Soil-based compost
☐ Climbing shrub

Clerodendrum is a vigorous shrub with lush green foliage and profuse, long-lasting flowers. Trained to canes it can twine to a height of 3m (10ft), but it can be kept lower by having the growing tips regularly pinched out.

Clerodendrum thomsoniae (bleeding heart vine, glory bower) is the most commonly grown species. Its oval, pointed leaves are deep green and glossy. The flowers appear in drooping sprays, up to 15cm (6in) long, from early summer to autumn. Each consists of five scarlet petals with long stamens backed by a pure white lantern-shaped calyx.

Cultivation
Clerodendrum likes bright filtered light and normal room temperatures. Maintain a humid atmosphere by placing the pot on moist pebbles and mist-spraying daily. Keep the compost thoroughly moist and feed fortnightly. During the winter rest, move to a cooler position around 13°C (55°F) and give enough water to stop the compost drying out.

Cut lateral shoots back by half or two-thirds in spring.
Propagation Grow from seed or take cuttings in spring.
Pests and diseases Trouble free.

CLIFFBRAKE FERN – see
Pellaea
CLIMBING ONION – see *Bowiea*

Clivia

Kaffir lily

Clivia miniata

☐ Height 45cm (1½ft)
☐ Temperature minimum 10°C (50°F)
☐ Bright light
☐ Soil-based compost
☐ Flowering perennial

Kaffir lily (*Clivia miniata*) is a stunning centrepiece with its circular heads of flame-coloured, bell-shaped flowers on upright stems. The dark green, glossy, strap-shaped leaves fan out around the stem, enhancing the floral display, which starts in early spring.

Cultivation
Kaffir lily thrives in bright light, out of direct sunlight at midday which may scorch the leaves. In summer maintain temperatures at 16-24°C (61-75°F) and keep the compost moist. In late autumn to early winter, rest the plant at temperatures of 10-13°C (50-55°F), keeping the compost just moist. When flower buds show in late winter, gradually raise the temperature to around 16°C (61°F) and increase the amount of water; feed fortnightly. Kaffir lilies flower best when pot-bound; repot only when roots appear on top of the compost.
Propagation Remove and pot up offsets from the brittle fleshy roots.
Pests and diseases Mealy bugs show as tufts of white waxy wool.

COCONUT PALM – see
Microcoelum

Codiaeum

croton, Joseph's coat

Codiaeum variegatum pictum

☐ Height up to 1m (3ft)
☐ Temperature minimum 13°C (55°F)
☐ Bright filtered light
☐ Soil-based compost
☐ Foliage plant

Grown for their superb range of foliage colour, markings and varying leaf shapes, crotons are popular house plants providing ornament throughout the year.

The only common species is *Codiaeum variegatum* and its variety *pictum* from which numerous hybrids have been bred. These shrubby plants have short-stalked, glossy, leathery leaves. They may be strap-shaped, lance-shaped, oval or deeply three-lobed. Other types have leaves which are twisted or have wavy edges. Leaf markings range from speckles and blotches to large patches of colour, while many forms have coloured veins.

Young leaves are lime green when they open and turn dark green before developing their more decorative markings. This can take up to two years.

Croton, also known as Joseph's coat, comes from Malaysia and Polynesia. It can be tricky to care for but is well worth the extra effort. Make sure it gets plenty of bright filtered light to encourage good leaf colouring.

The hybrids include 'Aucubifolium' which has glossy green, yellow-mottled leaves of a pointed oval shape. It resembles the outdoor spotted laurel (*Aucuba japonica* 'Maculata').

Coelogyne cristata

Coelogyne
coelogyne

☐ Height 15-30cm (6-12in)
☐ Temperature minimum 10-13°C (50-55°F)
☐ Bright but filtered light
☐ Orchid compost
☐ Epiphytic orchid

Coelogynes are excellent orchids to grow indoors, producing long-lasting sprays or spikes of large, often fragrant flowers.

The plants have rounded to flask-shaped pseudobulbs (swollen stems) from which grow two lance-shaped to oval leaves. The flowers range from green to yellowish brown to white and have prominent lips, usually marked with contrasting colours.

Because of their pendulous habit, these orchids are most effective when grown in specially designed orchid baskets or wired to slabs of bark or tree fern.

Popular species
Coelogyne cristata, up to 30cm (1ft) high, has glossy dark green, lance-shaped leaves up to 30cm (1ft) long. Drooping or arching spikes, 15-30cm (6-12in) long, carry up to seven pure white fragrant flowers measuring up to 10cm (4in) across. The lips are marked with orange to yellow at the centre. The species flowers in winter and spring.

Coelogyne massangeana, up to 30cm (1ft) high, has strongly veined, lance-shaped mid green leaves up to 45cm (1½ft) long. The pendent flower stems are up to 60cm (2ft) long and bear sprays of up to 20 flowers in spring and summer. They measure about

---

Codiaeum variegatum pictum

Cultivation
Crotons need a well-ventilated position in bright filtered light and constant temperatures of 18-21°C (64-70°F). Maintain humidity by standing pots on moist pebbles and mist-spraying occasionally. During active growth keep the compost thoroughly moist and feed fortnightly from early spring to autumn. During the winter rest, give only enough water to prevent the compost from drying out.

To control size and maintain a bushy form, cut back in early spring. Crotons produce a white sap when cut.

Propagation Take tip cuttings in early spring.

Pests and diseases Red spider mites may infest the foliage.

Codiaeum variegatum pictum

Coelogyne pandurata

Coffea
coffee plant

Coffea arabica

Coleus
flame nettle

Coleus blumei

5cm (2in) across and are pale yellow-buff; the lip is sepia-brown with yellow and white markings. *Coelogyne pandurata* (black orchid), up to 30cm (1ft) high, has glossy, narrow lance-shaped leaves up to 45cm (1½ft) long and bears arching sprays of bright pale green fragrant flowers up to 10cm (4in) across in summer and autumn. The lip is heavily marked with velvety black.

Coelogyne speciosa, up to 15cm (6in) high, has oblong to lance-shaped, glossy leaves up to 25cm (10in) long. The flower spikes bear two or three flowers up to 7.5cm (3in) wide. They are musk-scented and range in colour from buff green to pale salmon-pink. The frilled lips are marked with white, yellow and red-brown. The flowers appear at any time from spring to autumn.

Cultivation
Coelogynes need bright filtered light and temperatures of 18-24°C (64-75°F). Maintain a moist atmosphere by mist-spraying regularly. Keep the compost thoroughly moist during active growth and give an occasional foliar feed.

From late autumn to early spring give only enough water to prevent the compost from drying out. Rest the plants at temperatures of 10-16°C (50-61°F).

Propagation Divide and repot crowded plants in spring.

Pests and diseases Trouble free.

☐ Height up to 1.2m (4ft)
☐ Temperature minimum 13°C (55°F)
☐ Bright but filtered light
☐ Soil-based compost
☐ Foliage plant

Coffee plant (*Coffea arabica*) is commercially grown in coffee plantations, but it also makes a decorative house plant with its gleaming dark green leaves. They are heavily veined, roughly oval in shape and measure 5-15cm (2-6in) long. Mature specimens produce clusters of tiny white starry and fragrant flowers in summer. The blooms are sometimes followed by 12mm (½in) long berry-like fruits which turn from green through red to black.

'Nana' is a dwarf form ideal for growing indoors.

Cultivation
Coffee plants likes bright light but not direct sunlight and normal room temperatures. Maintain humidity by placing the pot on moist pebbles and mist-spraying at least twice a week. Keep the compost thoroughly moist during active growth and feed fortnightly.

During the winter rest give only enough water to prevent the compost from drying out. Keep at a minimum temperature of 13°C (55°F).

Propagation Grow from fresh seed in spring or take tip cuttings which are often difficult to root.

Pests and diseases Mealy bugs and scale insects may infest the leaves.

☐ Height 60-90cm (2-3ft)
☐ Temperature minimum 13°C (55°F)
☐ Bright light
☐ Soil-based compost
☐ Foliage plant

Flame nettle (*Coleus blumei*) is an easy-to-grow, decorative plant providing colourful foliage for the home throughout the year. It comes from Java.

The typical flame nettle leaf is pointed, coarsely toothed and oval with brightly coloured markings. But leaf shape varies from more rounded heart shapes to narrow lance shapes, while some varieties have deeply lobed foliage. Leaves generally have two or more colours in shades of light to dark green, red, pink, brown, orange, yellow and white.

Flame nettle bears spike-like clusters of blue or white, two-lipped flowers. They have little ornamental value and should be pinched out before they develop to

Coleus blumei, mixed seed strain

Coleus blumei 'Brilliancy'

encourage strong, bushy leaf growth.

Although coleus is a perennial, it is usually treated as an annual, grown from seed or cuttings in spring and discarded in autumn. By this stage plants usually look leggy and have lost leaves from around the base. They are difficult to overwinter.

Popular varieties

'Brilliancy' has bright red leaves edged yellow.

'Candidus' has pale green wavy-edged leaves with a white centre.

'Carefree' has green-edged lobed leaves, which are dark red, brownish pink and yellowish.

'Green Pennant' has cream-white leaves edged with bright green. The central vein is deep carmine.

'Sabre' has lance-shaped red, green and yellow leaves.

'Sunset' has pale green leaves with a pink patch at the centre.

Cultivation

Flame nettles thrive in bright light, including three to four hours a day direct sun, and prefer temperatures of 15-27°C (59-80°F). Maintain humidity, parti-

Coleus blumei 'Green Pennant'

cularly in warm rooms, by standing the pots on moist pebbles. Mist-spray regularly. During active growth keep the compost thoroughly moist and feed fortnightly.

Pinch out growing tips and flowering shoots regularly to maintain a bushy shape.

During any winter rest, maintain a minimum temperature of

13°C (55°F) and keep the compost just moist.

Propagation Grow from seed or take cuttings. Named and mixed seed selections are available.

Pests and diseases Mealy bugs form white waxy wool on stems and leaves.

Columnea

columnea, goldfish plant

Columnea gloriosa 'Purpurea'

Columnea microphylla

☐ Trails 45cm-1.8m (1½-6ft)
☐ Temperature minimum 13°C (55°F)
☐ Bright, but filtered light
☐ Peat-based compost
☐ Flowering plant

Columneas are spectacular plants from the steamy jungles of tropical America, where they trail in colourful streamers from the branches of trees. The showy, brilliantly coloured flowers are long-lasting and several species make highly decorative specimens for hanging baskets. Others are upright, with branching or arching stems equally profuse in bloom.

The fleshy, short-stalked leaves are generally mid to dark green and lance-shaped to oval or rounded. They measure up to 9cm (3½in) long and grow in opposite pairs. In most species each pair has one leaf which is larger than the other.

The flowers consist of a long tube flaring out into several lobes. The top lobe is bigger than the others and resembles a hood. Flowers come in bright shades of scarlet to orange and measure 5-9cm (2-3½in) long.

Popular species

Columnea x *banksii* has trailing stems up to 90cm (3ft) long. The fleshy, glossy leaves are dark green and the orange-red flowers have orange-marked throats. They measure 6-7.5cm (2½-3in) long and appear in winter and spring. White, violet-tinged berries may follow the flowers.

Columnea gloriosa has slender trailing stems 60cm-1.2m (2-4ft) long. The mid to dark green leaves are covered with reddish hairs and measure up to 3cm (1¼in) long. Profuse, bright scarlet flowers with orange marks on their throats appear from autumn to spring. They measure up to 7.5cm (3in) long. 'Purpurea' has deep purple-flushed leaves.

Columnea linearis is a shrubby, upright plant up to 45cm (1½ft) high. The narrow, lance-shaped leaves are deep glossy green and measure up to 9cm (3½in) long. In spring it bears profuse rose-pink flowers. They are covered with silky white hairs and are up to 4.5cm (1¾in) long with green calyces.

Columnea microphylla has slender trailing stems up to 1.8m (6ft) long. The oval to rounded leaves are light green and covered with purplish hairs. They are much smaller than the leaves of other species, generally measuring less than 12mm (½in) long. The profuse, bright orange-scarlet flowers are 5-7.5cm (2-3in) long and appear in spring.

Cultivation

Columneas need bright light but not direct sunlight. They tolerate normal room temperatures throughout the year. However, keep winter- and spring-flowering species at 13-16°C (55-61°F) in winter to encourage flowering.

Keep the compost moist and feed fortnightly. Columneas do not need a winter rest. Maintain a humid atmosphere by placing pots on moist pebbles.

Propagation Grow from seed in late winter to early spring or take tip cuttings in mid spring.

Pests and diseases Generally trouble free.

Conophytum

conophytum

Conophytum muscosipapillatum

☐ Height up to 7.5cm (3in)
☐ Temperature minimum 7°C (45°F)
☐ Bright light
☐ Cactus compost
☐ Flowering succulent

Conophytums are curious plants resembling smooth green pebbles, almost concealed in autumn beneath a sheet of narrow-petalled daisy-like flowers. They come from South and South-West Africa, where they resemble the stones among which they grow.

The plant bodies consist of two fleshy stemless leaves which are fused together. Some look like bunches of grapes, others are two-lobed and some are speckled or marbled. The flowers, and a new pair of leaves, emerge from a slit at the top, or between the lobes, and measure up to 5cm (2in) across. They come in shades of yellow, pink, purple and cream or white.

Popular species
Conophytum mundum, up to 4cm (1½in) high, has spherical dull green plant bodies studded with darker green dots. The flowers are yellow.
Conophytum muscosipapillatum is up to 7.5cm (3in) high. The grey-green plant bodies are covered with white down. They have flattened lobes which measure up to 4cm (1½in) high. The yellow

flowers are up to 6cm (2¼in) across.
Conophytum notabile is up to 5cm (2in) high. The grey-green plant bodies have two lobes and 2.5cm (1in) wide pinkish-red flowers that appear from mid spring to early summer.

Cultivation
Conophytums thrive in plenty of bright, direct sun in ordinary room temperatures. During active growth water moderately when the soil is dry and feed fortnightly. The winter rest extends from early winter to early summer when the bodies divide and shrivel. Keep them at a minimum temperature of 7°C (45°F) and give one good watering in early spring. *C. notabile* rests from late summer to mid spring.
Propagation Grow from seed in late spring. Alternatively, divide overcrowded clumps in summer.
Pests and diseases Mealy bugs show as tufts of white waxy wool. Root mealy bugs infest the roots and check growth. A physiological disorder due to over-watering may cause rotting.

COPPERLEAF – see *Acalypha*
CORALBERRY – see *Ardisia*

Cordyline

cordyline

Cordyline terminalis 'Atom'

☐ Height 90cm-1.2m (3-4ft)
☐ Temperature minimum 10°C (50°F)
☐ Bright or filtered light
☐ Soil-based compost
☐ Foliage plant

Cordylines are graceful palm-like shrubs grown for their handsome long narrow leaves.

They eventually become tree-like as lower leaves fall away, leaving a stem marked with scars of old leaf bases and topped with a dense cluster of tough leaves. They come in shades of grey-green to mid green with named varieties offering colourful striped foliage.

In summer *C. australis* and *C. indivisa* benefit from a spell outdoors. The species described come from New Zealand and tropical Asia. Some are similar to members of the genus *Dracaena*, particularly *C. indivisa*, which is commonly known as the blue dracaena. The sprays of white flowers are rarely produced on plants grown indoors.

Popular species
Cordyline australis (cabbage palm) is a slow-growing species up to 90cm (3ft) high. It has a dense, arching cluster of narrow lance-shaped to strap-shaped, grey-green leaves. They are up to 90cm (3ft) long and 5cm (2in) wide. Varieties include 'Purpurea' (purple-flushed leaves) and 'Rubra' (red-flushed leaves).
Cordyline indivisa (blue dracaena), up to 1.2m (4ft) high, has narrow lance-shaped leaves with a long point. They are mid green

Cordyline terminalis 'Red Edge'

Cotyledon
cotyledon

Cotyledon undulata

☐ Height up to 60cm (2ft)
☐ Temperature minimum 10°C (50°F)
☐ Bright light
☐ Cactus compost
☐ Succulent

Cotyledons are fascinating plants grown for their fleshy, sometimes frilly-edged leaves in pale shades of grey or grey-green. In summer mature plants bear clusters of drooping, long-stalked tubular flowers in shades of orange, yellow and red.

These plants originate from South Africa and tolerate the dry air of centrally heated rooms.

Popular species
Cotyledon orbiculata (pig's ears), up to 50cm (20in) high, has branching stems and fleshy, round, grey-green leaves with thin red edges. Clusters of yellow and red tubular flowers appear in summer.
Cotyledon undulata (silver ruffles), up to 60cm (2ft) high, has fleshy, white-grey leaves with prominent wavy edges. They measure up to 10cm (4in) long and have a white floury covering, particularly when young. Orange-yellow tubular flowers appear in summer.

Cultivation
Cotyledons need bright light and normal room temperatures. Water moderately when the top of the compost is dry; feed fortnightly. During the winter rest move to a cooler position with a minimum temperature of 10°C (50°F) and water sparingly.
Propagation Take tip cuttings in spring and early summer.
Pests and diseases Mealy bugs show as tufts of white waxy wool.

with red or yellow midribs and up to 1.2m (4ft) long.
Cordyline terminalis (goodluck plant, Ti tree), the most tender species, is up to 90cm (3ft) high. The lance-shaped, pointed, mid to deep green leaves have 15cm (6in) long stems and are red-flushed when young. A number of varieties are available with leaves variegated in shades of green, pink, red, purple and cream and white. They include 'Atom' with red-streaked leaves and 'Red Edge' with leaves edged with red.

Cultivation
C. australis and *C. indivisa* need bright light, including full sun, while *C. terminalis* prefers bright light out of direct sun. During active growth, ordinary room temperatures suit *C. terminalis*; the other species benefit from a spell outdoors in summer. Keep the compost thoroughly moist and feed once a fortnight.

During the winter rest, give only enough water to prevent the compost from drying out. Move *C. australis* and *C. indivisa* to a cooler place with a minimum temperature of 10°C (50°F).
Propagation Grow from seed in spring or detach suckers in late spring. Alternatively, take stem cuttings in late spring.
Pests and diseases Leaf spot shows as brown, purple-edged spots which are scattered with pinhead-sized black dots.

CORN PALM – see *Dracaena*

Crassula
crassula

Crassula arborescens 'Hummel's Sunset'

Crassula portulacea

☐ Height 10-90cm (4-36in)
☐ Temperature minimum 7°C (45°F)
☐ Bright light
☐ Cactus compost
☐ Succulent

Crassula is a diverse genus of plants, some upright and tree-like and some creeping, while others form mini-shrubs. All species have fleshy leaves which the plants use to store water. Chiefly grown as house plants for their succulent foliage, some species also flower spectacularly when mature.

Popular species
Crassula arborescens, syn. *Cotyledon arborescens* (Chinese jade), up to 90cm (3ft) high, is a shrub-

Crassula lycopodioides

by plant with rounded grey-green, red-edged leaves measuring about 5cm (2in) across. Mature plants may produce pinkish white flowers. 'Hummel's Sunset' has leaves with pinkish margins.
Crassula falcata, syn. *Rochea falcata* (airplane propeller plant), up to 60cm (2ft) high, has a fleshy stem and numerous blue-green leaves resembling aeroplane propellers. Profuse orange-red flowers appear in summer.
Crassula lycopodioides (rat-tail plant), up to 30cm (1ft) high, has tiny overlapping bright green leaves which densely clothe the stems. Minute yellow flowers appear in summer.
Crassula portulacea, syn. *C. argentea* (jade plant), up to 90cm (3ft) high, is a tree-like plant with a woody stem and bright green leaves which are roughly spoon-shaped and sometimes tinged red. Starry white flowers appear in spring.
Crassula rupestris (buttons-on-a-string, bead vine, rosary vine) is a creeping plant up to 10cm (4in) high. The round, thick, stalkless leaves are grey-green with red-brown edges. They grow in pairs

and look as though the stems pass straight through them. Yellowish flowers appear in spring and early summer.

Cultivation
Crassulas thrive in bright light with plenty of direct sunlight and temperatures over 16°C (61°F). During active growth water well when the compost is dry and feed fortnightly.

During the winter rest, move to a cooler position with temperatures as low as 7°C (45°F) and not exceeding 13°C (55°F); give only enough water to prevent the compost from drying out completely.
Propagation Root stem or leaf cuttings in spring or summer. Alternatively, grow from seed in spring. Plants may also be divided and repotted.
Pests and diseases Poor drainage or over-watering may cause plants to rot.

CREEPING CHARLEY – see *Pilea*
CREEPING FIG – see *Ficus*
CRETAN BRAKE – see *Pteris*
CROTON – see *Codiaeum*
CROWN CACTUS – see *Rebutia*
CROWN OF THORNS – see *Euphorbia*

Cryptanthus
earth star, starfish plant

Cryptanthus fosterianus

- ☐ Height 7.5-30cm (3-12in)
- ☐ Temperature minimum 18°C (64°F)
- ☐ Bright light
- ☐ Bromeliad compost
- ☐ Bromeliad

Earth stars form low-growing rosettes of tough leaves, often striped or cross-banded in attractive colours. These terrestrial bromeliads grow wild in rock fissures and on mossy tree roots. A collection of several different types can be wired to a tree branch.

Popular species
Cryptanthus acaulis, up to 7.5cm (3in) high, has a rosette of leaves which are mid green on top and covered with white scales beneath. *Cryptanthus bivittatus* forms a 7.5cm (3in) high rosette of narrow, toothed and undulating leaves. They are coloured greenish-brown, with two pink or red lengthways stripes.
Cryptanthus bromelioides, up to 30cm (1ft) high, has strap-shaped, finely toothed, wavy-edged leaves which are mid green. 'Tricolor' has lengthways cream, rose and green stripes.
Cryptanthus fosterianus, up to 7.5cm (3in) high, has wavy-edged, coppery green leaves with grey or buff cross bands.
Cryptanthus zonatus, up to 10cm (4in) high, is similar to *C. fosterianus* but with thinner green leaves cross banded with grey or buff. 'Zebvrinus' has bold silvery cross bands.

Cultivation
Earth stars need bright light, temperatures above 18°C (64°F) and high humidity. Place pots on moist pebbles. During active growth, give just enough water to moisten the compost slightly when it feels dry and give a weak liquid feed occasionally.
Propagation Detach and root offsets in spring.
Pests and diseases Trouble free.

Cryptanthus bromelioides 'Tricolor'

Ctenanthe
ctenanthe

Ctenanthe oppenheimiana 'Tricolor'

☐ Height 60-75cm (2-2½ft)
☐ Temperature minimum 13°C (55°F)
☐ Bright, filtered light
☐ Soil-based compost
☐ Foliage plant

Ctenanthes are grown for their boldly marked, handsome leaves often confused with two closely related genera, *Calathea* and *Maranta*. The species described come from Brazil.

Popular species
Ctenanthe lubbersiana is a robust and fast-growing species up to 75cm (2½ft) high. The oblong leaves have short pointed tips and are up to 20cm (8in) long. They are light to mid green with yellowish patches on top and pale green beneath.
Ctenanthe oppenheimiana, up to 75cm (2½ft) high, has lance-shaped leathery leaves measuring up to 30cm (1ft) long. The variety 'Tricolor' (never-never plant) is more popular than the species. It has dark green leaves with irregular blotches of creamy yellow covering one-third of the upper surface. The undersurface of the leaf is deep red, giving the whole leaf a reddish glow.

Ctenanthe setosa, up to 75cm (2½ft) high, has 45cm (1½ft) long, pointed-tipped leaves with downy purple stalks. They are pale green with dark green veins, picked out only on the upper surface.

Cultivation
Ctenanthes need bright light filtered through a translucent blind or curtain, at normal room temperatures. During active growth moisten the compost thoroughly when the top 12mm (½in) is dry and feed fortnightly. Good humidity is essential; stand pots on moist pebbles, and mist-spray frequently with tepid water.
During the winter rest, move to a cooler position with a minimum temperature of 13°C (55°F) and give only enough water to prevent the compost from completely drying out.
Propagation Take stem cuttings in spring. Alternatively, detach offsets from the parent plants and pot in a proprietary compost.
Pests and diseases Trouble free.

Cuphea
cuphea

Cuphea ignea

☐ Height 30-60cm (1-2ft)
☐ Temperature minimum 10°C (50°F)
☐ Bright light
☐ Soil-based compost
☐ Flowering shrub

Cuphea is a bushy plant prized for its colourful, tubular flowers produced almost continuously from spring until early autumn. It comes from tropical parts of the Americas.

Popular species
Cuphea hyssopifolia (false heather), up to 60cm (2ft) high, has wiry stems and narrow leathery leaves. Sprays of flowers with red and yellow tubes and tiny violet-blue petals appear in summer.
Cuphea ignea (cigar flower), up to 30cm (1ft) high, has mid green lance-shaped leaves. The flowers, which appear singly from spring to autumn, have red tubes tipped with white and black.

Cultivation
Cupheas need bright light and ordinary room temperatures. Maintain a humid atmosphere by placing the pots on moist pebbles. During active growth, water moderately when the compost is dry on top and feed fortnightly. During the winter rest keep at a temperature of 10-13°C (50-55°F) and water sparingly.
Propagation Take tip cuttings in spring or sow seeds in mid to late winter.
Pests and diseases Trouble free.

CURLY PALM – see *Howeia*

Cyanotis

cyanotis

Cyanotis somaliensis

☐ Trails up to 60cm (2ft)
☐ Temperature minimum 18°C (64°F)
☐ Bright light
☐ Soil-based or cactus compost
☐ Foliage plant

Cyanotis is an ideal plant for a hanging basket, with its trailing stems densely covered with oval to lance-shaped, fleshy leaves.

The three-petalled violet or blue flowers are rarely produced on plants grown indoors.

Popular species
Cyanotis kewensis (teddy-bear plant/vine) has short creeping stems covered with fine gingery brown hairs and 2.5cm (1in) long overlapping fleshy oval leaves. They are green on top and purple beneath.
Cyanotis somaliensis (pussy ears) has 5cm (2in) long, shiny green lance-shaped leaves edged with soft white hairs.

Cultivation
Cyanotis need bright light, including some direct sun and ordinary room temperatures throughout the year. To maintain humidity, keep the pots on trays of moist pebbles or in a saucer of water within the hanging basket. Alternatively, mist-spray regularly. Thoroughly moisten the compost when the top is dry and feed monthly. Do not wet the leaves when watering as this can cause unsightly marks.

The species listed do not need a winter rest.
Propagation Take tip cuttings in spring.
Pests and diseases Trouble free.

Cycas

sago palm

Cycas revoluta

☐ Height 90cm-1.2m (3-4ft)
☐ Temperature minimum 13°C (55°F)
☐ Bright light
☐ Soil-based compost
☐ Foliage plant

Sago palm (*Cycas revoluta*) is a handsome and arresting specimen plant with its long fronds arching from a pineapple-like base. Though palm-like it is not a true palm, but belongs to an ancient group of plants called cycads, which are among the most primitive of flowering plants.

The arching, dark green, deeply cut leaves look feathery but are quite stiff and hard. They grow in a rosette and measure up to 90cm (3ft) long. They are borne on 7.5-10cm (3-4in) stalks and divided into numerous needle-like leaflets arranged in a chevron pattern. The leaflets measure up to 15cm (6in) long. The base, which sits above the compost, has a rust-coloured felted covering and contains a reserve of water which the plant uses in droughts.

Sago palm is extremely slow-growing and often produces no more than one new leaf a year. It does not flower indoors.

Cultivation
To produce even one new leaf a year, sago palm needs bright light throughout the year, with or without direct sunlight. Do not attempt to grow in medium or poor light. It prefers warm room temperatures and good humidity, but tolerates temperatures as low as 13°C (55°F), as well as low humidity. During the active growth period, which lasts most of the year, give enough water to moisten the compost thoroughly when the top 12mm (½in) is dry. During any rest period that may occur – possibly because of inadequate winter light and low temperature – give only enough water to prevent the compost from drying out completely.
Propagation Sago palm is propagated commercially from seeds. They take a long time to germinate and it is easier to buy new plants.
Pests and diseases Mealy bugs and scale insects infest leaves and stems. A physiological disorder, due to underwatering or low temperatures, may cause browning of the foliage.

Cyclamen

cyclamen

Cyclamen 'Scarlet Aries'

☐ Height 15-23cm (6-9in)
☐ Temperature 13-18°C (55-64°F)
☐ Bright, filtered light
☐ Soil-based compost
☐ Flowering perennial

Cyclamen is one of the most popular house plants, providing beautiful flowers and attractive foliage. Most indoor types are derived from one species, *Cyclamen persicum*, which has numerous varieties offering a wide range of flower colour and leaf patterns.

The blooms appear from early autumn until early spring. They are carried on slender stems up to 23cm (9in) high above a mat of oval to roughly heart-shaped leaves which are dark green, variably patterned with silver.

The flowers, which are sometimes scented, especially in the miniature types, have sharply reflexed petals forming a shuttlecock shape. In the species they measure 2-4cm (1-1½in) long, but many varieties have petals up to 6cm (2½in) long. The petals are sometimes frilled and ruffled and pink, mauve, purple and red or white in colour. Some varieties are bicoloured.

Popular hybrids

'Aries' strain offers a range of bold colours, including scarlet.

Cyclamen 'Sierra White'

Cyclamen 'Fimbriata Salmon-Pink'

'Fimbriata' cyclamens have frilled and ruffled petals in a variety of colours, including salmon-pink.
'Sierra' cyclamens are pale-coloured, with the base of the petals stained a darker colour.

Cultivation

Cyclamens need bright light but out of direct sun in a cool position with temperatures of 13-18°C (55-64°F). They dislike the heat and dry air of centrally heated rooms. To maintain humidity, stand the pots on most pebbles. When the compost is dry, pour water into a saucer underneath the pot. Watering from the top of the compost may cause the corm to rot. Feed fortnightly.

Many cyclamens are discarded after flowering, but it is not difficult to bring them into bloom again. After flowering, move them to a cooler position, or outdoors. Continue to feed, but give less water. Stop watering and feeding when the leaves start to fade, usually in early summer. In late summer, start the corms into growth with renewed watering and repotting. Move to a brighter, warmer position when about six flowers are showing.

Propagation It is best to buy new plants as cyclamens are propagated from seed, a difficult process more suitable for experts.

Pests and diseases Grey mould causes spotting of the petals and rotting of leaves and leaf stalks. Diseased leaf tissues become covered with a grey velvet fungus. Physiological disorders, due to unsuitable cultural conditions, show as leaf discoloration. Soft rot may enter tissues.

Cymbidium

cymbidium

Cymbidium 'Annan Cooksbridge'

- ☐ Height up to 1.2m (4ft)
- ☐ Temperature minimum 15°C (59°F)
- ☐ Bright, filtered light
- ☐ Orchid compost
- ☐ Orchid

Cymbidiums belong to one of the most popular groups of orchids with their long winter and spring flowering season. Most are relatively easy to grow and are ideal for beginners.

The thousands of cymbidium hybrids have superseded the species. The range varies from year to year as new types are constantly introduced. They have strap-shaped leaves and arching or upright flower spikes. The blooms come in clear or dusky shades of pink to crimson or green, with contrasting lips, but most other colours, except blue or black, are available. The most popular types are miniature cymbidiums, which rarely grow much above 30cm (12in) high.

Popular hybrids

Cymbidium 'Annan Cooksbridge' is a miniature hybrid with upright spikes of deepest crimson, white-edged flowers measuring about 6cm (2½in) across. The lips are blotched with near black.
Cymbidium 'Cariga Tetra Canary' has upright spikes of bright yellow, green-shaded

Cyperus
umbrella sedge

Cyperus alternifolius

☐ Height 30cm-3m (1-10ft)
☐ Temperature minimum 10-16°C (50-61°F)
☐ Bright light
☐ Soil-based compost
☐ Foliage plant

Cymbidium 'Fort George Lewes'

flowers. The white-marked lips are edged with deep crimson.
Cymbidium 'Clarisse Carlton' has upright spikes of dusky pink, white-edged flowers. The white lips are rimmed and spotted with deep crimson and blotched yellow.
Cymbidium 'Elmwood' has arching spikes of cream flowers with pink shading, and yellow, red-marked lips.
Cymbidium 'Fort George Lewes' has upright spikes of green flowers up to 13cm (5in) across. The pseudobulb may produce two spikes, each with 14 flowers.

Cultivation
Cymbidiums need bright light out of direct sunlight in normal room temperatures. To maintain humidity, place the pots on moist pebbles; mist-spray daily when the temperature exceeds 18°C (64°F). Water moderately when the compost feels dry and feed fortnightly.

A brief rest in early winter improves flowering the following year. Move to a cooler position, around 15°C (59°F), and give less water. Do not feed.

Cymbidium 'Clarisse Carlton'

Propagation Divide and repot crowded plants in spring; cut the rhizomes into pieces, each with at least two pseudobulbs and roots. Pot up in a proprietary orchid compost. Do not water for three to four days after potting, but mist-spray the leaves.
Pests and diseases Scale insects make leaves and stems sticky. Orchid aphids produce white-fringed black scales on the underside of the leaves. Red spider mites occur in hot summers. Unsuitable conditions show as general discoloration of leaves.

Umbrella sedges are tall, delicate-looking plants, with narrow upright stems, topped by grassy bracts and tiny flowers.

Popular species
Cyperus alternifolius (umbrella grass), 60-75cm (2-2½ft) high, has arching, narrow leaf-like green bracts arranged like the spokes of an umbrella. Fluffy yellow flowers appear in mid summer, followed by brown seeds. Varieties include 'Gracilis' (up to 45cm/1½ft high) and 'Variegatus' (white striped leaves).
Cyperus papyrus (papyrus, Egyptian paper reed), up to 3m (10ft) high, has dark green stems crowned with globular heads of thread-like stems bearing fluffy, pale yellow-green flowers.

Cultivation
Umbrella sedges like full sun but tolerate light shade. Keep in temperatures over 16°C (61°F). Keep the compost thoroughly moist or ideally set the pots in containers of water.
Propagation Divide and pot up in spring. Alternatively, grow from seed.
Pests and diseases Trouble free.

Cyrtomium

holly fern

Cyrtomium falcatum

☐ Height up to 45cm (1½ft)
☐ Temperature minimum 10°C (50°F)
☐ Bright, filtered light
☐ Peat-based compost
☐ Fern

Holly fern (*Cyrtomium falcatum*) is a decorative foliage plant which tolerates a wide range of temperatures and is easy to grow in almost any situation. It makes a dramatic specimen plant raised on a pedestal.

The gracefully arching fronds are divided into toothed, glossy, deep green holly-like leaflets (pinnae). Spore cases are carried on the underside and are green at first but ripen to light brown. The base of the plant is a rhizome thickly covered with silvery, furry scurf.

Cultivation

Holly fern likes bright but filtered light and normal room temperatures. In temperatures over 21°C (70°F) stand the pot on moist pebbles to increase humidity. Moisten the compost thoroughly when the top 12mm (½in) is dry.

Though it does not need a winter rest, give less water if the temperature drops below 13°C (55°F) for more than a few days.

Propagation Divide in spring and pot up in an open, free-draining peat-based compost. Alternatively, sow spores.

Pests and diseases Scale insects occasionally infest stalks and fronds.

Cytisus

florists' genista

Cytisus x spachianus

☐ Height 30-45cm (1-1½ft)
☐ Temperature 7-16°C (45-61°F)
☐ Bright light
☐ Soil-based compost
☐ Flowering shrub

Florists' genistas are short-term house plants. They are shrubby with small, lobed leaves and spikes of yellow pea-shaped flowers.

They need cool conditions to flower indoors, and are generally bought in flower and discarded once the flowers have faded. However, they can be kept on a sheltered frost-free patio, then moved indoors again when the flowering season comes round.

Popular species

Cytisus canariensis, up to 45cm (1½ft) high, is a well-branched shrub with leaves divided into three mid green oval leaflets. Short spikes of fragrant yellow flowers appear at the tips of the green stems from mid spring to mid summer.

Cytisus x spachianus, syn. *C. fragrans*, is similar to *C. canariensis* but with dark green leaves and more profuse, rich yellow flowers.

Cultivation

Keep genista in the brightest, coolest place possible, preferably below 16°C (61°F). Water well when the compost feels dry.

Propagation Take cuttings in mid to late summer

Pests and diseases Trouble free.

Datura

datura

Datura sanguinea

☐ Height 1.8-2.4m (6-8ft)
☐ Temperature minimum 7°C (45°F)
☐ Bright light
☐ Soil-based compost
☐ Flowering shrub

The exotic datura is a climbing plant with huge pendent flowers of heady fragrance.

Thriving mature plants have a tree-like form with a mass of wavy-edged leaves. The trumpet-shaped flowers are white, pink, yellow or red-orange and are borne in summer and autumn.

Popular species

Datura x candida (angel's trumpets) can grow to 2.4m (8ft) high. The flowers are 25cm (10in) long and white, yellowish or pink. 'Plena' has double flowers.

Datura sanguinea, up to 1.8m (6ft) high, bears orange-red flowers with a yellow tube.

Cultivation

Daturas thrive in bright light, including some direct sun, in warm room temperatures; they are ideal for conservatories. Keep the compost moist and feed fortnightly during active growth. Give a winter rest around 7°C (45°F) and keep just moist.

Propagation Take heel cuttings.

Pests and diseases Red spider mite and whitefly may attack.

Davallia
davallia

Davallia fejeensis

☐ Height 30-60cm (1-2ft)
☐ Temperature minimum 10°C (50°F)
☐ Good, indirect light
☐ Peat-based compost
☐ Fern

Davallias are ornamental ferns providing a lush display of lacy foliage for hanging baskets and pots. Even the creeping rhizomes have ornamental interest, resembling the feet of hares, rabbits and squirrels with their furry and scaly covering.

Popular species
Davallia canariensis (deer's foot or hare's foot fern), up to 45cm (1½ft) high, has mid green, triangular fronds which arch over the side of the pot. The creeping rhizomes, said to resemble a deer's or hare's foot, are covered with brown scales.
Davallia fejeensis (rabbit's foot fern), up to 60cm (2ft) high, has bright green, broadly triangular fronds which can measure up to 60cm (2ft) long. The rhizomes are furry.
Davallia mariesii (squirrel's foot or ball fern), up to 45cm (1½ft) high, has lacy light green, trian-

gular fronds. The slender rhizomes are covered with red-brown scales and form decorative shapes.

Cultivation
Davallias like good light but not direct sunlight in normal room temperatures. Water liberally when the top of the compost is dry and feed once a month during active growth. Mist-spray regularly. During the winter rest period and at temperatures below 13°C (55°F), give only enough water to prevent the compost from drying out.
Propagation Divide the rhizomes and replant in early spring. Alternatively, sow spores.
Pests and diseases Trouble free.

DEER'S FOOT FERN – see *Davallia*
DESERT FAN PALM – see *Washingtonia*
DESERT PRIVET – see *Peperomia*
DEVIL'S IVY – see *Scindapsus*
DEVIL'S TONGUE – see *Ferocactus*

Dendrobium
dendrobium

Dendrobium nobile

☐ Height up to 60cm (2ft)
☐ Temperature minimum 10°C (50°F)
☐ Bright, filtered light
☐ Orchid compost
☐ Epiphytic orchid

Dendrobiums are among the most popular indoor orchids with their profuse colourful flowers held in elegant arching or drooping sprays.

The plants have elongated cane-like pseudobulbs (swollen stems storing food and water); the leaves are generally lance-shaped.

Flowers up to 10cm (4in) across are borne in spring. Colours range from white – sometimes suffused with pink or mauve – to golden yellow and shades of pink, cream and brown. The rounded lip may be stained with a contrasting colour and is sometimes covered with tiny hairs, giving it a furry appearance.

The genus is enormous, with species originating from cold mountain regions to jungles. As with other orchids, hybrids are becoming increasingly popular.

Popular species
Dendrobium aureum, syn. *D. heterocarpum*, has creamy yellow flowers with a buff-brown lip. They have a pleasant fragrance and appear earlier than the blooms of most other species.
Dendrobium fimbriatum has drooping sprays of up to 20 light orange-yellow flowers. The lip is

Dieffenbachia

dumb cane

Dieffenbachia 'Camilla'

☐ Height 45cm-1.5m (1½-5ft)
☐ Temperature minimum 16°C (61°F)
☐ Bright, filtered light
☐ Soil-based compost
☐ Foliage plant

Dendrobium infundibulum

deeply fringed and a deeper shade of orange. Each bloom measures about 5cm (2in) across. The variety 'Oculatum' is similar to the species but is more robust. The flowers have a dark maroon-brown blotch on the lip.

Dendrobium 'Gatton Sunray' is a hybrid with pale yellow, scented flowers. The lip is covered with short hairs, giving it a furry appearance, and the throat is stained maroon-brown.

Dendrobium infundibulum has white papery 10cm (4in) wide flowers with a yellow stained lip. The long-lasting flowers have a papery texture.

Dendrobium nobile is one of the most popular species. It has white, rose-purple-tipped flowers with a maroon stain on the lip. They are about 5cm (2in) wide.

Dendrobium pierardii has pale mauve-pink almost translucent petals and a cup-shaped white lip. This species has a drooping habit but can be trained up a pole.

Dendrobium wardianum has white flowers with purple-tipped petals and lip. The throat is bright yellow with two deep maroon spots at the base.

Cultivation

Dendrobiums need bright filtered light and temperatures of 16-21°C (61-70°F). During active growth water moderately, feed fortnightly and mist-spray to maintain humidity. Gradually stop feeding and watering as growth slows (leaf tips may turn yellow) in autumn. During the winter rest, maintain a minimum night temperature of 10-13°C (50-55°F).

Propagation Divide and repot when new growths start to put out roots.

Pests and diseases Aphids may infest the leaves and/or flowers.

DEVIL'S BACKBONE – see *Kalanchoë*

One of the most attractive – and somewhat demanding – foliage house plants, dumb cane's range of marbled and spotted foliage provides ornament for the home throughout the year. The plants can grow up to 1.5m (5ft) tall, though many species are more compact.

Dumb cane contains a poisonous sap which can irritate the eyes or skin wounds. If it gets into the mouth it causes painful swelling of the tongue.

Popular species

Dieffenbachia amoena, 60cm-1.2m (2-4ft) high, has oblong, glossy dark green leaves marbled with white along the side veins. Mature plants may have leaves up to 60cm (2ft) long and 20cm (8in) wide.

Dieffenbachia x *bausei* is a hybrid up to 90cm (3ft) high. The broadly lance-shaped leaves, which reach 30cm (1ft) long, are yellow-green, with dark green and white spots and marks, and dark green edges.

Dieffenbachia bowmannii is up to 1.2m (4ft) high. The narrow leaves, up to 60cm (2ft) long, are dark green with light green markings along the side veins.

Dionaea

Venus fly trap

Dionaea muscipula

☐ Height up to 15cm (6in)
☐ Temperature minimum 7°C (45°F)
☐ Bright but filtered light
☐ Lime-free potting compost
☐ Carnivorous perennial

The carnivorous Venus fly trap (*Dionaea muscipula*) is a fascinating plant to watch when an insect lands on a leaf. The leaf, fringed with 'teeth' and hinged in the middle, immediately closes up and remains shut for about two weeks, slowly digesting its meal.

In good light, the leaves are bright green on the outside and red on the inside.

Venus fly trap, which comes from South Carolina, USA, can be difficult to grow indoors. It needs plenty of warmth and moisture, and is an ideal specimen for a bottle garden.

Cultivation

Venus fly trap needs bright light but no direct sunlight and temperatures over 13°C (55°F). Keep the compost constantly moist. Place the pot on moist pebbles and mist-spray daily or keep under a glass cover. Feed occasionally with minute scraps of meat, cheese or dead flies.

During the winter rest period keep the compost thoroughly moist in temperatures over 7°C (45°F). Do not feed.

Propagation Divide the roots or sow seeds in spring.

Pests and diseases A physiological disorder, due to insufficient moisture or warmth, causes wilting and death.

Dieffenbachia 'Exotica'

Dieffenbachia 'Camilla' up to 45cm (1½ft) high, has cream oval leaves edged with dark green.

Dieffenbachia 'Exotica', also known as leopard lily, is up to 45cm (1½ft) high. The pointed oval leaves are up to 25cm (10in) long and are dark green with whitish splashes.

Dieffenbachia imperialis, up to 1.5m (5ft) high, is a robust plant. The leathery oval leaves, up to 60cm (2ft) long, are dark green with pale green, grey and yellowish markings.

Dieffenbachia maculata, syn. *D. picta*, up to 1.2m (4ft) high, is the most popular species, with numerous varieties. It bears oblong to oval leaves, dark green with ivory-white markings. Varieties include 'Rudolphe Roehrs' (yellow-green, dark green margins and veins).

Cultivation

Dumb canes need bright but filtered light, temperatures not below 16°C (61°F) and high humidity. Stand pots on moist pebbles and mist-spray regularly. When the top of the compost is

Dieffenbachia amoena

dry, water well. Feed fortnightly during active growth.

Propagation Take tip cuttings or stem sections from the lower stem in late spring.

Pests and diseases Mealy bugs may infest the leaf stalks.

Dizygotheca
false aralia

Dizygotheca elegantissima

☐ Height 1.2-1.8m (4-6ft)
☐ Temperature minimum 16°C (61°F)
☐ Bright but filtered light
☐ Soil-based compost
☐ Foliage shrub

False aralia (*Dizygotheca elegantissima*) bears delicate foliage, its long-stalked leaves divided into numerous narrow, deeply toothed leaflets. They are coppery red when young, later maturing to dark green, almost black.

Formerly known as *Aralia elegantissima*, dizygotheca is often grown in multiple arrangements for its contrast to other foliage plants.

Cultivation
False aralia needs bright light out of direct sunlight and constant warm room temperatures. Maintain high humidity by placing the pot on moist pebbles and mist-spray daily. Water moderately when the top of the compost is dry and feed fortnightly during active growth. The winter night minimum is 16°C (61°F).
Propagation Grow from seed or buy new plants.
Pests and diseases Trouble free.

DONKEY'S TAIL – see *Sedum*
DOVE ORCHID – see *Oncidium*

Dracaena
dracaena

Dracaena deremensis 'Bausei'

☐ Height 45cm-1.8m (1½-6ft)
☐ Temperature minimum 16°C (61°F)
☐ Bright but filtered light
☐ Soil-based compost
☐ Foliage shrub

Dracaenas make elegant centrepieces for any well-lit room with their arching, beautifully marked leaves. As the plants mature, older leaves fall away, leaving a slender trunk marked with scars where each leaf was attached. They are often confused with cordylines.

Healthy specimens grown in ideal conditions may eventually reach small tree-like proportions, but they are extremely slow-growing. They never flower as indoor pot plants.

Popular species
Dracaena deremensis, up to 1.2m (4ft) high, bears tufts of sword-shaped leaves up to 45cm (1½ft) long. The leaves are glossy dark green with two lengthways silver stripes. Popular varieties, in preference to the species, include 'Bausei' (white and dark green stripes) and 'Warneckii' (dark green margins, two white stripes separated by a central dark green stripe).

Dracaena draco (dragon tree), up to 1.2m (4ft) high, has tough, mid green, sword-shaped leaves up to 45cm (1½ft) long. This species is particularly slow-growing and tolerates lower temperatures than other dracaenas.

Dyckia
dyckia

Dracaena surculosa

Dracaena marginata 'Tricolor'

Dracaena fragrans (corn palm), up to 1.2m (4ft) high, is similar to *D. deremensis*, but with broader, arching leaves. Varieties include: 'Lindenii' (broad creamy gold margins, narrow green and gold centre); 'Massangeana' (green margins, wide yellow central stripe); and 'Victoria' (cream-yellow margins, silvery grey-green central stripe).

Dracaena hookeriana, up to 1.2m (4ft) high, bears glossy green, leathery, sword-shaped leaves up to 75cm (2½ft) long. The variety 'Variegata' has white-striped leaves.

Dracaena marginata, up to 1.8m (6ft) high, has tufts of narrow green, red-edged leaves up to 40cm (16in) long; it is the easiest species to grow. Varieties include 'Tricolor' (similar to the species but with additional red stripes) and 'Variegata' (cream stripes).

Dracaena sanderiana (ribbon plant), up to 45cm (1½ft) high, bears narrow lance-shaped, grey-green leaves up to 20cm (8in) long with silver or ivory margins. Of erect habit, the species sometimes branches.

Dracaena surculosa, syn. *D. godseffiana* (gold-dust dracaena), up to 60cm (2ft) high, has branching stems and elliptic, dark green leaves heavily sprinkled with creamy spots. In the variety 'Florida Beauty' the spots are larger and merge together.

Cultivation

Dracaenas thrive in bright light out of direct sunlight and need warm humid conditions at warm room temperatures. With the exception of *D. draco*, the plants drop their leaves if temperatures drop below 18°C (64°F). Place the pots on moist pebbles and mist-spray regularly. Keep the soil damp and feed fortnightly during the growing season. During the winter rest, keep at a minimum night temperature of 16°C (61°F). Repot only when necessary; most dracaenas can stay for several years in quite small pots.

Propagation Take stem or tip cuttings or basal shoots in spring or summer.

Pests and diseases Leaf spot fungus attacks the leaves, producing pale brown irregular spots with a purple border and pinpoint-sized black dots. Mealy bugs may infest stems and check growth. Root mealy bugs invade the roots. Scale insects form round white or pearl-grey scales on the leaves and stems.

DUMB CANE – see
Dieffenbachia
EARTH STAR – see *Cryptanthus*
EASTER CACTUS – see
Rhipsalidopsis
EASTER LILY – see *Lilium*

Dyckia fosteriana

- ☐ Height 15cm (6in)
- ☐ Temperature minimum 10°C (50°F)
- ☐ Bright light
- ☐ Bromeliad compost
- ☐ Flowering bromeliad

An easily grown bromeliad, *Dyckia fosteriana* is a low, stemless rosette plant with rigid, heavily spined leaves. They are grey-green in colour but appear metallic-bronze in bright light. Bell-shaped, orange-yellow flowers are borne in spring. Unlike other bromeliads, dyckia produces flower stalks from the side, not the centre, of mature rosettes which do not die after flowering but spread to form large clumps.

Cultivation

Dyckia thrives in bright light, in full sun, and in the dry air of centrally heated rooms. It grows throughout the year, with no apparent rest period. It will tolerate temperatures as low as 10°C (50°F). Dyckia benefits from an outdoor spell in summer. Keep the compost moist but not saturated – at low temperatures water moderately only. Feed monthly in spring and summer.

Propagation Detach and pot up offsets in late spring.

Pests and diseases Trouble free.

Echeveria

echeveria

Echeveria harmsii

Echeveria derenbergii

- ☐ Height 7.5-30cm (3-12in)
- ☐ Temperature minimum 13-15°C (55-59°F)
- ☐ Bright light
- ☐ Cactus compost
- ☐ Flowering succulent

Echeverias are intriguing plants for a sunny window-sill with their plump leafy rosettes and bell-shaped flowers.

The fleshy leaves come in shades of green, grey-green and blue-green and are sometimes edged with red; they are usually smooth and covered with a waxy bloom. The bell-shaped flowers rise above the rosettes on stiff stalks and range from red to orange and yellow.

Popular species

Echeveria affinis has almost stemless rosettes up to 7.5cm (3in) high. The pointed oblong to lance-shaped leaves range from bright green to brownish or greenish black. Deeper leaf colouring is due to bright light. Red flowers appear on 30cm (1ft) high stems from summer to autumn.

Echeveria derenbergii (painted lady) forms a cluster of almost stemless rosettes, each up to 7.5cm (3in) high. The broad, spoon-shaped leaves are grey-green with red edges. Sprays of orange flowers appear on 7.5cm (3in) high stems in early summer.

Echeveria harmsii is a shrub-like plant up to 30cm (1ft) high. The stems are tipped with narrow spoon-shaped leaves which are bright green and faintly red-edged. Red, yellow-tipped flowers, up to 5cm (2in) long, appear on long stalks in spring and summer.

Echeveria peacockii forms a cluster of rosettes, each up to 10cm (4in) high. They have blue-green, oblong leaves with a white waxy covering. Sprays of red flowers appear on a stem up to 30cm (1ft) high in summer.

Cultivation

Echeverias thrive in bright light, including direct sunlight, in nor-

Echeveria peacockii

mal room temperatures. Moisten the compost sparingly when it feels dry and feed fortnightly. Avoid watering the foliage. During the winter rest, move plants to a cooler position with temperatures of 10-15°C (50-59°F) and water only enough to keep the compost from drying out completely.

Propagation Detach and pot up rosettes or take leaf cuttings in summer.

Pests and diseases Mealy bugs often shelter in the leaf rosettes.

Echinocactus

golden ball cactus, barrel cactus

Echinocactus grusonii

☐ Height up to 25cm (10in)
☐ Temperature minimum 5-13°C (41-55°F)
☐ Bright light
☐ Cactus compost
☐ Cactus

Grown for their fierce yellow spines, golden ball cacti are long-lived, tolerant house plants thriving on sunny window sills.

These desert cacti generally form a single globular stem in shades of green or blue-green. The stem has numerous ribs bearing woolly areoles (cushion-like pads). Clusters of strong yellow spines grow radially from the areoles, the central spines sometimes measuring more than 12mm (½in) long.

The species described come from Mexico, where old plants can reach a height of 90cm (3ft). However, they are all extremely slow-growing and take at least ten years to achieve the dimensions quoted here.

Popular species

Echinocactus grusonii reaches a height and spread of 23cm (9in), though it can eventually grow much larger. The single green, almost circular stem has numerous ribs with clusters of prominent, sharp yellow spines. The shorter spines arch back from the areoles while the thicker central ones stick straight out. The crown of the stem is topped with yellow-white wool. Mature plants bear tubular yellow flowers on the upper part of the body in late spring, but specimens grown indoors are unlikely to bloom.
Echinocactus horizonthalonius has a single blue-grey, flattened globular stem which eventually grows to about 25cm (10in) high. It has seven to thirteen ribs bearing clusters of straight or curved thick yellow spines. Pink flowers, about 5cm (2in) across, appear on young plants in summer.

Cultivation

Echinocacti need full sun and thrive in normal room temperatures. During active growth, water moderately when the compost is dry and feed monthly. Move established plants outdoors to a sunny spot in summer.

Move the plants to a cooler position in winter with temperatures of 5-13°C (41-55°F). Give only enough water to prevent the compost from drying out completely.
Propagation New plants must be raised from seed sown in early summer.
Pests and diseases Trouble free.

Echinocereus

echinocereus

Echinocereus blanckii

☐ Height 5-25cm (2-10in)
☐ Temperature minimum 7-10°C (45-50°F)
☐ Bright light
☐ Cactus compost
☐ Cactus

Grown for their swollen prostrate or upright stems and vivid funnel-shaped flowers in summer, echinocereus species are tolerant plants for a sunny position. They bloom profusely from an early age.

Popular species

Echinocereus blanckii, up to 15cm (6in) high and 30cm (1ft) across, has prostrate blue-green cylindrical and bristly stems. The flowers are reddish violet.
Echinocereus knippelianus is a rounded blue-green plant up to 5cm (2in) high. It has white bristly spines and bears purplish flowers.
Echinocereus pectinatus (hedgehog cactus) forms a squat column up to 25cm (10in) high, densely covered with spines. It bears scented, deep pink flowers.

Cultivation

Echinocereus likes full sun and normal room temperatures. During active growth, water moderately when the compost is dry.

During the winter rest, keep in a light position, ideally with a temperature of about 7°C (45°F). Water sparingly.
Propagation Grow from seed or take cuttings.
Pests and diseases Mealy bugs show as tufts of white waxy wool.

Echinopsis

sea urchin cactus, thistle globe

Echinopsis eyriesii

☐ Height up to 20cm (8in)
☐ Temperature minimum 4-10°C
(40-50°F)
☐ Bright light
☐ Cactus compost
☐ Cactus

Sea urchin cactus is a delightful plant with long-tubed, white, pink or yellow flowers in summer. The ribbed body is cylindrical or globular with sharp spines.

Popular species

Echinopsis eyriesii is globular, later cylindrical. The dark green stem has about 15 prominent ribs with clusters of small dark brown spines. The nocturnal pure white, fragrant flowers are about 20cm (8in) long.

Echinopsis multiplex has a mid green, globular stem with about 12 sharp ribs and stout brown spines. The 15cm (6in) long pink flowers open in the evening.

Cultivation

The plants prefer direct sunlight in ordinary room temperatures. Water moderately when the compost is dry and feed fortnightly. In winter, rest the plants at a maximum of 10°C (50°F). Give less water.

Propagation Detach and pot up offsets. Or grow from seed.

Pests and diseases Mealy bugs show as tufts of white waxy wool.

EGYPTIAN PAPER REED – see *Cyperus*
EGYPTIAN STAR CLUSTER – see *Pentas*
ELEPHANT'S EAR – see *Caladium* and *Philodendron*

Epidendrum

epidendrum

Epidendrum stamfordianum

☐ Height 60cm-1.2m (2-4ft)
☐ Temperature 13-21°C (55-70°F)
☐ Bright but filtered light
☐ Orchid compost
☐ Epiphytic orchid

Epidendrums belong to one of the largest orchid groups, with fragrant, long-lasting blooms for much of the year. Several species have been reclassified in the genus *Encyclia*.

The genus is roughly divided into two groups: plants with pseudobulbs (swollen stems) and leathery leaves, and plants with thin, cane-like stems, fleshy leaves and no pseudobulbs. The flowers are often elegant, with narrow, gracefully spread petals in shades of orange, red, yellow, mauve and green.

Popular species

Epidendrum cochleatum (cockle-shell orchid), up to 90cm (3ft) high, has oval pseudobulbs and two mid green, strap-shaped leaves. It bears upright flower spikes about 30cm (1ft) high from mid winter to summer, though flowers may appear at other times. The pale green blooms are about 10cm (4in) wide with drooping petals and an upright, shell-shaped deep purple and yellow lip. The sprays usually consist of four to seven flowers.

Epidendrum radicans is up to 1.2m (4ft) high, and 60cm (2ft)

Epiphyllum

orchid cactus

Epidendrum radicans

across, with a cane-like stem and fleshy, oblong mid green leaves. Dense clusters of 2.5cm (1in) wide flowers in brilliant shades of red, orange and yellow are produced at any time of year. The lip is sometimes a different colour.

Epidendrum stamfordianum, 60cm (2ft) high, has club-shaped pseudobulbs and narrow leathery leaves. The 4cm (1½in) long greenish yellow flowers appear in arching sprays from winter to spring. The petals are spotted with red and the fringed lip is yellow-white.

Cultivation

Epidendrums need bright indirect light and temperatures above 18°C (64°F). Keep the compost moist during active growth and maintain good humidity by placing the pots on moist pebbles.

Maintain a minimum night temperature of 13°C (55°F) throughout the year, and keep cane-stemmed plants moist. During the brief rest period, give types with pseudobulbs just enough water to prevent them from shrivelling.

Propagation Divide the pseudobulbs and repot in spring. Alternatively, take cuttings of cane-stemmed types in spring.

Pests and diseases Scale insects may infest leaves and stems.

Epiphyllum 'Ackermanii'

☐ Height up to 60cm (2ft)
☐ Temperature minimum 10-13°C (50-55°F)
☐ Bright but filtered light
☐ Cactus compost
☐ Epiphytic cactus

The beautiful flowers and plump, leaf-like stems of the orchid cacti have made them some of the most popular flowering plants for the home. The plants have a trailing habit and are ideal for hanging baskets, though they may also be staked and grown upright in pots.

The flattened or twisted, mid to dark green stems have wavy or notched edges with clusters of tiny, bristle-like spines; from a distance the stems resemble a row of plump leaves. They grow up to 60cm (2ft) long.

The flowers, which appear in late spring to summer, are bell-shaped with numerous pointed petals; they are often fragrant, especially white-flowered types.

Most of the orchid cacti in cultivation are hybrids between *Epiphyllum*, *Heliocereus* and *Selenicereus*. They have a wide range of colourful flowers which open during the day and measure up to 15cm (6in) across. They come in shades of red, orange, yellow, purple and pink, but not blue.

Hybrids of *E. cooperi* have white or yellow blooms which open at night at the base of the stems and can measure up to 10cm (4in) across. The flowers are often heavily scented but are less profuse than the flowers of *E.* 'Ackermanii' hybrids.

Orchid cacti are epiphytes from the tropical forests of South America, where they enjoy moist conditions and filtered light.

Episcia

episcia

Episcia cupreata

Epiphyllum cooperi

Popular hybrids

'Ackermanii' has profuse bright red flowers which may appear at any time of year. They measure 10cm (4in) across.

'Autumn' has coral-pink flowers.

'King Midas' has golden yellow flowers with a darker centre and darker outer petals.

'London Glory' produces profuse dark red to purple flowers.

'Reward' has yellow flowers. The inner petals are cream with yellow stripes and the outer petals are pure yellow.

'Truce' has flowers with white inner petals and pale green outer petals.

Cultivation

Orchid cacti need good light but not direct sun, and thrive on east-facing window-sills. Keep at a daytime temperature of 21°C (70°F) and maintain good humidity on moist pebbles or with saucers of water beneath hanging baskets. During active growth, moisten the compost thoroughly when the top feels dry, and feed fortnightly. During the winter rest move to a cooler position with temperatures over 10°C (50°F) and keep the compost just moist.

Repot annually after flowering and move outdoors in a shaded position in summer.

Propagation Take stem cuttings from late spring to summer. Dry for a few days before potting up.

Pests and diseases A physiological disorder shows as irregular corky or rusty looking spots on the stems. A viral disease causes yellow or purple spots.

☐ Trailing stems to 45cm (1½ft)
☐ Temperature minimum 16°C (61°F)
☐ Bright light
☐ Peat-based compost
☐ Flowering perennial

Prized for their prettily marked foliage and colourful flowers, episcias make a fine display in hanging baskets.

The trailing stems are up to 45cm (1½ft) long and, where they touch the compost, root to form a spreading carpet of plantlets which are easily detached and potted up for propagation.

The hairy oval leaves are embossed or puckered and generally have toothed edges. The lobed flowers, which are sometimes fringed, are in shades of red, white and yellow. The main flowering season is from spring to autumn.

Popular species and hybrids

Episcia cupreata (flame violet) has dark green leaves with the veins often marked with silver. The flowers are red and yellow. Varieties are available with leaves of silver variegations or a coppery flush.

Episcia 'Cygnet' has velvety light green leaves with scalloped edges. The flowers are white with prominent purple spots in the throat and a deeply fringed mouth.

Episcia dianthiflora (lace flower) has velvety rounded leaves with purple or brown veins. The white flowers have frilled petals.

Episcia lilacina has embossed leaves ranging from coppery green to pale green with a reddish flush. The flowers have lilac lobes and a yellow throat.

Episcia reptans (flame violet) has embossed dark or bronze-green leaves with silvery veins. The flowers are rosy red with blood red hairy throats.

Cultivation

Episcias need bright light with several hours a day of direct sun though away from scorching midday sun in summer. They do best at temperatures of 21-24°C (70-75°F). Maintain high humidity by placing the pots over moist pebbles and mist-spraying regularly. Alternatively, grow in a terrarium. Keep the compost thoroughly moist during active growth and give a weak feed at every watering. *E.* 'Cygnet' likes thoroughly moist compost.

A winter rest is unnecessary, but if the temperature falls below 16°C (61°F), give less water.

Propagation Detach plantlets. Alternatively, divide and pot up the roots or take cuttings.

Pests and diseases Aphids may infest young leaves, making them sticky and sooty.

Euphorbia

euphorbia

Euphorbia pulcherrima

Euphorbia obesa

☐ Height 13cm-1.5m (5in-5ft)
☐ Temperature minimum 13°C (55°F)
☐ Bright or filtered light
☐ Soil-based compost; cactus compost
☐ Flowering shrubs; succulents

A large genus which includes shrubs, perennials and succulents, *Euphorbia* offers a range of widely varying house plants. Among them are species as diverse as the popular poinsettia (*E. pulcherrima*), grown for its colourful winter bracts, the spherical, cactus-like *E. obesa*, and crown of thorns (*E. milii*), a thorny flowering shrub.

The true flowers of euphorbias are tiny and barely noticeable. But they are often surrounded by brilliantly coloured, showy bracts which persist for a long time.

Foliage differs greatly between the species, ranging from the large veined leaves of poinsettia to the tiny, sparse leaves of milk bush (*E. tirucalli*). Some succulent types have no true leaves, but have modified stems instead.

Most euphorbias exude a poisonous milky or gum-like sap (latex) when cut which can cause skin irritation. It is advisable to keep euphorbias out of the reach of young children.

Popular species

Euphorbia fulgens (scarlet plume), a shrubby tree-like species, grows up to 1.2m (4ft) high. The thin arching branches bear mid to bright green lance-shaped leaves. Sprays of flowers are surrounded by showy, scarlet bracts and appear from late autumn to late winter.

Euphorbia milii, formerly known as *E. splendens* (crown of thorns), is a dense semi-succulent shrub up to 60cm (2ft) high with thorny stems. The bright mid green, lance-shaped to oval leaves are borne only on new shoots. Old stems are always leafless. The tiny flowers are each surrounded by two large kidney-shaped red or yellow bracts and appear in clusters. The main flowering season is in winter, but flowers may appear at other times.

Euphorbia obesa (Turkish temple) is a spherical, succulent plant which becomes cylindrical with age. It grows slowly to 13cm (5in) high, and has up to eight ribs. The stem is grey-green with brown-purple stripes and bands, giving it a chequered appearance. Minute, sweetly scented, bell-shaped, green to yellow flowers appear at the crown in summer.

Euphorbia pseudocactus is a cactus-like succulent eventually growing up to 1.5m (5ft) high and 75cm (2½ft) across. The bright green to dark green, thorny stems are arranged rather like a candelabra and have three to five horny ridges with indentations between.

Euphorbia pulcherrima (poinsettia) is a popular sub-shrubby species usually bought for Christmas display and discarded after flowering. Up to 60cm (2ft) high, it has bright to mid green oval, often shallowly lobed leaves. The tiny flowers appear at the top of the branching stems, surrounded by showy red, leaf-shaped bracts which last from early to late winter. Varieties with pink, white or pale green bracts are also available. Although usually a short-term plant, poinsettia can, with care, be induced to flower for a second and third year.

Euphorbia tirucalli (milk bush) is a shrubby succulent up to 1.2m (4ft) high. It has narrow branching, finger-like stems. The minute leaves soon disappear.

Cultivation

E. milii enjoys bright, sunny light in warm room temperatures. Water well when the compost is dry at the top and feed fortnightly during active growth. During the winter rest, keep at a cooler temperature not below 13°C (55°F) and give less water.

E. pulcherrima needs bright but filtered light in draught-free

Exacum
German violet

Exacum affine 'Midget Blue'

Euphorbia milii

Euphorbia pseudocactus

☐ Height up to 30cm (1ft)
☐ Temperature minimum 16°C (61°F)
☐ Bright, filtered light
☐ Soil-based compost
☐ Short-term flowering plant

warm rooms. Water only when the compost is dry at the top.

Succulent euphorbias need bright light at normal room temperatures. During active growth, keep the compost moist and feed fortnightly. During the winter rest, keep in a cooler position at 10°C (50°F) and not below 5°C (41°F). Water sparingly when dry.
Propagation Grow from seed or take cuttings; dip cut ends in powdered charcoal to stop milky sap and allow cuttings to dry for a few days before rooting.
Pests and diseases Trouble free.

EUROPEAN FAN PALM – see *Chamaerops*

German violet (*Exacum affine*), also known as Arabian or Persian violet, is a bushy little plant decked with profuse mauve-purple, delicately scented flowers.

The plant grows 23-30cm (9-12in) high, with shiny oval, mid to deep green leaves. The cup-shaped flowers, which have conspicuous yellow stamens, appear from summer to autumn.

German violet is a temporary plant, usually grown as an annual and discarded after flowering. Named varieties include 'Blithe Spirit' (white flowers); 'Midget Blue' (dwarf form similar to the species); and 'Starlight Fragrance' (fragrant mauve flowers).

Cultivation
German violet enjoys bright light but not direct sun in the middle of the day. Keep at normal room temperatures and maintain humidity by placing the pot on moist pebbles and mist-spraying regularly. During active growth, keep the compost thoroughly moist, but not wet, and feed fortnightly. Dead-head frequently to prolong the flowering season.

After flowering, either discard the plant or overwinter at a minimum temperature of 16°C (61°F). Give less water, but do not let the compost dry out completely.
Propagation Grow from seed sown in spring.
Pests and diseases Trouble free.

EYELASH BEGONIA – see *Begonia*
FALSE ARALIA – see *Dizygotheca*
FALSE CASTOR OIL PLANT – see *Fatsia*
FALSE HEATHER – see *Cuphea*
FALSE JERUSALEM CHERRY – see *Solanum*

x *Fatshedera*

tree ivy

x Fatshedera lizei

☐ Height 60cm-1.8m (2-6ft)
☐ Temperature minimum 10°C (50°F)
☐ Bright, indirect light
☐ Soil-based compost
☐ Foliage shrub

Tree ivy (x *Fatshedera lizei*) is an excellent plant for warm and cool rooms with its large, ornamental leaves and tough constitution.

The plant, which is a hybrid between ivy (*Hedera*) and *Fatsia japonica*, can be trained up a pole or allowed to trail from a basket.

The glossy deep green leaves are ivy-shaped and up to 20cm (8in) across. 'Variegata' has cream-white markings on the leaves.

Cultivation

Tree ivy prefers indirect light but tolerates a partially shaded position. It thrives at normal room temperatures and tolerates dry conditions. During active growth, water moderately when the top of the compost is dry and feed fortnightly.

During the winter rest move to a cooler position with a minimum temperature of 10°C (50°F) and keep the compost just moist. The less tolerant 'Variegata' requires a minimum winter temperature of 16°C (61°F).

Tree ivy can be stood outdoors in a partially shaded position during the summer months.

Propagation Take tip cuttings in spring.

Pests and diseases Aphids, scale insects and red spider mites can be troublesome.

Fatsia

false castor oil plant

Fatsia japonica

☐ Height up to 1.5m (5ft)
☐ Temperature minimum 7°C (45°F)
☐ Bright indirect light
☐ Soil-based compost
☐ Foliage shrub

False castor oil plant (*Fatsia japonica*) is a handsome foliage plant which looks ornamental throughout the year.

It has rich and glossy, mid to deep green leaves with paler undersides. They are divided into seven to nine coarsely toothed, oblong to lance-shaped lobes. Each leaf measures up to 23cm (9in) across.

It is a hardy, evergreen outdoor shrub which in autumn bears globular heads of white flowers followed by glossy black berries. Indoor pot plants rarely flower unless they are kept in a cool conservatory.

Pot-grown specimens are unlikely to achieve a height and spread of more than 90cm (3ft). Plants grown in large tubs in a cool conservatory may grow up to 1.5m (5ft) high and 1.2m (4ft) across.

Varieties include 'Moseri' (more compact than the species, larger leaves) and 'Variegata' (white-edged leaves).

Cultivation

False castor oil plant thrives in bright light out of direct sunlight, in a well-ventilated position with normal room temperatures. Maintain humidity by standing the pot on moist pebbles and mist-spraying regularly. Keep the compost thoroughly moist and feed fortnightly.

During the winter rest move to a cooler position with a temperature of about 7°C (45°F) and keep the compost just moist.

Propagation Detach suckers or basal shoots in early to mid spring and root as cuttings. Alternatively, grow from seed in mid spring.

Pests and diseases Mealy bugs, covered with tufts of white wool, may infest leaf bases.

Faucaria

faucaria

Faucaria tigrina

- ☐ Height 10-15cm (4-6in)
- ☐ Temperature minimum 10°C (50°F)
- ☐ Bright light
- ☐ Cactus compost
- ☐ Flowering succulent

Faucarias are dwarf succulents with handsome fleshy leaves arranged in pairs to form a star-shaped, near stemless rosette. The triangular leaves are dark green and edged with fierce-looking but soft teeth. In autumn, large daisy-like flowers, which open in the afternoon, are borne on even young plants.

Popular species
Faucaria tigrina (tiger jaw) has rigid 2.5cm (1in) wide leaves that taper to a point. They are grey-green with white markings. The flowers are golden yellow and up to 5cm (2in) wide.
Faucaria tuberculosa resembles *F. tigrina* but has smaller leaves with tiny white tubercles on the upper surfaces. The flowers are smaller.

Cultivation
Faucarias need bright light, including full sun, and ordinary room temperatures. They require a definite winter rest around 10°C (50°F). During growth, water freely to keep the compost moist, and feed once a month; in winter water sparingly.
Propagation Divide and pot up overgrown clumps in spring.
Pests and diseases Trouble free.

Ferocactus

ferocactus

Ferocactus latispinus

- ☐ Height up to 15cm (6in)
- ☐ Temperature minimum 10°C (50°F)
- ☐ Bright light
- ☐ Cactus compost
- ☐ Cactus

Though ferocacti rarely grow more than 15cm (6in) high as indoor plants, they make impressive additions to a collection of cacti with their rounded bodies, protected by an armoury of spines.

They are desert cacti, easy to care for but unlikely to flower.

Popular species
Ferocactus acanthodes has a greyish green oval to cylindrical stem with up to 23 ribs. The areoles (cushion-like pads) bear curved reddish or yellow interlacing spines and central straight spines.
Ferocactus latispinus (fish-hook cactus, devil's tongue) has a greyish-green, globular stem with 8 to 20 ribs. The areoles bear red or white spines and a red central spine curved like a fish-hook and slightly flattened.

Cultivation
Ferocacti thrive in full sun in normal room temperatures. During active growth, water moderately when the compost is dry and feed monthly. In autumn and winter, keep at a temperature around 10°C (50°F) and water sparingly.
Propagation Grow from seed.
Pests and diseases Mealy bugs appear as tufts of white waxy wool at the base of the spines. Root mealy bugs infest roots.

Ficus

fig

Ficus benjamina

- ☐ Height 15cm-3m (6in-10ft)
- ☐ Temperature minimum 7-16°C (45-61°F)
- ☐ Bright, indirect or medium light
- ☐ Soil- or peat-based compost
- ☐ Foliage plants

Ficus is a large genus that includes a wide range of indoor evergreen shrubs and small trees, from the popular rubber plant to the trailing creeping fig.

The plants are grown for their leaves, which are often glossy and come in shades of green or with interesting variegations.

Popular species
Ficus benghalensis (banyan tree) is a tree-like plant up to 1.8m (6ft) high. The broad, leathery, dark green oval leaves are 20cm (8in) long with yellowish veins.
Ficus benjamina (weeping fig) is a graceful, bushy plant generally up to 1.8m (6ft) high, though it can grow much taller. It has slender slightly drooping branches with glossy dark green oval leaves. They are slender-pointed and up to 10cm (4in) long.
Ficus deltoidea, syn. *F. diversifolia* (mistletoe fig), is a slow-growing bushy plant up to 60cm (2ft) high. The rounded leaves, up to 7.5cm (3in) long, are bright or dark green above, pale green or fawn below. It bears clusters of berry-like, inedible yellow fruits throughout the year.
Ficus elastica (rubber plant), a tree-like plant, is rarely grown, having been superseded by named varieties. Up to 3m (10ft) high,

Ficus triangularis 'Variegata'

and *F. triangularis*. A night temperature of 7°C (45°F) is sufficient for *F. deltoidea* and *F. pumila*.
Propagation Take tip cuttings of small-leaved species. Increase large-leaved types by air layering.
Pests and diseases Mealy bugs and scale insects may be troublesome. Inadequate watering may cause leaf discoloration.

FIDDLE-LEAF – see *Philodendron*
FIRE DRAGON PLANT – see *Acalypha*
FISH-HOOK CACTUS – see *Ferocactus*
FISHTAIL PALM – see *Caryota*

Ficus elastica 'Doescheri'

the rubber plant is usually unbranched, with glossy deep green, oblong to oval leaves up to 30cm (1ft) long. Varieties include: 'Black Prince' (black-green leaves); 'Decora' (dark green foliage); 'Doescheri' (green leaves with ivory and white markings, young leaves tinted pink); 'Robusta' (large leaves); and 'Tricolor' (cream-variegated leaves, sometimes flushed pink).
Ficus lyrata (fiddle-leaf fig) is an upright, bushy or tree-like plant up to 1.2m (4ft) high. It has violin-shaped, dark green leaves with wavy edges. They are slightly puckered, with yellow veins, and often over 30cm (1ft) long.
Ficus pumila, syn. *F. repens* (creeping fig), can be grown as a trailing or climbing plant. It has stems up to 60cm (2ft) long. The pointed oval leaves are dark green with prominent veins and up to 2.5cm (1in) long.
Ficus triangularis is an upright, bushy plant up to 1.2m (4ft) high. It has deep green, glossy, almost triangular leaves 7.5-10cm (3-4in) across. 'Variegata' has leaves edged with creamy white.

Cultivation
Most species enjoy indirect sun in normal room temperatures. Place the pots on moist pebbles and mist-spray regularly to maintain humidity. During the growing season, keep the compost moist and feed fortnightly. *F. pumila* should never be allowed to dry out. During the winter rest, keep the soil just moist, at 16°C (61°F) for *F. elastica* and *F. lyrata*, 13-16°C (55-61°F) for *F. benjamina*

Ficus pumila

83

Fittonia

painted net leaf

Fittonia verschaffeltii argyroneura

Fittonia verschaffeltii

☐ Height up to 15cm (6in)
☐ Temperature minimum 13°C (55°F)
☐ Medium light
☐ Peat-based compost
☐ Foliage plant

Painted net leaf (*Fittonia verschaffeltii*) is a compact plant grown for its ornamental leaves, handsomely patterned with a network of coloured veins. It can be difficult to grow as it requires constant warmth, high humidity and moist but not wet compost. It often succeeds best in a bottle garden or enclosed terrarium.

The plant has creeping stems and oval dark green leaves with carmine veins. The leaves measure up to 10cm (4in) long.

Painted net leaf reaches no more than 15cm (6in) in height, but can spread about 23cm (9in) across with the stems sometimes trailing over the edge of the pot.

The most widely available variety is *F. v. argyroneura* (silver net leaf or mosaic plant), which has leaves with ivory-white veining. The variety 'Minima' or 'Nana' is similar, but smaller, with leaves only 2.5cm (1in) long.

Cultivation

Painted net leaf needs medium light or partial shade in summer, as direct sun through glass easily scorches the leaves. In winter, move the plant to a well-lit position. Keep in a room with temperatures over 18°C (64°F) throughout the year. Water sparingly at all times to keep the compost moist – if the roots dry out, the leaves drop. During active growth feed at half strength every fortnight. To maintain humidity, place the pot on moist pebbles.

Pinch out flower stems as they appear to encourage bushy growth.

Propagation Fittonias lose their attractiveness with age; propagate regularly from tip cuttings in spring.

Pests and diseases Trouble free.

FLAME NETTLE – see *Coleus*
FLAME VIOLET – see *Episcia*
FLAMING KATY – see
Kalanchoë
FLAMING SWORD – see *Vriesea*
FLAMINGO FLOWER – see
Anthurium
FLOWERING MAPLE – see
Abutilon

Fortunella

fortunella, kumquat

Fortunella japonica 'Variegata'

☐ Height up to 1.2m (4ft)
☐ Temperature minimum 13-16°C
  (55-61°F)
☐ Bright light
☐ Soil- or peat-based compost
☐ Flowering and fruiting shrub

Fortunella is a handsome shrub or small tree related to *Citrus* species. Attractive in leaf, it also bears scented flowers and colourful fruits (kumquats).

Popular species

Fortunella japonica has spiny stems set with elliptic, thick and leathery, dark green leaves. The heavily scented flowers in spring and summer are followed by orange fruits up to 3cm (1¼in) across. 'Variegata' has white-flecked leaves.
Fortunella margarita has almost thornless stems and lance-shaped leaves up to 10cm (4in) long. The oval dark orange fruits are up to 4cm (1½in) long.

Cultivation

Fortunellas need direct sun and normal room temperatures. Maintain humidity by placing the pots on moist pebbles. During active growth keep the compost thoroughly moist and feed fortnightly. During the winter rest, at 13-16°C (55-61°F), water sparingly. Prune lightly in spring.
Propagation Grow from seed or take tip cuttings.
Pests and diseases Red spider mites and scale insects may attack.

FRECKLE FACE – see *Hypoestes*

Freesia

freesia

Freesia x *hybrida* variety

☐ Height up to 45cm (18in)
☐ Temperature minimum 5°C (41°F)
☐ Bright light
☐ Soil-based compost
☐ Flowering corm

Prized for their sweetly scented, delicate flowers, freesias (*Freesia* x *hybrida*) are delightful plants for a sunny window-sill.

Reaching up to 45cm (18in) high, they have mid green, narrowly lance-shaped leaves on narrow branching stems. In summer or winter to spring they bear one-sided spikes of funnel-shaped, upward-facing flowers up to 5cm (2in) long. Numerous hybrids, with single or double flowers in shades of mauve, pink, red, yellow and cream or white, are available.

Cultivation

Pot summer-flowering freesias in mid spring, and winter- to spring-flowering types in early autumn to early winter in a proprietary potting compost. They like bright light and cool temperatures around 16°C (61°F). Keep moist during active growth and feed

Freesia x *hybrida* variety

fortnightly. Dry off the corms when the leaves start to turn yellow and rest them at temperatures around 5°C (41°F).
Propagation Remove and pot up offset corms.
Pests and diseases Aphids may infest stems and leaves. Red spider mites cause mottling and webbing of the foliage.

FRIENDSHIP PLANT – see *Billbergia*

Fuchsia

fuchsia

Fuchsia 'Golden Dawn'

☐ Height 60cm (2ft) or more
☐ Temperature minimum 7°C (45°F)
☐ Bright light
☐ Soil-based compost
☐ Deciduous flowering shrub

Popular plants for pots and hanging baskets, outdoors and in the greenhouse, fuchsias can also be grown as house plants. Well known for their drooping clusters of tubular or bell-shaped flowers, fuchsias come in vivid colours of scarlet, crimson, mauve, purple and pink, as well as pure white and pastel shades. They are often

Fuchsia 'Swingtime'

in various colour combinations, though some are self-coloured.

The leaves are oval to lance-shaped and usually mid green. Varieties with gold, white or yellow variegations are available.

There are hundreds of named varieties, single or double-flowered, borne on upright or trailing shrubs or on specially trained standards. Low-growing, small-flowered types are the most suitable indoors.

Cultivation
Buy young plants in spring and place them in bright light with at least three hours of direct sun daily. Pot on as necessary, using a soil-based proprietary compost. Good humidity is essential – stand the pots on moist pebbles and

mist-spray daily. Cool temperatures around 16°C (61°F) are best – in hot rooms, flower buds and leaves drop prematurely.

Water freely during active growth to keep the compost moist; feed weekly.

After flowering, discard the plants or prune them back by half and overwinter them at 7-10°C (45-50°F); water sparingly. In spring, trim the woody stems and start the fuchsias into growth by moving them into better light and normal room temperatures; resume frequent watering and spraying.

Propagation Take tip cuttings in early autumn or spring.

Pests and diseases Aphids and whiteflies infest leaves and stems.

Fuchsia 'Leonora'

Gardenia
gardenia

Gardenia jasminoides 'Fortuniana'

- Height 60-120cm (2-4ft)
- Temperature minimum 16-18°C (61-64°F)
- Bright, filtered light
- Peat-based compost
- Flowering shrub

Gardenia (*Gardenia jasminoides*) is grown for its beautiful white saucer-shaped flowers, which can fill a room with their fragrance.

The shrub generally grows about 60cm (2ft) high as a pot plant and has dark glossy green, lance-shaped to oval leaves. They are up to 10cm (4in) long and make a perfect foil for the flowers, which appear during late spring and summer.

The variety most often seen as a pot plant is 'Fortuniana', with waxy double flowers more than 7.5cm (3in) across in summer and autumn. The variety 'Veitchiana' can be brought into flower in winter.

Cultivation
To produce the best display of flowers, gardenia needs bright light out of direct sunlight in constant room temperatures of 16-18°C (61-64°F) while flower buds are forming. Maintain high humidity by standing the pots on moist pebbles and mist-spraying daily with tepid, lime-free water. During active growth, water moderately when the compost is dry and feed fortnightly. Give less water during the winter rest.

To bring 'Veitchiana' into flower in winter, pinch out flower buds in spring and summer.

Propagation Take tip cuttings in early spring.

Pests and diseases Aphids infest young shoots, making plants sticky and sooty. Red spider mites infest the underside of leaves, mealy bugs infest stems. Bud drop is generally caused by a sudden change in temperature.

GARLAND FLOWER – see *Hedychium*

Gasteria
gasteria

Gasteria maculata

- Height 5-20cm (2-8in)
- Temperature minimum 10°C (50°F)
- Medium light
- Cactus compost
- Succulent

Gasterias are attractive foliage plants with tough, fleshy leaves arranged in two ranks. They are marked with flecks, spots or warts. Long arching stems of red tubular flowers may appear at any time.

Popular species
Gasteria liliputana, up to 7.5cm (3in) high, has lance-shaped leaves. They are dark green, heavily flecked with white.
Gasteria maculata, up to 20cm (8in) high, has dark green leaves with white flecks and spots.
Gasteria verrucosa (wart gasteria), up to 15cm (6in) high, has tapering dark green leaves arranged in pairs and heavily marked with grey or white warts.

Cultivation
Gasterias need filtered light and thrive on north-facing sills in normal room temperatures. During active growth, water moderately when the top of the compost is dry. Feeding is unnecessary. During the winter rest, keep at 10°C (50°F). Water sparingly.
Propagation Detach and pot up offsets in summer.
Pests and diseases Mealy bugs show as tufts of white waxy wool. Root mealy bugs infest the roots.

GENISTA – see *Cytisus*
GERMAN IVY – see *Senecio*
GERMAN VIOLET – see *Exacum*
GINGER-WORT – see *Hedychium*

Glechoma

ground ivy

Glechoma hederacea 'Variegata'

☐ Height 10cm (4in)
☐ Temperature minimum 5°C (41°F)
☐ Medium light
☐ Soil-based compost
☐ Foliage plant

Ground ivy (*Glechoma hederacea,* syn. *Nepeta hederacea*) is a hardy outdoor perennial used for ground cover. As a pot plant, it is usually represented by the variety 'Variegata'. This has trailing stems, often 60cm (2ft) long, and is suitable for a hanging basket.

The small, pale to mid green, white-variegated leaves are kidney-shaped with rounded teeth and soft hairs. Small flower spikes of blue hooded flowers are borne in summer.

Cultivation
Glechoma does best in medium light, such as near a north-facing window, and in ordinary room temperatures. Water moderately and feed every fortnight during active growth; at the winter rest, a temperature of 5°C (41°F) is sufficient, with enough water to prevent the compost from drying out completely.
Propagation Divide and pot up crowded plants in early or mid spring. Alternatively, take cuttings from basal shoots.
Pests and diseases Generally trouble free.

Gloriosa

glory lily

Gloriosa rothschildiana

☐ Height up to 1.8m (6ft)
☐ Temperature minimum 10-15°C (50-59°F)
☐ Bright filtered light
☐ Soil-based compost
☐ Flowering climber

Grown for its colourful flowers, glory lily rapidly climbs a trellis or moss pole to make a spectacular feature.

The flowers, which appear from early to late summer, resemble Turk's-cap lilies with narrow reflexed petals.

Gloriosa rothschildiana has crimson flowers with yellow wavy edges. *G. superba* has yellow flowers turning orange then red. The edges of the petals are crimped. Both species have glossy, mid green lance-shaped leaves and die down after flowering.

Cultivation
Glory lilies need bright light out of direct sun in normal room temperatures. During active growth, keep the compost moist and feed fortnightly. Stop watering when the top growth dies down. For the winter rest, keep dry at 10-15°C (50-59°F); start the tubers into growth in spring.
Propagation Remove and pot up offsets when repotting in spring.
Pests and diseases Over-watering causes discoloured patches on leaves.

GLORY BUSH – see *Tibouchina*
GLOXINIA – see *Sinningia*
GOAT'S HORN CACTUS – see *Astrophytum*
GOLDEN BALL CACTUS – see *Echinocactus* and *Notocactus*
GOLDEN FEATHER PALM – see *Chrysalidocarpus*
GOLDEN HUNTER'S ROBE – see *Scindapsus*
GOLDEN TRUMPET – see *Allamanda*
GOLDFISH PLANT – see *Columnea*
GOOD LUCK PALM – see *Chamaedorea*
GOODLUCK PLANT – see *Cordyline*
GOOSEFOOT PLANT – see *Syngonium*
GRAPE IVY – see *Cissus*

Grevillea
silk oak

Grevillea robusta

☐ Height 90cm-1.8m (3-6ft)
☐ Temperature minimum 7°C (45°F)
☐ Bright filtered light
☐ Peat-based compost
☐ Foliage plant

Silk oak (*Grevillea robusta*) is grown for its light, fern-like foliage. It makes a handsome specimen shrub and a good foil for large-leaved and flowering plants.

The evergreen foliage is mid to deep green, deeply divided and covered with silky hairs. The young leaves are tinged bronze.

Cultivation
Silk oak thrives in bright light out of direct sun, in a well-ventilated position with normal room temperatures. To maintain humidity, stand the pots on moist pebbles. During active growth, keep the compost moist and feed fortnightly; the plant benefits from an outdoor spell in summer. During the winter rest, keep at 7-10°C (45-50°F) and give less water. Fast-growing silk oak can be pruned by up to half in early spring.
Propagation Grow from seed.
Pests and diseases Trouble free.

Guzmania
guzmania

Guzmania lingulata

☐ Height 30-40cm (12-16in)
☐ Temperature minimum 16°C (61°F)
☐ Bright, filtered light
☐ Bromeliad compost
☐ Bromeliad

One of the most popular bromeliads, guzmania is highly decorative with its colourful flowers and bracts, and its dense rosette of narrow, arching leaves.

Most guzmanias flower in late winter or early spring, but the bracts – which conceal the true flowers – last for many weeks and are often more showy than the flowers. The smooth-edged glossy leaves form a water-holding reservoir at the centre of the rosette.

Popular species
Guzmania lingulata, syn. *G. cardinalis*, up to 30cm (1ft) high, has shiny bright green, rather narrow leaves up to 45cm (1½ft) long. The flower stem is topped by crimson bracts; they are triangular with a cluster of yellow-white flowers at the centre. The flowers are short-lived but the bracts remain colourful for many weeks.
Guzmania monostachya, syn. *G. tricolor*, up to 40cm (16in) high, has narrow, slightly arching leaves. The long-stalked flower spike is topped with small green, white-tipped bracts with vertical brown-purple stripes. The white flowers are hidden by the bracts.

Guzmania sanguinea

Guzmania sanguinea, up to 30cm (1ft) high, has lance-shaped, arching, red-tinged leaves and a central boss of pale yellow or white flowers.

Cultivation
Guzmanias need bright, filtered light, high humidity and temperatures above 18°C (64°F); water the compost moderately and keep the rosette filled up; feed every two weeks during active growth. Mist-spray regularly.
Propagation Detach and pot up well-rooted offsets in spring or summer.
Pests and diseases Trouble free.

Gymnocalycium

gymnocalycium, chin cactus

Gymnocalycium baldianum

☐ Height 5-10cm (2-4in)
☐ Temperature minimum 5°C (41°F)
☐ Bright light
☐ Cactus compost
☐ Cactus

Chin cacti earned their popular name from the chin-like indentations beneath each areole (cushion-like pad). The plant bodies are generally bluish-green, the spines curved and often attractively coloured. Large flowers are borne on even tiny plants in summer.

Popular species

Gymnocalycium baldianum, syn. *G. venturianum*, forms a solitary stem up to 7.5cm (3in) high. The broad ribs have pronounced 'chins', and the spines are white or yellow. The flowers are usually brilliant red.

Gymnocalycium denudatum (spider cactus) forms a slightly flattened stem up to 10cm (4in) high. It has broad ribs with thick grey, brown-tipped spines and white flowers.

Gymnocalycium mihanovichii is up to 7.5cm (3in) high, with sharply angled ribs sometimes marked with red, and thin, yellow spines. The flowers are green-yellow or pink. The numerous varieties have red, creamy yellow or black stems. Lacking chlorophyll they are grafted on to a green cactus base.

Gymnocalycium quehlianum has a flattened blue-green stem up to 5cm (2in) high, with broad ribs and pronounced 'chins' beneath woolly areoles. The thin yellow spines are brown at the base; the flowers are white, tinged red.

Cultivation

Gymnocalyciums need bright light and sun and ordinary room temperatures. During active growth water plentifully, keeping the compost thoroughly moist. Feed fortnightly. Rest the plants at about 5°C (41°F) and water just enough to prevent the stems from shrivelling.

Propagation Grow from seed in spring. Coloured varieties of *G. mihanovichii* must be bought.

Pests and diseases Mealy bugs may form colonies.

Gymnocalycium quehlianum

Gynura

velvet plant

Gynura aurantiaca

☐ Height 90cm-1.5m (3-5ft)
☐ Temperature minimum 13°C (55°F)
☐ Bright light
☐ Soil-based compost
☐ Foliage plant

Delightful climbing or trailing plants, gynuras offer unusual foliage with their deep green, purple-felted leaves.

The small orange spring flowers smell unpleasant and are best removed.

Popular species

Gynura aurantiaca is a bushy plant up to 90cm (3ft) high. Stems and leaves have a velvety covering of bright violet-purple hairs. The leaves are sometimes lobed.

Gynura procumbens, syn *G. sarmentosa*, is a trailing or twining weak-stemmed species 1.2-1.5m (4-5ft) high. The toothed leaves have a purple main vein. Pinch out shoot tips to encourage bushy growth.

Cultivation

Velvet plants like bright light with some direct sun and ordinary room temperatures with good humidity. During active growth, keep the compost moist and feed fortnightly. During the winter, rest the plants at around 13°C (55°F) and keep them barely moist.

Propagation Take tip cuttings in spring.

Pests and diseases Trouble free.

Haemanthus
blood lily

Haemanthus katharinae

☐ Height 23-45cm (9-18in)
☐ Temperature minimum 13°C (55°F)
☐ Bright light
☐ Soil-based compost
☐ Flowering bulb

The South African blood lilies are bulbous plants with exotic globular flowers. They are easy to grow as indoor pot plants and have lance-shaped to oblong, fleshy and usually stalkless leaves.

Popular species
Haemanthus albiflos, up to 30cm (1ft) high, bears 5cm (2in) wide flower heads, white and resembling shaving brushes. They are borne in summer and early autumn.
Haemanthus coccineus, up to 30cm (1ft) high, produces heads of red flowers and bracts in late summer to early autumn. The leaves appear after the flowers.
Haemanthus katharinae, up to 30cm (1ft) high, has salmon-red, spherical flower heads up to 15cm (6in) wide in mid summer.
Haemanthus multiflorus, up to 45cm (1½ft) high, bears 15cm (6in) wide spherical heads of red flowers in mid spring.

Cultivation
Blood lilies need bright light with some direct sun in ordinary room temperatures. During active growth, water moderately and feed fortnightly.

Haemanthus coccineus

Rest the bulbs in winter at temperatures above 13°C (55°F).
Propagation Some species produce offsets which can be potted up in spring; others must be raised from seed.
Pests and diseases Mealy bugs may infest the plants.

HAMMOCK FERN – see *Blechnum*
HARE'S FOOT FERN – see *Polypodium* and *Davallia*
HART'S TONGUE FERN – see *Asplenium*

Hamatocactus
strawberry cactus

Hamatocactus setispinus

☐ Height 15cm (6in)
☐ Temperature minimum 4-10°C (40-50°F)
☐ Bright light
☐ Cactus compost
☐ Flowering cactus

The strawberry cactus (*Hamatocactus setispinus* syn. *Ferocactus setispinus*) is a desert plant that flowers while still young. Slow-growing, it reaches a height of 15cm (6in), the single-stemmed, globular plant body having narrow, notched ribs. They are set with areoles that bear clusters of thin brown radial spines and thicker central hooked spines.

Cup-shaped, 10cm (4in) wide cream to yellow flowers are borne at the crown in summer and early autumn; they are followed by red berries.

Cultivation
Strawberry cactus needs as much bright light and sun as possible in order to flower. It thrives at ordinary room temperatures and needs a winter rest at 10°C (50°F). During the growing season, water moderately, letting the compost dry out between waterings, and feed every two weeks. In winter, water just enough to prevent shrivelling.
Propagation Sow seed in spring.
Pests and diseases A sticky gum on the areoles causes black mould; rinse it off with tepid water.

Haworthia

haworthia, pearl plant

Haworthia attenuata

☐ Height 2.5-15cm (1-6in)
☐ Temperature minimum 5-10°C (41-50°F)
☐ Bright light
☐ Cactus compost
☐ Succulent

Haworthias are fascinating foliage plants with thick, fleshy leaves and conspicuous markings.

The leaves form rosettes, usually low and compact, though some species are upright with rows of overlapping rosettes. Some haworthias have hard, tough leaves; others are soft with translucent areas.

Sprays of small bell-shaped flowers may appear in summer, but they are not showy and usually removed.

Haworthias use their fleshy leaves to store food and water and can withstand a considerable amount of neglect.

Popular species
Haworthia attenuata, up to 10cm (4in) high, forms a rosette of tapering dark green leaves with white warts.
Haworthia cuspidata forms clusters of 7.5cm (3in) wide rosettes. The pale green leaves are about 2.5cm (1in) long with short and pointed, transparent tips.
Haworthia margaritifera (pearl plant), up to 7.5cm (3in) high, has rosettes of dark green lance-shaped leaves thickly covered with white warts.
Haworthia maughanii, up to

2.5cm (1in) high, has rosettes of almost vertical, cylindrical mid green leaves. The leaf tips are flat and almost transparent, allowing light to reach the plant's inner tissues. In the wild, the entire plant is buried, save for the leaf tips.
Haworthia reinwardtii, up to 15cm (6in) high, has an upright stem clothed in dark green lance-shaped leaves covered with white warts.
Haworthia tesselata (wart plant, star window plant) forms star-shaped rosettes up to 5cm (2in) high. The greenish brown, toothed leaves are roughly triangular and marked with a network of white veins.
Haworthia truncata is similar to *H. maughanii*, but the leaves are arranged in rows.

Cultivation
Haworthias like bright but filtered light, at ordinary room temperatures. During active growth, water moderately when the top of the compost is dry and feed monthly. The plants need a definite winter rest at around 10°C (50°F); water only to prevent the compost from drying out.
Propagation Grow from seed or detach and pot up offset rosettes.
Pests and diseases Mealy bugs produce conspicuous tufts of white wool. Root mealy bugs infest roots.

HEARTS-ON-A-STRING – see *Ceropegia*

Hedera

ivy

Hedera canariensis 'Gloire de Marengo'

☐ Height 60cm-3m (2-10ft)
☐ Temperature minimum 7-10°C (45-50°F)
☐ Bright or filtered light
☐ Soil-based compost
☐ Foliage climbing or trailing plants

One of the best known and most tolerant foliage climbers, ivy is a useful and easily grown plant offering a range of leaf colours and markings. It is versatile enough to serve a variety of purposes.

Ivies look attractive trailing from hanging baskets with other foliage or flowering plants. They can be trained up moss poles, or planted in large troughs to scramble up trellis.

The leathery leaves range in form from the typical 'ivy' shape of common ivy (*H. helix*) with three to five lobes, to oval, heart or diamond shapes with some varieties offering leaves which are arrow-shaped. Leaf colours include dark and mid green, silvery or grey-green, gold, yellow, pink and white.

Ivies can grow up to 3m (10ft) high indoors, but they tolerate hard pruning and can be trimmed to shape at any time.

Popular species and varieties
Hedera canariensis (Canary

Hedera helix 'Glacier'

Hedera helix 'Shamrock'

Hedychium
ginger-wort

Hedychium gardnerianum

Island ivy) has bright green, leathery lobed leaves measuring 10-15cm (4-6in) across. The variety 'Gloire de Marengo', syn. 'Variegata', has leaves which are light green in the centre, paling to silvery green with white margins. The leaves are less deeply lobed than the species.

Hedera colchica (Persian ivy) has dark green, leathery, oval or heart-shaped leaves which are 20-25cm (8-10in) wide and 15cm (6in) long. The young growth is covered with yellow down. 'Dentata' has thin, widely toothed, dark green, purple-tinted leaves larger than the species; 'Dentata Variegata' is similar but edged with cream-yellow.

Hedera helix (common ivy) has glossy dark green, heart-shaped leaves, sometimes with silver markings along the veins. The species is rarely grown having been superseded by numerous ornamental varieties. These include: 'Buttercup' (slow-growing, rich yellow leaves); 'Chicago' (five-lobed, pointed leaves); 'Chicago Variegata' (small, grey-green cream-edged leaves); 'Glacier' (silvery edged leaves); 'Goldchild' (yellow leaf edges); 'Ivalace' (glossy green leaves, crinkled and wavy leaf edges); 'Kolibri' (small, grey-green and creamy white leaves); 'Little Diamond' (diamond-shaped small leaves edged creamy white); 'Manda's Crested' (curly-leaved, star-shaped, soft pale green); 'Marmorata' (leaves mottled cream and grey); 'Sagittifolia' (grey-green, arrowhead leaves,

edged white); and 'Shamrock' (mid green, sharply pointed lobed leaves, prominent veins).

Cultivation
Ivies prefer a well-ventilated position in bright but filtered light. Variegated types need some direct sun to maintain good leaf colouring. Green-leaved ivies will tolerate poor light but grow lanky. During active growth the ideal temperature range is 16-18°C (61-64°F); at higher temperatures increase humidity by placing the pots on moist pebbles and mist-spraying regularly. Keep the compost just moist and feed monthly.

During the winter rest move to a well lit but cooler position with a temperature around 10°C (50°F); water sparingly.

Stems may be cut back to half their length in spring to encourage strong, leafy growth. To encourage bushy rather than trailing or climbing growth, pinch out growing tips.

Propagation Take cuttings of tips or side-shoots in summer.

Pests and diseases Scale insects infest the undersides of leaves and make the plants sticky and sooty. Mites cause a fine light mottling of upper leaf surfaces. Leaf spot shows as brown spots. Red spider mites cause a fine webbing on the underside of the leaves.

HEDGEHOG CACTUS – see *Echinocereus*

☐ Height 90cm-1.2m (3-4ft)
☐ Temperature minimum 7°C (45°F)
☐ Bright filtered light
☐ Soil-based compost
☐ Flowering plant

Grown for their spikes of orchid-like often fragrant flowers, ginger-worts bring a touch of the exotic to the home.

Popular species
Hedychium coccineum (red/scarlet ginger lily), up to 1.2m (4ft) high, has narrow, lance-shaped mid green leaves up to 45cm (1½ft) long. Spikes of red flowers appear from summer on. *H. gardnerianum* is similar but with yellow flowers.

Hedychium coronarium (garland flower, butterfly ginger), up to 90cm (3ft) high, has mid green lance-shaped leaves up to 60cm (2ft) long. Spikes of scented white flowers appear in summer.

Cultivation
Ginger-worts need bright light but out of direct sun, at ordinary room temperatures. Grow in large tubs and, during active growth, water moderately and feed fortnightly. During the winter rest move to a position with a temperature around 7°C (45°F). Keep barely moist.

Propagation Divide and repot the rhizomatous roots in spring.

Pests and diseases Trouble free.

Heliocereus

heliocereus, sun cactus

Heliocereus serratus

☐ Height 30-90cm (1-3ft)
☐ Temperature 16-24°C (61-75°F)
☐ Bright light
☐ Cactus compost
☐ Cactus

Grown for their beautiful funnel-shaped flowers and sprawling four-angled stems, heliocereus, also known as sun cactus, are ideal cacti for displaying in hanging baskets by sunny windows.

Popular species
Heliocereus serratus, syn. *Cereus serratus*, up to 30cm (1ft) high, has branching stems with yellow spines. The flowers, borne in late spring and summer, are red with mauve shading inside.
Heliocereus speciosus, syn. *Cereus speciosissimus* and *C. speciosus*, has branching stems up to 90cm (3ft) long and up to 5cm (2in) thick; they have yellow to brown spines. The flowers are bright scarlet with a bluish sheen in the throat.

Cultivation
Heliocereus need bright light, including some direct sun at ordinary room temperatures throughout the year. During active growth in spring and summer, keep the compost thoroughly moist and feed fortnightly. In autumn and winter water moderately when the top half of the compost is dry.
Propagation Take stem cuttings in spring or summer.
Pests and diseases Trouble free.

HELXINE – see *Soleirolia*

Heliotropium

heliotrope

Heliotropium x *hybridum*

☐ Height 30cm (12in)
☐ Temperature minimum 7-10°C (45-50°F)
☐ Bright filtered light
☐ Soil-based compost
☐ Short-term flowering plant

The strongly scented heliotrope (*Heliotropium* x *hybridum*) can perfume an entire room with its deep violet or white flowers. Most heliotropes are hybrids; they are available as pot plants or as named seed selections and much used for outdoor bedding schemes, when they are grown as annuals and discarded at the end of the season.

As indoor pot plants, heliotropes can be grown as perennials. They reach a height of about 30cm (12in), with branching stems clothed with oblong, dark green and wrinkled leaves. Dense globular heads of tiny forget-me-not-like flowers are borne in the leaf axils from late spring until autumn.

Cultivation
Grow heliotropes in bright but filtered light, at ordinary room temperatures; in warm positions, increase humidity by standing the pots on moist pebbles. Water freely during active growth and feed every 10 days.

Overwintered plants should be rested at a temperature of 7-10°C (45-50°F) and kept barely moist. Large plants can be cut hard back in early spring to encourage branching and early flowers.
Propagation Take stem cuttings in early spring or late summer. Or sow seed in late winter.
Pests and diseases Whiteflies may be troublesome at high humidity.

Heptapleurum

parasol plant

Heptapleurum arboricola 'Variegata'

☐ Height up to 1.8m (6ft)
☐ Temperature minimum 16°C (61°F)
☐ Bright light
☐ Soil-based compost
☐ Foliage shrub

Parasol plant (*Heptapleurum arboricola*) is a popular and easily grown shrub with leaves divided into leaflets arranged in a circle like a parasol.

It grows up to 1.8m (6ft) high with an unbranched stem, but can take on a more bushy, spreading form if the growing tips are pinched out.

Popular varieties
'Geisha Girl' has slender stems and shiny dark green leaves.
'Hayata' has grey-green leaves with pointed leaflets.
'Variegata' has cream-white variegated leaves.

Cultivation
Parasol plants need bright light with some direct sun, and a minimum temperature of 16°C (61°F) throughout the year. Water moderately when the top of the compost is dry. Maintain humidity by placing the pots on moist pebbles and mist-spraying regularly. Feed fortnightly in spring and summer.
Propagation Take stem or tip cuttings in spring.
Pests and diseases Trouble free.

HERRINGBONE PLANT – see *Maranta*

Hibiscus

hibiscus

Hibiscus rosa-sinensis

Hibiscus rosa-sinensis

☐ Height 45cm-1.8m (1½-6ft)
☐ Temperature minimum 13°C (55°F)
☐ Bright filtered light
☐ Soil-based compost
☐ Flowering shrub

Prized for its glossy leaves and exotic, rather papery funnel-shaped flowers, hibiscus is a well-branched colourful flowering shrub for a brightly lit position.

The flowers come in shades of red, orange, yellow and pink or white and can measure up to 15cm (6in) across. Individual flowers are short-lived, but are quickly followed by others. The main flowering season is from summer to autumn, but thriving plants may produce occasional blooms at other times of the year.

Popular species

Hibiscus rosa-sinensis (rose of China) is the most popular species for growing indoors. It grows quickly, eventually attaining a height and spread of up to 1.8m (6ft) unless heavily pruned. It has dark green, broadly oval leaves which are toothed, pointed and sometimes shallowly lobed. From early summer to early autumn it

bears profuse but short-lived flowers as much as 13-15cm (5-6in) across. They are scarlet in the type species, but varieties and hybrids come in semi-double and double forms, in shades of pink, apricot, yellow and orange and white. The variety 'Cooperi' has smaller crimson flowers and narrower leaves variegated with cream and crimson.

Hibiscus schizopetalus (Chinese lantern), a shrub up to 1.8m (6ft) high and across, has slender, rather arching stems which may need support. The leaves are glossy green and the drooping flowers are orange-red with reflexed, fringed petals. They appear from late summer to early autumn.

Cultivation

Hibiscus needs bright light out of direct sunlight in normal room temperatures. Maintain humidity by standing the pot on moist pebbles; mist-spray regularly, but avoid wetting opening flowers. During active growth keep the compost constantly moist and feed fortnightly.

During the winter rest keep in

a cooler position with a minimum temperature of 13°C (55°F). Give only enough water to prevent the compost from drying out.

Repot annually in early spring, using a proprietary soil-based potting compost. To keep the plants within bounds and to encourage large blooms cut back hard in early spring, up to 15cm (6in) of the base. Left unpruned, the plants produce more profuse but smaller flowers.

Propagation Take tip or heel cuttings in spring or summer.

Pests and diseases Aphids may infest young shoots, flower buds and flowers, making them sticky and sooty. Mealy bugs cause conspicuous tufts of white waxy wool on stems and leaves. Over-dry conditions and/or low night temperatures may cause bud-drop. A physiological disorder may cause yellowing of the leaves. Small black spots may appear and leaves fall prematurely. Inadequate light leads to a poor show of flowers.

Hippeastrum

hippeastrum

Hippeastrum 'El Toreador'

☐ Height 45-75cm (1½-2½ft)
☐ Temperature minimum 10°C (50°F)
☐ Bright light
☐ Soil-based compost
☐ Flowering bulb

Hippeastrum 'Appleblossom'

Hippeastrum 'Orion'

The beautiful hippeastrum has a reputation for being difficult to bring into flower after its first year. But with enough light and correct watering, the huge, funnel-shaped blooms will provide an exotic and elegant feature year after year.

Most hippeastrums are hybrids. The flowers, which measure up to 15cm (6in) wide, are in shades of red, pink and orange or white. They may be all one colour, striped or with contrasting shadings, sometimes with a greenish throat. They open in small clusters of two to four in spring, either just before or at the same time as the leaves.

The strap-shaped leaves are mid to dark green and measure up to 45cm (1½ft) long.

Hippeastrums are often incorrectly called amaryllis, after a different but related genus belonging to the same family.

Popular hybrids
'Appleblossom' has white flowers shaded rose-pink with green shading at the centre.
'El Toreador' is deep scarlet.
'Lady Jane' bears orange double flowers.
'Orion' has scarlet flowers with a cream-white stripe down the centre of each petal.
'White Lady' is pure white with green shading at the throat.

Cultivation
Hippeastrums need bright light, including direct sunlight, and growing temperatures around 18°C (64°F). Water moderately when the top of the compost is dry and feed fortnightly; during flowering keep the compost moist.

Reduce watering after flowering and move to a cooler position at 10°C (50°F). Stop watering when the top growth dies down. Repot only when bulbs are congested; start into growth by resuming watering in autumn.
Propagation Remove and pot up offset bulbs.
Pests and diseases Mealy bugs may infest bulbs and leaves.

HOLLY FERN – see *Cyrtomium* and *Polystichum*
HOT WATER PLANT – see *Achimenes*

Howeia

howea

Howeia belmoreana

☐ Height up to 3m (10ft)
☐ Temperature minimum 13°C (55°F)
☐ Bright light
☐ Soil-based compost
☐ Palm

Howeia is a popular indoor palm which can achieve tree-like proportions in a large, well-lit room.

The leaves grow from a single central stem and are divided into numerous leaflets, giving a delicate frond-like appearance.

As pot plants howeias can grow up to 3m (10ft) in large containers though they take many years to do so. The plants are sometimes listed under *Kentia*.

Popular species
Howeia belmoreana (curly palm), up to 3m (10ft) high, has dark green, upright leaves divided into numerous lance-shaped leaflets. The leaves measure up to 45cm (1½ft) long and across on stalks up to 45cm (1½ft) long.

Howeia forsteriana (Kentia palm, sentry palm, paradise palm) is up to 2.4m (8ft) high. It is similar to *H. belmoreana* but the leaves are more arching and divided into fewer leaflets.

Cultivation
Howeias need bright or medium light in ordinary room temperatures. During active growth keep the compost thoroughly moist and feed fortnightly.

During the winter rest move to a well-lit position with temperatures of 10-13°C (50-55°F) and water moderately until new growth starts. Pot on every two years in spring.
Propagation Grow from seed.
Pests and diseases Trouble free.

Hoya

wax plant

Hoya carnosa

☐ Height 23cm-3m (9in-10ft)
☐ Temperature minimum 10°C (50°F)
☐ Bright light
☐ Soil-based compost
☐ Climbing or trailing shrubs

Ideal for indoor trellises or hanging baskets, wax plants climb or trail their stems clothed with fleshy evergreen leaves and clusters of waxy flowers.

Hoyas are tolerant of indoor conditions provided good light and humidity are available.

The star-shaped, highly fragrant flowers are white, pale yellow or flesh-pink and generally appear in summer. When mature, the flowers glisten with sticky nectar. Sometimes, nectar is produced in such large quantities that it drips on to the floor.

Popular species
Hoya australis is a climbing plant which quickly reaches a height up to 3m (10ft). It has rich green oval or rounded leaves. In summer it bears clusters of about 15 white fragrant flowers with red centres. *Hoya bella* (miniature wax plant), 23-30cm (9-12in) high, has slightly pendulous branches and is suitable for a hanging basket. The fleshy, heart-shaped pale green leaves sometimes have silvery spots. The fragrant, white waxy flowers, which may appear at any time from mid spring to early autumn, are borne in clusters about 5cm (2in) wide. Each flower has a rose-crimson or purple centre.

Hoya carnosa, a climber up to 3m (10ft) high, bears fleshy, oval mid

Hoya carnosa

green leaves. White to flesh-pink, fragrant flowers appear in clusters up to 7.5cm (3in) across from mid spring to early autumn. The scent of the flowers is strongest in the evening when it can fill a living room with a powerful sweet perfume. This species, which climbs by aerial roots, sometimes forms an entire new stem before any leaves develop on it. 'Variegata' is a form with cream-edged leaves.

Hoya multiflora can be trained as a climbing plant or as a shrub. Up to 90cm (3ft) high, it has bright green leaves marked with silver. The pale yellow fragrant flowers have a white or pale brown centre and appear in loose clusters in late summer.

Cultivation
Wax plants need bright light, including at least three to four hours a day of direct sun at temperatures of 16-24°C (61-75°F). However, *H. bella* dislikes direct sun in summer. Maintain humidity by standing the pots on moist pebbles and mist-spraying regularly. During active growth, water moderately when the top of the compost feels dry and feed fortnightly.

During the winter rest, move to a cooler position with temperatures around 10°C (50°F). Provide canes, wire hoops or trellis to support climbing species and tie the stems in as required.

Hoya multiflora

Propagation Take tip or stem cuttings in summer.
Pests and diseases A physiological disorder, usually due to overwatering, causes the leaves to turn brown.

HUNTSMAN'S HORN – see *Sarracenia*

Hyacinthus
Dutch hyacinth

Hyacinthus orientalis Dutch hybrids

☐ Height 15-25cm (6-10in)
☐ Temperature maximum 16°C (61°F)
☐ Bright light
☐ Soil- or peat-based compost, bulb fibre
☐ Flowering bulb

The Dutch hyacinth (*Hyacinthus orientalis*) is one of the best-loved house plants, offering welcome colour and delicious scent in winter and spring.

The strap-shaped leaves appear first, soon followed by tightly clustered, sweetly scented flower spikes up to 25cm (10in) high. The individual flowers are bell-shaped and in shades of blue, pink, red, creamy yellow or white. Double-flowered types have looser flower spikes. Multiflora types have several spikes of flowers to each bulb but with fewer flowers on each spike. Miniature hyacinths grow up to 15cm (6in) high. Specially prepared bulbs are offered in summer and early autumn for flowering at Christmas.

Popular hybrids
'**Ann Mary**' has rose-red to salmon flowers.
'**Blue Princess**' bears several stems (multiflora) of pale porcelain-blue flowers.
'**Carnegie**' has white flowers.
'**City of Haarlem**' has primrose-yellow flowers.
'**Delft Blue**' has dense spikes of pale blue, mauve-flushed flowers.
'**Lady Derby**' has shell-pink flowers.

Hydrangea

hydrangea

Hyacinthus orientalis 'Lady Derby'

'L'Innocence' is pure white.
'Orange Queen' has orange to salmon-red flowers.
'Ostara' has large, purple-tinted mid blue flower spikes.
'Pink Pearl' is deep hydrangea-pink, lightly scented.

Cultivation

Plant hyacinth bulbs in autumn in moist compost, with half the bulb exposed above the surface. Place in a dark, cool position with temperatures ideally below 10°C (50°F) for six to ten weeks. Prepared bulbs are the earliest to flower.

When leaf tips are about 2.5cm (1in) high, move the plants gradually into better light. When the flower buds appear, move to a bright position with some direct sun, with temperatures up to 16°C (61°F). Keep the compost moist, not wet throughout.

Hyacinths can also be grown in water, in special glasses with constricted necks. Fill the glasses with water to just below, but not touching, the bulb.

Hyacinths are temporary house plants. After flowering, either discard or plant them in the garden.
Propagation Buy new bulbs.
Pests and diseases Aphids may infest leaves and stems. Rot diseases may destroy the bulbs. Mites may destroy flower buds.

Hydrangea macrophylla, lace-cap and mop-head varieties

☐ Height 30-60cm (1-2ft)
☐ Temperature maximum 16°C (61°F)
☐ Bright filtered light
☐ Alkaline or lime-free potting compost
☐ Flowering shrub

Hydrangeas are short-term house plants bought in bud and kept indoors for the eight short weeks they are in bloom. They provide a magnificent display in a well-lit, cool room or conservatory.

The oval mid green leaves are toothed, sometimes minutely so. Most pot-grown hydrangeas are up to 60cm (2ft) high and across.

The massive heads of four- or five-petalled flowers are white, blue, pink, purple or red.

Most indoor hydrangeas are varieties of *H. macrophylla*, chiefly the hortensia or mop-headed varieties, though lace-cap types, with flattened flower heads, are also available.

Apart from white, flower colour is affected by the acidity of the compost; blue varieties produce pink flowers in an alkaline compost, while pink varieties turn blue in an acidic compost.

Hortensias (mop-heads), the most common indoors, have rounded heads of sterile flowers composed of bracts rather than petals. Lace-cap hydrangeas have flat heads with tiny fertile flowers on the inside and sterile florets with coloured sepals round the outside. Variegated forms of mop-head or lace-cap hydrangeas are sometimes available, with creamy-yellow edged leaves.

Cultivation

Hydrangeas need bright but filtered light, and cool temperatures up to 16°C (61°F). Keep the compost thoroughly moist and feed fortnightly.

When the flowers have faded, either discard the plants or plant them out in shady, sheltered positions outdoors.
Propagation Take tip cuttings in early autumn, for growing as outdoor shrubs.
Pests and diseases Aphids may infest stems and leaves. Red spider mites may cause mottling of the foliage.

Hymenocallis
spider lily

Hymenocallis caribaea

- ☐ Height up to 45cm (1½ft)
- ☐ Temperature minimum 5°C (41°F)
- ☐ Bright light
- ☐ Soil-based compost
- ☐ Flowering bulb

Grown for its lovely white flowers with graceful narrow petals and trumpet-like corolla, spider lilies are elegant plants for the greenhouse or for cooler parts of the home.

Each bulb produces a clump of mid green, arching, strap-shaped leaves, and a sturdy, upright stem carrying up to six flowers.

The white, sometimes fragrant blooms resemble the hoop petticoat daffodil and are up to 15cm (6in) across.

Popular species
Hymenocallis caribaea is an evergreen species with broadly strap-shaped leaves, and fragrant white flowers in summer.
Hymenocallis x *festalis*, up to 45cm (1½ft) high, is deciduous. The white flowers, with long, narrow reflexed petals, appear from spring to early summer or later.

Cultivation
Spider lilies need bright but filtered light, in temperatures around 16°C (61°F). During active growth, keep the compost moist and feed fortnightly.

During winter move plants to a cooler position, at 5°C (41°F), and keep the compost just moist. *H. caribaea* requires moist compost throughout the year.

Plant so that the neck of each bulb is just above the surface of the compost.
Propagation Remove offset bulbs.
Pests and diseases Mealy bugs show as tufts of white waxy wool.

Hypocyrta
clog plant

Hypocyrta glabra

- ☐ Height 20cm (8in)
- ☐ Temperature minimum 15°C (59°F)
- ☐ Medium light
- ☐ Peat-based compost
- ☐ Flowering plant

The clog plant (*Hypocyrta glabra*) is a so-called gesneriad originating from steamy tropical jungles. It thrives at high humidity and makes a charming pot plant; it can also be grown in a hanging container, spreading its arching stems clothed with fleshy, dark green and glossy leaves that resemble those of box.

In summer, the plant is studded with curious-shaped, waxy orange flowers.

Cultivation
Clog plant needs a lightly shaded position, away from bright light, in ordinary to warm room temperatures which should not fall below 15°C (59°F) in winter. It requires high humidity – stand the pot on moist pebbles and mist-spray frequently except during flowering. Keep the compost moist throughout the year and feed fortnightly during active growth. Pinch out the growing tips to encourage a branching habit.
Propagation Root tip cuttings taken in mid spring.
Pests and diseases Generally trouble free.

Hypoestes
polka dot plant, freckle face

Hypoestes phyllostachya

- ☐ Height up to 38cm (15in)
- ☐ Temperature minimum 15°C (59°F)
- ☐ Bright filtered light
- ☐ Soil-based compost
- ☐ Foliage plant

Polka dot plant (*Hypoestes phyllostachya*) is grown for its prettily spotted foliage and makes an attractive feature in a sunny spot.

The pointed oval leaves are olive green, heavily spotted or marbled with pink. They measure about 6cm (2½in) long. Small lilac flowers appear in spring, but they are inconspicuous and generally removed as soon as they appear.

The variety 'Splash' has particularly large pink spots which often merge.

Cultivation
Polka dot plant likes bright filtered light and temperatures of 16-24°C (61-75°F). During active growth, water moderately when the top of the compost is dry and feed fortnightly. During the brief winter rest, at a temperature not below 15°C (59°F), water sparingly.

Cut back in spring to prevent straggly growth.

Plants bought from a nursery have invariably been treated with a growth regulating hormone to maintain low, compact growth. In the home they grow taller and less compact and are best replaced after a couple of years.
Propagation Take tip cuttings from spring to late summer.
Pests and diseases Trouble free.

Impatiens

busy Lizzie

Impatiens walleriana hybrid

☐ Height 15-90cm (6in-3ft)
☐ Temperature minimum 13°C (55°F)
☐ Bright filtered light
☐ Soil-based compost
☐ Flowering plant

Popular for their easy cultivation and handsome flowers which appear for many months of the year, busy Lizzies are favourites among indoor gardeners.

The species, which have long-spurred, scarlet, carmine or yellow flowers, can grow straggly, but there is a wide choice of neater hybrids, including compact types. They offer a range of flower colour – red, pink, white and bicoloured and striped blooms.

Leaves are generally elliptic and pointed and come in different shades of green and bronze.

Popular species and hybrids

Impatiens petersiana, up to 90cm (3ft) high, is correctly named *I. walleriana petersiana*. The stems and pointed leaves are bronze-red. It bears carmine 2.5-4cm (1-1½in) wide flowers throughout summer and autumn.

Impatiens repens is a creeping plant suitable for hanging baskets, its stems trailing up to 60cm (2ft). The small leaves are roughly kidney-shaped, and the yellow 4cm (1½in) wide flowers have a long backward-pointing spur; they appear in the summer.

Impatiens walleriana, syn. *I. holstii* or *I. sultani*, is a shrubby plant up to 60cm (2ft) or more high. It has bright green leaves and pale green, slightly translucent, succulent stems. Bright scarlet flowers appear mainly from mid spring to mid autumn

Impatiens 'New Guinea' hybrids

Impatiens walleriana, double-flowered hybrid

and measure up to 4cm (1½in) across. The species is the parent of many hybrids, some only 15-23cm (6-9in) high. Most bloom when young, with flowers in shades of red, pink and white. Striped, bicoloured and double-flowered types are available. Foliage, mid to dark green, is sometimes tinted bronze.

Impatiens 'New Guinea' hybrids offer a wider range of foliage colour, including variegated types with leaves in shades of green, red, yellow and bronze. Flowers can measure 7.5cm (3in) across and come in shades of pink, red, purple, orange and white.

Cultivation

Busy Lizzies need bright light, but out of direct sunlight, in temperatures above 13°C (55°F). Maintain humidity by standing the pots on moist pebbles and mist-spraying regularly. During active growth, water moderately when the top of the compost is dry, and feed fortnightly.

Busy Lizzies are often discarded after a year as they grow leggy. Encourage bushiness by pinching out growing tips. Staking may be necessary.

Propagation Tip cuttings taken in summer root easily in water; alternatively, grow from seed.

Pests and diseases Aphids may make the plants sticky and sooty. Red spider mites cause mottling and bronzing of the leaves.

INCH PLANT – see *Tradescantia*

Iresine

beefsteak plant, bloodleaf

Iresine herbstii 'Brilliantissima'

☐ Height up to 60cm (2ft)
☐ Temperature minimum 16°C (61°F)
☐ Bright light
☐ Soil-based compost
☐ Foliage perennial

Beefsteak plant (*Iresine herbstii*) makes an interesting feature for a sunny window-sill or the conservatory with its unusual foliage in shades of red or green.

Also known as bloodleaf, the plant forms a soft-stemmed shrub up to 60cm (2ft) high. The stems are red and bear oval to rounded leaves which are sometimes notched at the tips, and puckered. They measure up to 10cm (4in) long and are deep purple-red with the network of veins picked out in paler red.

The variety 'Aureoreticulata' (chicken gizzard) has green leaves with the pattern of veins marked out in yellow or paler green. 'Brilliantissima' has scarlet-veined, plum-red leaves.

Beefsteak plant grows rapidly but tends to become straggly with age. Propagation is easy, and old plants are often discarded after taking cuttings.

Cultivation

Beefsteak plants thrive in bright light, including three or four

Iresine herbstii 'Aureoreticulata'

hours daily direct sun in year-round temperatures of 16-24°C (61-75°F). Maintain humidity by standing the pots on moist pebbles and mist-spraying regularly. During active growth, keep the compost thoroughly moist and feed fortnightly. During the brief winter rest, at 16°C (61°F), keep the compost just moist.

Pinch out growing tips regularly to encourage bushy growth.

Propagation Take tip cuttings in spring.

Pests and diseases Scale insects may form colonies on the underside of the leaves. Lack of light leads to poor leaf colour.

Iris

iris

Iris danfordiae

☐ Height 10-15cm (4-6in)
☐ Temperature 7-13°C (45-55°F)
☐ Bright light
☐ Soil-based compost
☐ Flowering bulb

The dainty irises, with their superb range of blue, yellow or white flowers, make attractive indoor plants, flowering in late winter and early spring. They are perfectly hardy plants suitable for potting in autumn and bringing into a cool position to flower indoors earlier than in the open garden. After flowering and when the foliage has withered, dry off the bulbs and plant in the garden in early autumn.

The flowers appear from early winter to spring. They have three upward-pointing petals (standards) and three outer petals (falls) which arch out at an angle to the standards. The falls are spotted or marked with contrasting colours.

Popular species

Iris danfordiae, up to 10cm (4in) high, bears honey-scented flowers in mid to late winter before the leaves appear. They are vivid lemon-yellow with smaller standards than other species. The black or greenish spotted falls stand out horizontally.

Iris histrioides 'Major', up to 10cm (4in) high, bears bright royal blue flowers, up to 9cm (3½in) across, from early winter. The falls have an orange crest-like marking surrounded by white.

Iris reticulata 'Harmony'

The leaves are only 2.5cm (1in) high when the flowers appear.

Iris reticulata, up to 15cm (6in) high, bears deep purple-blue flowers from late winter to early spring. They measure 6-7.5cm (2½-3in) across and the falls have a distinct orange marking. The leaves extend above the blooms at flowering time. Hybrids include: 'Cantab' (pale blue); 'Harmony' (deep royal blue); 'J.S. Dijt' (purple-red, vigorous); 'Natasha' (near-white, pale grey falls, standards ageing to soft blue); and 'Pauline' (petunia-violet with white markings).

Cultivation

Pot iris bulbs 2.5cm (1in) deep in moist compost in early to mid autumn. Keep in a cool position at temperatures of 7-13°C (45-55°F).

When the developing buds begin to show colour, move the pots to a bright position with temperatures up to 18°C (64°F). Keep the compost moist. After the flowers have faded, feed monthly until the foliage has withered.

Propagation Buy new bulbs.

Pests and diseases Aphids may infest plants, making them sticky and sooty.

IVY – see *Hedera*
JACOBEAN LILY – see *Sprekelia*
JACOB'S COAT – see *Acalypha*
JADE TREE – see *Crassula*

Jasminum

jasmine

Jasminum officinale

☐ Height 90cm (3ft) or more
☐ Temperature minimum 10°C (50°F)
☐ Bright light
☐ Soil-based compost
☐ Flowering climber

Prized for their sweetly scented flowers, jasmines do best on cool window-sills, with their lax stems trained up canes or wire hoops.

Popular species

Jasminum mesnyi, syn. *J. primulinum*, is a rambling species which should be tied to a support. It has dark green leaves and bears semi-double yellow, unscented flowers throughout spring.

Jasminum officinale (common white jasmine), a climber with twining stems, has mid green leaves and bears clusters of white flowers from summer to autumn. 'Aureovariegatum' has cream-yellow blotched leaves.

Jasminum polyanthum (pink jasmine) has twining stems and dark green leaves. Strongly fragrant, white flowers open from pink buds in winter and spring. The species flowers while quite young.

Cultivation

Jasmines need bright light, including direct sun, in temperatures around 16°C (61°F). During

Jasminum mesnyi

active growth, keep the compost thoroughly moist and feed fortnightly. When the flowers fade, cut the stems hard back and move to a cooler position with temperatures of 10-13°C (50-55°F).

Propagation Take tip or heel cuttings in summer or early autumn.

Pests and diseases Aphids may infest young shoots. Mealy bugs show as tufts of white waxy wool.

JERUSALEM CHERRY – see *Solanum*
JOSEPH'S COAT – see *Codiaeum*
KAFFIR LILY – see *Clivia*

Kalanchoë
kalanchoë

Kalanchoë pumila

Kalanchoë tomentosa

☐ Height 20-90cm (8in-3ft)
☐ Temperature minimum 10°C (50°F)
☐ Bright light
☐ Soil-based compost
☐ Succulent

Kalanchoës are succulent plants, some grown for their attractive foliage, others, including the popular *K. blossfeldiana*, for their clusters of long-lasting flowers.

Most kalanchoës are upright or bushy shrubs, but the prostrate *K. pumila* makes an excellent specimen for a hanging basket. All do well on a sunny window-sill and are easy to grow.

Kalanchoës have plump lance-shaped to oval leaves with plain, wavy or scalloped edges and are sometimes velvety; they serve as water-storing organs, and the plants are tolerant of the dry air in centrally-heated rooms. Leaf colour ranges from silvery green to mid green and some species have brown-blotched or brown-edged foliage.

The individual flowers are tubular and come in shades of red, pink, orange, purple and yellow; they are carried in dense clusters.

Popular species
Kalanchoë beharensis (velvet leaf), up to 60cm (2ft) high, forms a single stem with velvety, dull green leaves. They are triangular to lance-shaped with wavy edges and a shallow central indentation.
Kalanchoë blossfeldiana (flaming Katy), up to 30cm (1ft) high, is an upright bushy plant. The oval, pale to mid green fleshy leaves have wavy edges. Scarlet tubular flowers appear in clusters from winter to spring, though flowers may appear at other times. Varieties with pink, orange, yellow and cream flowers are also available.
Kalanchoë daigremontiana, syn. *Bryophyllum daigremontianum* (devil's backbone), is up to 90cm (3ft) high. The narrow triangular, toothed, mid green leaves are spotted with reddish brown and measure up to 20cm (8in) long. Plantlets appear along the leaf margins.
Kalanchoë pumila, up to 20cm (8in) high, is suitable for a hanging basket. It has small, coarsely toothed lance-shaped leaves on weak arching, pink-tinged stems coated with a white meal. Clusters of pale pink flowers appear in mid to late winter.
Kalanchoë tomentosa (pussy ears, panda plant), up to 45cm (1½ft) high, has woolly, silvery green oblong leaves with brown edges.

Cultivation
Kalanchoës need bright light, including direct sun and ordinary room temperatures. During active growth, water moderately when the top of the compost is dry, and feed fortnightly.

During the winter rest, move to a cooler position at about 10°C (50°F) and keep the compost just moist. *K. blossfeldiana* is usually discarded after flowering, but can be given a short rest when the flowers have faded until new growth appears; it rarely flowers indoors again.
Propagation Take stem or leaf cuttings in spring. *K. daigremontiana* is increased from plantlets.
Pests and diseases Mealy bugs produce tufts of white waxy wool. Root mealy bugs may infest the root system and check growth.

KANGAROO VINE – see *Cissus*
KENTIA PALM – see *Howeia*

Kalanchoë blossfeldiana

Kohleria

kohleria

Kohleria bogotensis

☐ Height up to 90cm (3ft)
☐ Temperature minimum 10°C (50°F)
☐ Bright light
☐ Peat-based compost
☐ Flowering plant

The colourful kohlerias are rhizomatous plants that will flower throughout the year on a sunny window-sill.

Popular species

Kohleria bogotensis, up to 60cm (2ft) high, has velvety dark green oval leaves, sometimes mottled with silver-green and red. The drooping bell flowers have orange upper petals and yellow, red-spotted lower petals.
Kohleria eriantha, up to 90cm (3ft) high, bears narrow oval dark green leaves covered with reddish brown hairs. It bears scarlet flowers with yellow spots.

Cultivation

Kohlerias need bright light with some direct sun and normal room temperatures. Maintain humidity by placing pots on moist pebbles. During active growth, water moderately when the compost is dry and feed fortnightly. Below 10°C (50°F) the plants become dormant and should be kept dry.
Propagation Divide the rhizomes or take stem cuttings.
Pests and diseases Trouble free.

KUMQUAT – see *Fortunella*
LACE FLOWER – see *Episcia*

Lachenalia

lachenalia

Lachenalia aloides

☐ Height 15-30cm (6-12in)
☐ Temperature minimum 4-7°C (40-45°F)
☐ Bright light
☐ Soil-based compost
☐ Flowering bulb

Lachenalias are charming South African plants, providing a fine display of long-lasting winter colour, with their spikes of drooping, tubular flowers. They come in shades of yellow, purple and red, often with green and red markings. The plants die down after flowering.

Popular species

Lachenalia aloides, syn. *L. tricolor* (Cape cowslip), up to 30cm (1ft) high, bears yellow flowers with green and red markings. Varieties include: 'Aurea' (orange-yellow without markings) and 'Nelsonii' (bright yellow, green-tipped).
Lachenalia bulbifera, syn. *L. pendula*, 15-25cm (6-10in) high, has deep purple, red or yellow flowers with red and green tips.

Cultivation

Lachenalias need bright light including direct sun in tempera-

Lachenalia bulbifera

tures of 15-18°C (59-64°F). During active growth, keep the compost moist and feed fortnightly. When the flowers have faded, reduce watering; keep dry during dormancy and restart into growth in late summer.
Propagation Detach and pot up bulbils when growth restarts in summer.
Pests and diseases Basal rot may affect the bulbs. Ink disease shows as small brown spots.

Laelia

laelia

Laelia anceps

Laelia purpurata

☐ Height 15-60cm (6in-2ft)
☐ Temperature minimum 10°C (50°F)
☐ Bright light
☐ Orchid compost
☐ Epiphytic orchid

Grown for their magnificent wide-spreading flowers in shades of rose, lilac, purple and white, laelias make a magnificent feature, sometimes for several months.

The elongated pseudobulbs usually produce only one strap-shaped or oblong leaf each. The flowers appear in autumn or winter.

Popular species
Laelia anceps, up to 45cm (1½ft) high, has oblong to lance-shaped leaves. The upright flower stems arch at the tips and are up to 60cm (2ft) long. Each bears a spray of two to five 10cm (4in) wide flowers in early to mid winter. They are deep rose-lilac with a rich velvety purple lip and a purple-veined yellow throat. There are numerous varieties, including forms with white petals, and hybrids between this species and cattleya orchids.

Laelia cinnabarina, up to 45cm (1½ft) high, has a single narrow oblong leaf; the upright or arching flower stem bears sprays of 6cm (2½in) wide flowers. They are orange-red with a darker lip and appear in winter.

Laelia pumila, up to 15cm (6in) high, is a dwarf species with one oblong leaf. In autumn each flower stem bears one, or sometimes two, blooms up to 10cm (4in) across. They are bright rose-purple with a deep crimson-purple, yellow throated lip.

Laelia purpurata, up to 60cm (2ft) high, bears one oblong leaf and sprays of up to nine flowers, each up to 18cm (7in) across, from late spring to mid summer. The crinkly edged petals are white, flushed with rose. The large lips have yellow throats with purple veins; the central lobe is deep purple with a crinkled, narrow white margin.

Cultivation
Laelias need bright light, but away from strong midday sun. Daytime temperatures around 16°C (61°F) and 10°C (50°F) at night are ideal. Maintain high humidity by placing the pots on moist pebbles and mist-spray occasionally.

During active growth, water moderately when the compost is dry on top. During the rest period,

Laelia cinnabarina

after flowering or in winter, water sparingly, giving just enough water to prevent the pseudobulbs from shrivelling.

Propagation Divide and repot the plants when new growing points begin to develop roots in late winter to early spring. Alternatively, divide after flowering. Each division should have a growing point.

Pests and diseases Trouble free.

x *Laeliocattleya*

laeliocattleya

x *Laeliocattleya* 'Oriental Prince' x 'Olympica'

x *Laeliocattleya* 'Marienette Posie'

- ☐ Height up to 60cm (2ft)
- ☐ Temperature minimum 13°C (55°F)
- ☐ Bright light
- ☐ Orchid compost
- ☐ Epiphytic orchid

Laeliocattleyas are hybrids between *Laelia* and *Cattleya* and numerous forms exist with splendid blooms in shades of purple, mauve and yellow and white. The lips are often stained with a contrasting colour and the petals may be crimped or plain.

The large colourful, often fragrant flowers are mainly produced in autumn and winter.

Popular hybrids

'Chitchat Tangerine' bears sprays of delicate, narrow-petalled orange-yellow flowers in summer. They measure up to 5cm (2in) across and have rusty orange spotted lips.

'Culminant La Tuilerie' bears pink 15-18cm (6-7in) wide flowers in spring. The pink-edged lip is a darker pink.

'Marienette Posie' has white petals with a white-edged, deep purple lip splashed with yellow. The edges of the lip and petals are crimped.

'Marietta' has 13cm (5in) wide red-purple flowers with a deep purple, yellow-marked lip. The edges of the lip and petals are attractively crimped.

x *Laeliocattleya* 'Chitchat Tangerine'

'Oriental Prince' x **'Olympica'** bears 15-20cm (6-8in) wide flowers in autumn. The lavender-mauve petals have crimped edges and the large, frilly-edged lips are purple.

'Patricia Purves' bears deep mauve-purple flowers in spring. They are 15-18cm (6-7in) across.

Cultivation

Laeliocattleyas need bright light, but out of strong midday sun. They enjoy daytime temperatures above 18°C (64°F) with cooler temperatures around 13°C (55°F) at night. Maintain humidity by placing the pots on moist pebbles and mist-spraying occasionally. During active growth, water moderately when the compost feels dry on top and feed at every third or fourth watering. During the rest period, water sparingly, giving just enough water to stop the pseudobulbs shrivelling.

Propagation Divide and repot the plants when they become congested, in late winter to early spring. Alternatively, divide after flowering.

Pests and diseases Trouble free.

Lantana
yellow sage

Lantana camara

☐ Height up to 90cm (3ft)
☐ Temperature minimum 10°C (50°F)
☐ Bright filtered light
☐ Soil-based compost
☐ Flowering shrub

Yellow sage (*Lantana camara*) is popular for its colourful and fragrant globular flower heads during spring and summer.

The 5cm (2in) wide flower heads often contain individual blooms in several different shades: they start out white-yellow and change to brick-red as they mature. The pointed oval leaves are mid to deep green.

Varieties have flowers predominantly in shades of yellow, pink, red and white, but all change colour as they age.

Yellow sage can be kept to a height of 30cm (12in) by frequent pinching out of shoot tips.

Cultivation
Yellow sage likes bright light out of direct sun in normal room temperatures. Maintain humidity by standing the pot on moist pebbles and mist-spraying occasionally. During active growth, keep the compost thoroughly moist and feed fortnightly. During the winter rest, keep the compost barely moist at a temperature of about 10°C (50°F).
Propagation Take stem cuttings in summer.
Pests and diseases Trouble free.

Lapageria
Chilean bellflower

Lapageria rosea

☐ Height up to 3m (10ft)
☐ Temperature minimum 7°C (45°F)
☐ Bright light
☐ Lime-free compost
☐ Flowering climber

Chilean bellflower (*Lapageria rosea*) is often grown as a greenhouse or conservatory climber, but it also makes a fine house plant with its glossy dark green foliage and rose-crimson flowers.

The drooping, bell-shaped flowers appear from summer to autumn. They measure up to 7.5cm (3in) long and are borne on twining stems which can be trained up canes.

Cultivation
Chilean bellflower thrives in bright light, including direct sun, and in normal room temperatures. Maintain humidity by standing the pot on moist pebbles. During active growth, keep the compost thoroughly moist and feed fortnightly. During the winter rest, keep barely moist at a temperature of 7°C (45°F).
Propagation Sow seed in spring.
Pests and diseases Aphids may infest young shoots.

LEADWORT – see *Plumbago*
LEMON – see *Citrus*

Licuala
Queensland fan palm

Licuala spinosa

☐ Height up to 1.2m (4ft)
☐ Temperature minimum 13°C (55°F)
☐ Bright filtered light
☐ Peat- or soil-based compost
☐ Foliage plant

The Queensland fan palm (*Licuala spinosa*, syn. *L. horrida*) is an elegant foliage plant, producing several stems from the crown and bearing thorny, slender-stalked fronds made up of radiating, wedge-shaped and pleated or ribbed leaflets that terminate in blunt tips.

It is a slow-growing palm that tolerates fairly low light levels and will grow adequately in the same pot size for several years.

Cultivation
Queensland fan palm prefers good light out of direct sun but will tolerate a lightly shady position. It needs ordinary to warm room temperatures and thrives in a humid atmosphere – stand the pot on moist pebbles and mist-spray the foliage daily during active growth. Water freely and feed every fortnight from spring to autumn. During the winter rest, water moderately and keep at a temperature of 13°C (55°F).
Propagation Sow seed in spring.
Pests and diseases Scale insects and mealy bugs may attack the foliage.

Lilium

lily

Lilium Mid-Century Hybrid

☐ Height 60cm-1.2m (2-4ft)
☐ Temperature maximum 16°C (61°F)
☐ Bright light
☐ Peat- or soil-based compost
☐ Flowering bulb

The beautiful lilies, with their outstanding flowers in all colours of the rainbow except blue, are rewarding plants to grow in a cool part of the home.

The usual flowering time is mid summer to early autumn, but with careful cultivation some lilies can be forced to flower from mid spring.

Popular species and hybrids

Lilium auratum (golden-rayed lily), up to 1.2m (4ft) high, bears fragrant bowl-shaped flowers up to 30cm (1ft) across in late summer to early autumn. They are brilliant white with a golden yellow ray or band on each petal and raised, deep purple and yellow spots. The species needs lime-free compost.

Lilium longiflorum (Easter lily), up to 90cm (3ft) high, has heavily fragrant, white trumpet-shaped flowers up to 18cm (7in) long. They usually appear in mid to late summer.

Lilium regale (regal or royal lily), up to 90cm (3ft) high, bears loose clusters of fragrant white, funnel-shaped flowers in mid summer. They are up to 13cm (5in) long with pale yellow centres and rose-purple shaded backs.

Lilium speciosum, up to 90cm (3ft) high, bears sprays of fragrant, bowl-shaped white flowers up to 13cm (5in) long in late summer to early autumn. They have recurved petals, heavily shaded with crimson.

Mid-Century Hybrids have 10-15cm (4-6in) wide flowers carried singly or in clusters. They are outward-facing, upright or pendent and come in shades of yellow, orange, crimson and red and are spotted with maroon or brown.

Cultivation

Plant lily bulbs in pots in autumn and keep in a cool, dark position with a maximum temperature of 10°C (50°F). Keep the compost just moist.

When top growth appears, move to a bright position, without direct sunlight, at a maximum temperature of 16°C (61°F).

Alternatively, to encourage early flowering, move to a warmer place with temperatures of 18-21°C (64-70°F) and feed fortnightly. When the buds show colour, stop feeding and reduce the temperature to 16°C (61°F).

To bring *L. longiflorum* and Mid-Century Hybrids into flower in spring, pot treated bulbs in winter and force them at a temperature of 20°C (68°F) in good light. After flowering, move pots to a sheltered position outdoors and keep the compost moist. Repot in autumn.

Bulbs can be forced only once.
Propagation Detach bulblets when repotting in autumn.
Pests and diseases Aphids make plants sticky and sooty.

LIPSTICK VINE – see
Aeschynanthus

Lithops

living stones

Lithops karasmontana

☐ Height 2.5-4cm (1-1½in)
☐ Temperature minimum 10°C (50°F)
☐ Bright light
☐ Cactus compost
☐ Succulent

As the common name suggests, living stones resemble stones, except in autumn when yellow or white daisy flowers appear from slits at the top of the plant bodies. These consist of pairs of swollen, fleshy leaves fused together. They come in shades of green, grey and brown and may be marbled or marked with a network of lines or spots.

Popular species

Lithops erniana, up to 2.5cm (1in) high, is grey with a network of red-brown lines. It bears white flowers. The species *L. karasmontana* is similar.

Lithops lesliei, 4cm (1½in) high, is light to pale brown with brownish spots. It bears yellow, pink-tinged flowers.

Cultivation

Living stones need bright light including direct sun and normal room temperatures. During active growth, water sparingly; feeding is unnecessary. After flowering, rest the plants at about 10°C (50°F), stop watering until the old leaves have shrivelled and been replaced by new leaves.
Propagation Divide congested clumps in summer.
Pests and diseases Mealy bugs show as tufts of white waxy wool. Root mealy bugs may check growth.

LIVING STONES – see *Lithops*

Lobivia

lobivia

Lobivia pentlandii

☐ Height 10-15cm (4-6in)
☐ Temperature minimum 2°C (35°F)
☐ Bright light
☐ Cactus compost
☐ Cactus

Lobivias are spiny, globular desert cacti, with 5cm (2in) wide, funnel-shaped and colourful flowers in summer.

Lobivia is an anagram of Bolivia, the native habitat of these cacti.

Popular species

Lobivia allegraiana, up to 15cm (6in) high, is bright green and bears pink or red flowers.
Lobivia aurea, syn. *Echinopsis aurea* (golden lily cactus), up to 10cm (4in) high, bears profuse bright yellow flowers.
Lobivia hertrichiana (cob cactus), up to 10cm (4in) high, has a dark green, strongly spined plant body and bears scarlet flowers.
Lobivia pentlandii, up to 10cm (4in) high, has pink to orange-red flowers.

Cultivation

Lobivias need bright light including direct sun, and ordinary room temperatures. During active growth, water moderately when the compost feels dry, and feed fortnightly. During the winter rest, keep at a temperature below 10°C (50°F) and give only enough water to prevent the compost from drying out completely.
Propagation Grow from seed in early spring or detach and pot up offsets.
Pests and diseases Mealy bugs and root mealy bugs may infest the plants.

LOLLIPOP PLANT – see
Pachystachys

Lycaste

lycaste

Lycaste 'Wyldfire Wheatley'

☐ Height 23-30cm (9-12in)
☐ Temperature minimum 10°C (50°F)
☐ Bright filtered light
☐ Orchid compost
☐ Epiphytic orchid

Lycastes are Central American orchids prized for their colourful flowers, often strongly fragrant, and borne over several weeks. The tough, veined leaves are deep green and oblong to lance-shaped. The flowers are carried singly, each pseudobulb producing several stems. The sepals are generally larger than the petals. They offer a wide range of flower colour, including shades of orange, yellow, green, pink, red and cream.

These orchids do well on a draught-free, well-lit window-sill.

Popular species and hybrids

Lycaste aromatica bears fragrant orange-red flowers in winter and spring. They measure 5cm (2in) across and are offset by leaves as long as 45cm (18in).
Lycaste cruenta bears deep golden-orange to chrome-yellow flowers on 15cm (6in) tall stems in spring. They measure up to 6cm (2½in) across and have a spicy fragrance.
Lycaste deppei bears long-lasting flowers up to 10cm (4in) wide in mid spring to early summer. They have pale green sepals, lightly flushed and mottled with red, while the petals are white. The lip is chrome-yellow with red marks and spots. The stems are about 13cm (5in) long.
Lycaste virginalis, syn. *L. skinneri*, bears fragrant flowers, up to 15cm (6in) across, usually in autumn and winter. They have white, pink flushed sepals and

Lycaste deppei

pure white petals flushed or spotted with rose-red and crimson. The stems are up to 25cm (10in) long. 'Alba' is pure white.
Lycaste 'Wyldfire Wheatley' is a hybrid with rounded russet-red flowers. The small red petals are edged and spotted with white.

Cultivation

Lycastes need bright light out of direct sun, and daytime temperatures around 18°C (64°F) and good humidity. During active growth, water moderately when the compost is dry and feed fortnightly. During the winter rest, give only enough water to prevent the pseudobulbs from shrivelling.

Water carefully as the leaves may develop brown spots if water is dropped on them.
Propagation Divide the rhizomes and pot up in spring.
Pests and diseases A virus disease causes a mosaic pattern of light green on the foliage.

MADAGASCAR JASMINE – see
Stephanotis
MADAGASCAR PERIWINKLE –
see *Catharanthus*
MAIDENHAIR FERN – see
Adiantum

Mammillaria

mammillaria

Mammillaria plumosa

Mammillaria bocasana

- ☐ Height 5-20cm (2-8in)
- ☐ Temperature minimum 5-10°C (41-50°F)
- ☐ Bright light
- ☐ Cactus compost
- ☐ Cactus

One of the few cacti with flowers which are followed by decorative fruit, mammillarias also have attractive spines. Most species flower readily as pot plants. The cup-shaped flowers often form a ring around the top of the plants and are followed by small fig-like fruits, in shades of pink and red.

Popular species

Mammillaria bocasana (powder puff cactus) has roughly globular stems, up to 5cm (2in) high. They are blue-green, covered with a network of fine white spines and silky hairs. A longer red or yellow, hooked spine projects from the centre of each areole. Cream flowers appear in early summer, followed by purple berries.

Mammillaria densispina has clusters of slow-growing, round or cylindrical stems up to 15cm (6in) high. They are dark green, densely covered with yellow radial spines and long red central spines which later turn brown. In summer, purple-red and yellow flowers freely encircle the tips of the stems.

Mammillaria elegans has slow-growing cylindrical, pale green stems up to 20cm (8in) high. Smaller offshoots grow from the base. White spines cover the surface of the stems, with longer central spines projecting from the areoles. The violet-red or carmine flowers appear in mid to late summer.

Mammillaria erythrosperma has globular dark green stems up to 5cm (2in) high which rapidly form a cushion-like clump up to 15cm (6in) across. Each stem has glossy spines radiating from the areoles in a starry shape, and three or four central yellow spines. In summer deep pink flowers appear, followed by red fruits.

Mammillaria gracilis var. *fragilis* produces a cushion-like cluster of slender cylindrical stems 5cm (2in) high. They are bright green, covered with short white radial spines and longer, brown-tipped central spines. White flowers appear in summer.

Mammillaria hahniana (old lady cactus) has a flattened globular stem up to 10cm (4in) high which eventually produces offsets. The grey-green stems are covered with spines resembling long white hairs. Purplish red flowers appear in late spring.

Mammillaria plumosa (feather cactus) is slow-growing, producing clusters of globular stems, 5-7.5cm (2-3in) high. They are deep green, completely hidden by interlocking feathery white spines. This species only occasionally produces its greenish-white flowers.

Mammillaria prolifera forms a clump of roughly cylindrical stems, up to 6cm (2½in) high. They are dark green with bristly white radial spines giving a woolly appearance. The areoles also bear yellow central spines. The yellow, green-flushed flowers in late spring are followed by pink-red fruits.

Mammillaria zeilmanniana (rose pincushion) has clusters of 5cm (2in) high globular stems which are pale green and glossy. The areoles bear white radial spines and brown central spines. Profuse deep violet-red flowers appear in summer.

Cultivation

Mammillarias need bright light, including direct sun, at ordinary room temperatures. During active growth, water moderately when the compost feels dry, and feed fortnightly.

During the winter rest, keep almost dry, at a temperature at or below 10°C (50°F).

Propagation Sow seeds in spring. Alternatively, divide clusters from late spring to late summer.

Pests and diseases Mealy bugs may produce conspicuous tufts of white waxy wool. Root mealy bugs infest roots and check growth.

Maranta
prayer plant

Maranta leuconeura 'Kerchoveana'

☐ Height 15-20cm (6-8in)
☐ Temperature minimum 13°C (55°F)
☐ Bright filtered light
☐ Soil-based compost
☐ Foliage plant

A decorative foliage plant, prayer plant (*Maranta leuconeura*) takes its common name from the manner in which the leaves stand upright at night, like hands in prayer.

The oval leaves are emerald-green marked with purple-brown blotches when young. As they mature, the leaves become grey with darker blotches.

Popular varieties include: 'Erythroneura' (herringbone plant, more upright than the species, longer dark green leaves, dark crimson midribs and veins); 'Kerchoveana' (rabbit foot, light green leaves, dark brown blotches); and 'Massangeana' (smaller leaves, ivory midribs and veins).

Cultivation
Prayer plant needs filtered light and temperatures of 18-21°C (64-70°F) throughout the year. Maintain humidity by placing the pot on moist pebbles and mist-spray regularly. During active growth,

Maranta leuconeura 'Erythroneura'

keep the compost moist; feed fortnightly.

During the winter the temperature should not fall below 13°C (55°F) at night. Water moderately when the compost feels dry.
Propagation Divide the rhizomes in spring or take cuttings.
Pests and diseases Trouble free.

MARMALADE BUSH – see *Streptosolen*

Microcoelum
coconut palm

Microcoelum weddelianum

☐ Height up to 1.2m (4ft)
☐ Temperature minimum 16°C (61°F)
☐ Bright filtered light
☐ Soil-based compost
☐ Foliage plant

The dwarf coconut palm (*Microcoelum weddelianum*), sometimes offered as *Cocos* or *Syagrus weddeliana*, is a graceful plant with glossy dark green leaf fronds that emerge from a short stout base. The palm fronds, along central ribs covered with black scales, are divided into numerous narrow leaflets arranged in herringbone fashion.

The palm, which never flowers indoors, eventually grows to 1.2m (4ft) high, with fronds as much as 90cm (3ft) long.

Cultivation
The coconut palm needs good light, out of direct sun, and constant temperatures above 16°C (61°F). It will not tolerate dry air, and humidity should be maintained by standing the pot on permanently moist pebbles and by mist-spraying frequently.

During active growth, water moderately when the compost feels dry, and feed monthly.
Propagation Increase by seed is the only, extremely slow, method.
Pests and diseases Trouble free.

MILK BUSH – see *Euphorbia*

Miltonia
pansy orchid

Miltonia 'Rouge California Plum'

☐ Height 23-45cm (9-18in)
☐ Temperature minimum 16°C (61°F)
☐ Medium light
☐ Orchid compost
☐ Epiphytic orchid

Pansy orchids – so called because their sweetly scented, velvety flowers are shaped like a pansy – make striking house plants if the right conditions can be provided.

The blooms, which can measure up to 10cm (4in) across, appear singly or in spikes, usually in late spring and summer. They come in shades of purple, plum, red-brown and white. The petals are often blotched or edged with pink, white, yellow or purple, and the lip is marked with a contrasting colour.

The long leaves are strap-shaped and the pseudobulbs are generally about 10cm (4in) high.

Most pansy orchids are hybrids, with exceptionally large and colourful flowers.

Popular species and hybrids
Miltonia roezlii has bluish green leaves up to 30cm (1ft) long. It bears flower spikes with three to five blooms up to 10cm (4in) wide in early summer. The flowers are white with an orange-yellow disc on the lip and a purple blotch on each petal. 'Alba' has white flowers with a yellow blotch at the base of the lip.

Miltonia spectabilis

Miltonia 'Rouge California Plum' is a hybrid with spikes of white-edged, plum-red flowers. The petals have wavy edges.

Miltonia spectabilis has yellowish green leaves. In autumn it bears a profusion of flowers on stalks up to 25cm (10in) long. They are white, flushed pink with the lip marked rose-purple. The variety 'Moreliana' has plum-coloured flowers with bright purple lips.

Miltonia warscewiczii produces a single leaf about 15cm (6in) long. In winter to spring it bears spikes of flowers on stalks up to 30cm (1ft) long. The reddish brown blooms measure about 4cm (1½in) long and have yellow-tipped, wavy-edged petals. The white-tipped lip is rose-purple with a brown blotch.

Cultivation
Pansy orchids do best in medium light and temperatures of 16-21°C (61-70°F). To maintain high humidity, place the pots on moist pebbles and mist-spray regularly. Keep the compost moist and give a liquid feed at every third or fourth watering during the growing season.

Propagation Divide the rhizomes in spring or summer.

Pests and diseases Scale insects may infest leaves and stems.

Mimosa
sensitive plant, humble plant

Mimosa pudica

☐ Height up to 60cm (2ft)
☐ Temperature minimum 18°C (64°F)
☐ Bright light
☐ Soil-based compost
☐ Foliage plant

Sensitive plant (*Mimosa pudica*) is grown for its leaves, which, when touched, rapidly close up and droop. This fascinating plant regains its shape after a short period. The leaves fold naturally at night.

The light green foliage, on hairy and spiny stems, is divided into numerous narrow leaflets, giving a delicate ferny appearance. In mid to late summer the plant bears fluffy rounded heads of tiny pink flowers. The flower heads measure 5-7.5 (2-3in) across.

Sensitive plant, also known as humble plant or touch-me-not, is a short-lived shrub generally discarded after flowering.

Cultivation
Sensitive plant needs bright light, including direct sun, at ordinary, warm room temperatures. Maintain humidity by placing the pot on moist pebbles. Water moderately when the top of the compost is dry, and feed fortnightly.

Propagation Grow from seed.

Pests and diseases Trouble free.

Mimulus
monkey flower

Mimulus aurantiacus

- ☐ Height up to 45cm (1½ft)
- ☐ Temperature minimum 5°C (41°F)
- ☐ Bright light
- ☐ Soil-based compost
- ☐ Flowering shrub

The colourful monkey flower is easy to grow and provides a long-lasting display of curiously shaped blooms. The species most suitable for indoor cultivation is *Mimulus aurantiacus*, syn. *M. glutinosus* or *Diplacus glutinosus*.

It has sticky mid to dark green lance-shaped leaves and bears 5cm (2in) wide trumpet-shaped flowers from mid spring to mid autumn. They come in shades of yellow, crimson, and pale buff.

Cultivation
Monkey flower needs bright light, including direct sun in normal room temperatures. During active growth, water moderately when the compost feels dry, and feed fortnightly.

During the winter rest, maintain a minimum temperature of 5°C (41°F) and give less water.
Propagation Take cuttings.
Pests and diseases Trouble free.

MIND-YOUR-OWN-BUSINESS – see *Soleirolia*
MISTLETOE CACTUS – see *Rhipsalis*
MISTLETOE FIG – see *Ficus*
MONKEY PLANT – see *Ruellia*
MONK'S HOOD – see *Astrophytum*

Monstera
Swiss cheese plant

Monstera deliciosa

- ☐ Height 1.2-4.5m (4-15ft)
- ☐ Temperature minimum 10°C (50°F)
- ☐ Bright filtered light
- ☐ Soil-based compost
- ☐ Foliage plant

The popular Swiss cheese plant (*Monstera deliciosa*) makes a magnificent indoor feature with its glossy perforated and deeply incut leaves.

The young leaves of this long-lived shrub are heart-shaped and entire. The perforations develop as the leaf matures. In ideal conditions, the largest leaves can reach 90cm (3ft) long and 60cm (2ft) across. 'Variegata' has cream to yellowish green markings.

The cream-yellow flower spathes rarely appear on plants grown indoors.

Cultivation
Swiss cheese plant thrives in bright filtered light in ordinary room temperatures. Maintain humidity by standing the pot on moist pebbles and mist-spraying regularly. During active growth, water moderately when the compost feels dry and feed fortnightly.

During the winter rest, maintain a minimum temperature of 10°C (50°F) and give less water.

Stake plants over 30cm (1ft) high and train aerial roots into the compost or a stout moss-covered pole.
Propagation Take tip cuttings with at least one mature leaf. Alternatively, air-layer the stems.
Pests and diseases A physiological disorder due to incorrect watering causes brown or yellow blotches on the leaves.

MOONSTONES – see *Pachyphytum*
MOSAIC PLANT – see *Fittonia*
MOSS FERN – see *Selaginella*
MOTHER-IN-LAW'S TONGUE – see *Sansevieria*
MOTHER-OF-THOUSANDS – see *Saxifraga* and *Tolmiea*
MOUSE PLANT – see *Arisarum*

Musa

banana

Musa acuminata

- ☐ Height 1.2-1.8m (4-6ft)
- ☐ Temperature minimum 10-16°C (50-61°F)
- ☐ Bright filtered light
- ☐ Soil-based compost
- ☐ Foliage plant

The banana plant makes an exotic indoor plant with its lush foliage and ornamental fruits.

The single stem bears broadly lance-shaped, mid green leaves up to 90cm (3ft) long. Drooping spikes of leathery bracts and yellow tubular flowers may appear in summer, followed later by fruits.

Popular species

Musa acuminata 'Dwarf Cavendishii', syn. *M. cavendishii*, is up to 1.8m (6ft) high. The drooping flower spike has purple bracts and may be followed by small edible bananas.

Musa velutina, up to 1.2m (4ft) high, has red flower bracts. The fruits are inedible.

Cultivation

Musas need bright filtered light and temperatures over 16°C (61°F). Maintain high humidity by standing the pots on moist pebbles and mist-spraying often. During active growth, keep the compost thoroughly moist and feed fortnightly. During the winter rest at 10°C (50°F) – 16°C (61°F) for *M. velutina* – keep the compost just moist.

Propagation Detach and pot up rooted suckers in spring.

Pests and diseases Trouble free.

Musa velutina, fruits

Narcissus

narcissus, daffodil

Narcissus 'Paper White'

- ☐ Height up to 45cm (1½ft)
- ☐ Temperature up to 16°C (61°F)
- ☐ Bright light
- ☐ Soil- or peat-based compost or bulb fibre
- ☐ Flowering bulb

Daffodils and other narcissi are easy to grow indoors and provide a splendid display of colour in winter and spring.

One of the most widely seen garden narcissi is the rich yellow 'King Alfred' with its large trumpets and broad, slightly pointed petals. But there is a vast choice of narcissi in many shades of yellow, as well as cream and white, often with contrasting corollas. Petals may be rounded or reflexed and double forms are also available. Flowers are usually carried on a single stem, though in some types one stem bears two or more blooms.

The most popular indoor narcissi are the Tazetta and Poetaz groups, which can be forced into flower in mid winter. Both types usually have several flowers on each stem.

Any narcissi can be grown indoors but for best results choose short-stemmed, early flowering types which tolerate indoor light. However, even on a sunny window-sill the stems will be more elongated than on identical types outdoors. For even growth, turn the pots regularly.

Popular species

Narcissus bulbocodium (hoop-pet-

Narcissus 'Flower Drift'

Narcissus 'February Gold'

ticoat daffodil), 5-15cm (2-6in) high, bears yellow flowers. The cup is about 2.5cm (1in) long and the insignificant petals are very narrow.

Narcissus cyclamineus, 15-20cm (6-8in) high, has rich gold pendent flowers. The trumpet is up to 5cm (2in) long and the 4cm (1½in) long petals sweep up and back. This species, so named because its flowers are reminiscent of the cyclamen, is the parent of many hybrids known as cyclamineus narcissi.

Narcissus triandrus 'Albus' (angel's tears narcissus) has pendent cream-white flowers with cup-shaped coronas and reflexed, back-swept petals.

Popular varieties

'Chinese Sacred Lily' is a bunch-flowered variety with sweetly scented white flowers; the short broad cup is orange-yellow.

'February Gold', a cyclamineus narcissus, has golden yellow flowers with a slightly darker trumpet.

'Flower Drift' is double-flowered with rounded white petals and pale yellow cups tipped with deep orange.

'Geranium' is a popular tazetta narcissus. It has four to six flowers to a stem, with broad pure white petals and a short bright orange-scarlet cup.

'Jumblie' has two or three golden yellow flowers on each stem. The petals are reflexed and the trumpets are tinted orange.

'Paper White' has several small sweetly scented flowers on each stem. The petals are white with a short trumpet.

'Peeping Tom' has golden yellow pendent flowers with long narrow trumpets and back-swept petals.

'Rip van Winkle' has scented double yellow flowers.

'Scarlet Gem' has several flowers per stem. The petals are deep golden yellow and the short shallow bowls are orange-red.

'Silver Chimes' has up to ten flowers on each stem. The petals are pure white and the short cup is palest yellow.

'Tête-à-tête' has two or more pendent buttercup-yellow flowers per stem. The petals are swept back.

'Yellow Cheerfulness' has fully double, sweetly scented bunched flowers, pale yellow deepening towards the centre.

Cultivation

Pot narcissi bulbs in early autumn in moist compost. The bulbs should be planted with the top half above the compost and almost, but not quite, touching. Place the pots in a cool dark position with temperatures under 10°C (50°F) and keep the compost moist.

When flower buds appear, move the pots to a bright position in direct sun and at temperatures up to 16°C (61°F). Keep the compost moist.

Alternatively, grow the bulbs in shallow bowls of pebbles. Arrange the bulbs so that their necks are level with the surface of the pebbles. Keep the container filled with water to just below the base of the bulbs.

Forced tazetta and poetaz narcissi cannot be brought into flower again and should be discarded. Hardy types can be moved back to a cool position after the flowers have faded. Feed fortnightly until the leaves fade. Store the bulbs in a cool dark place until autumn or plant out in the garden.

Propagation All narcissi are increased from offset bulbs. For a good indoor display of flowers, buy fresh bulbs every year.

Pests and diseases Trouble free.

Neoregelia

neoregelia

Neoregelia carolinae 'Tricolor'

☐ Height up to 30cm (1ft)
☐ Temperature minimum 10°C (50°F)
☐ Bright light
☐ Bromeliad compost
☐ Epiphytic bromeliad

Neoregelias are grown for their decorative leafy rosettes which undergo dramatic colour changes at flowering time. These easy-to-grow bromeliads have strap-shaped leaves up to 30cm (1ft) long, often with spiny edges. Foliage colours range from bright green to dark green, sometimes attractively striped. During flowering, which can happen at any time of year, the leaves become suffused with attractive shades of red or pink, usually at the centre of the foliage rosette, but sometimes at the leaf tips.

At the centre of each leaf rosette is a water-holding reservoir, from which the blue, 2.5cm (1in) wide flowers appear, surrounded by a ruff of bracts.

Popular species

Neoregelia carolinae grows up to 30cm (1ft) high. It has narrow, shiny, bright green leaves with pointed tips. At flowering time the centre becomes bright red or purple. The variety 'Tricolor' (blushing bromeliad) has ivory-white striped leaves which turn pink as the plant ages.

Neoregelia spectabilis (painted fingernail), up to 30cm (1ft) high, has leathery dark green leaves with white bands beneath. At the tip of each leaf is a red spot resembling a painted fingernail. The centre of the plant turns rose-red at flowering time. The bracts are purple-brown.

Cultivation

Neoregelias thrive in bright light, including direct sunlight, in ordinary room temperatures. Maintain good humidity by placing the pots on moist pebbles and by mist-spraying daily. During active

Neoregelia spectabilis

growth, water moderately and keep the water reservoir filled. Feed monthly.

During the winter rest, maintain a minimum temperature of 10°C (50°F) and give less water.

Propagation Remove offsets from the base in spring and pot up in bromeliad compost.

Pests and diseases Trouble free.

Nephrolepis

sword fern

Nephrolepis exaltata

- ☐ Height up to 1.2m (4ft)
- ☐ Temperature minimum 10°C (50°F)
- ☐ Bright, filtered light
- ☐ Peat-based compost
- ☐ Fern

Popular indoor foliage plants, sword ferns are noted for their clumps of delicately arching leaf fronds. They are fast-growing plants with pale to dark green fronds divided into attractive herringbone or lacy patterns, and are ideal for pedestals or hanging baskets.

Popular species

Nephrolepis cordifolia, up to 60cm (2ft) high, has nearly upright pale green fronds with closely set pinnae arranged like a ladder. The variety 'Plumosa' is more upright, with frilled pinnae. *Nephrolepis exaltata* has pale green fronds, 1.2-1.8m (4-6ft) long. Varieties include: 'Bostoniensis' (Boston fern, wider fronds, faster-growing than the species); 'Elegantissima' (bright green, feathery fronds); 'Rooseveltii' (darker green, wavy fronds); and 'Teddy Junior' (up to 45cm/1½ft long, darker green, wavy fronds).

Cultivation

Sword ferns like bright light out of direct sunlight in ordinary room temperatures and good humidity. During active growth, keep the compost moist and feed fortnightly. A winter rest is unnecessary but at low temperatures (10°C/50°F) give less water.

Propagation Divide clumps or pot up young rooted plantlets.

Pests and diseases Trouble free.

Nerium

oleander, rose bay

Nerium oleander

- ☐ Height up to 1.8m (6ft)
- ☐ Temperature minimum 7°C (45°F)
- ☐ Bright light
- ☐ Soil-based compost
- ☐ Flowering shrub

Oleander (*Nerium oleander*) is a tender evergreen shrub, grown for its clusters of fragrant blooms.

The flowers, which are borne in clusters from early summer to mid autumn, are pink, but white, orange and red varieties, including double-flowered forms, are available.

The mid green or greyish, narrowly lance-shaped leaves are leathery and borne on sparsely branched stems.

Cultivation

Oleander likes bright light, including direct sun, in normal room temperatures. During active growth, keep the compost moist and feed fortnightly. During the winter rest, move to a cooler position with temperatures of 7-16°C (45-61°F) and give less water.

Oleander benefits from a summer spell outdoors in a sheltered, sunny position.

After flowering, shorten flowering shoots by up to half to promote a good show of blooms the following year. Prune lateral shoots to shape.

Propagation Take tip cuttings in early summer.

Pests and diseases Scale insects often cluster on the undersides of leaves. Mealy bugs cause conspicuous tufts of white waxy wool and make plants sticky.

Nerium oleander, flowers

Nertera
bead plant

Nertera granadensis

☐ Height 5-7.5cm (2-3in)
☐ Temperature 10-16°C (50-61°F)
☐ Bright light
☐ Soil- or peat-based compost
☐ Berrying perennial

The decorative bead plant (*Nertera granadensis*) forms a prostrate mat of tiny leaves, almost completely covered in autumn and winter by tiny bright orange bead-like fruits.

It has closely matted stems bearing broadly oval, mid green leaves. Insignificant, greenish yellow flowers appear in early summer, followed by the fruits, which are fully developed by late summer and remain on the plant for several months.

Cultivation
Bead plant thrives in bright light, including three to four hours of direct sun every day, and temperatures of 10-16°C (50-61°F). Maintain humidity by placing the pot on moist pebbles. Mist-spray daily when the flower buds appear and until the fruits have developed.

During active growth, water moderately when the compost is dry on top. Feed monthly from flowering until the fruits are mature. During the short winter rest, give less water, but do not allow the compost to dry out completely.

Bead plants set fruit best in the open; in early summer move plants to a sheltered position outdoors and leave them there until the fruits have formed.

Propagation Divide old clumps in spring. Alternatively, take tip cuttings.

Pests and diseases Trouble free.

Nidularium
nidularium

Nidularium fulgens

☐ Height 25-45cm (10-18in)
☐ Temperature minimum 13°C (55°F)
☐ Bright, filtered light
☐ Bromeliad compost
☐ Epiphytic bromeliad

The regular outline of a mature nidularium has an almost sculptural look, making it an eye-catching feature.

Nidularium, which comes from Brazil, has strap-shaped, usually glossy leaves forming an arching rosette. The foliage is light to dark green, sometimes with darker green marks and sometimes flushed with brown or red.

Just before flowering, the centre of the rosette becomes highly colourful. A flower head of white or bluish flowers, surrounded by bracts, appears from the centre.

The rosette begins to die when the flowers fade, but may take two years to do so.

Popular species
Nidularium billbergioides, up to 25cm (10in) high, has sword-shaped, bright green leaves with spiny teeth. The upright flowering stem bears yellow, green tipped bracts, partially hiding the white flowers.
Nidularium fulgens (blushing bromeliad) is up to 30cm (1ft) high. The arching, shiny light green leaves are flecked with darker green and the edges are indented. The flower head bears three-petalled, violet-blue flowers and red bracts.
Nidularium innocentii (bird's nest bromeliad), up to 45cm (1½ft) high, has strap-shaped, finely toothed, metallic green leaves. They are overlaid with purple-brown on top and wine-red beneath. The white flowers, which usually appear in autumn, are surrounded by orange-red, sometimes green-tipped bracts. Varieties include 'Striatum' with wide yellow stripes on the leaves and rose-red bracts.

Cultivation
Nidulariums thrive in bright but filtered light in ordinary room temperatures. Maintain high humidity by placing the pots on moist pebbles and mist-spraying daily.

Give only enough water to prevent the compost from drying out, but keep the rosettes filled with fresh water. Use rainwater where possible. During active growth, feed monthly.

During the winter rest, move to a cooler position with a minimum temperature of 13°C (55°F). Water sparingly, enough to stop the compost drying out completely.

Propagation Remove offsets from the rosette bases, allowing them to dry for a few days before potting up in bromeliad compost.

Pests and diseases Trouble free.

NORFOLK ISLAND PINE – see *Araucaria*

Notocactus
golden ball cactus

Notocactus scopa

Notocactus leninghausii

x Odontioda
odontioda

x *Odontioda* 'Dalmar Lyoth Bacchus'

☐ Height up to 90cm (3ft)
☐ Temperature minimum 5-10°C (41-50°F)
☐ Bright light
☐ Cactus compost
☐ Cactus

An attractive addition to a collection of cacti, golden ball cactus thrives on a sunny window-sill with the minimum of attention.

The swollen, bristly plant body is globular or cylindrical and often forms clumps. In spring or summer, large funnel-shaped, bright yellow flowers appear at the top of the plants.

Popular species
Notocactus apricus forms a clump of light green globular stems, each up to 7.5cm (3in) high. Each areole (cushion-like pad) along the prominent ribs bears up to 20 bristly, curved grey spines and four larger red-yellow central spines. The yellow, red-tinged flowers are up to 10cm (4in) long.
Notocactus leninghausii has a light green cylindrical body which can grow up to 90cm (3ft) tall. Mature specimens form offsets clustered around the base. The areoles bear up to 15 bristly pale yellow, radial spines and four golden yellow central spines about 2.5cm (1in) long. In summer the plant may produce 2.5cm (1in) wide lemon-yellow flowers, but the species is chiefly grown for its shape and its spines.

Notocactus ottonis, up to 10cm (4in) high, has a bright green, globular or cylindrical stem, with offsets produced around the base. The white woolly areoles bear up to 18 yellow-brown spines and three or four larger red-brown central spines. Mature plants bear 10cm (4in) long yellow flowers.
Notocactus scopa has a pale green globular to cylindrical stem up to 18cm (7in) high. On young specimens the areoles are white and woolly, but later they bear bristly white spines and three or four stronger red-brown spines. The plant produces yellow, 5cm (2in) wide flowers in spring.

Cultivation
Golden ball cacti thrive in bright light, including direct sunlight, and normal room temperatures. During active growth, water moderately when the top of the compost is dry and feed fortnightly. During the winter rest, keep in a cooler position, ideally at a temperature of 10°C (50°F) and give only enough water to prevent the compost from drying out completely.
Propagation Take offsets in spring and summer or grow from seed.
Pests and diseases Mealy bugs cause conspicuous tufts of white waxy wool.

OAK, SILKY – see *Grevillea*

☐ Height up to 90cm (3ft)
☐ Temperature minimum 10°C (50°F)
☐ Bright filtered light
☐ Orchid compost
☐ Epiphytic orchid

With their bold flower forms and exciting colour range, odontiodas make fine specimen plants for indoor display.

These epiphytic orchids are hybrids between *Odontoglossum* and *Cochlioda*, though their blooms and cultivation needs most resemble those of *Odontoglossum*. Flower size and colour come from cochliodas, and further hybridization has occurred between odontiodas and odontoglossums.

The long-lasting flowers are borne in upright spikes or arching sprays, most commonly between autumn and late spring. Individual blooms have broad petals which usually overlap, and the edges are often crimped.

Flower colour includes a fine range of reds, white – often with palest mauve to deepest purple markings – and shades of yellow, sometimes with red or chestnut-brown markings.

The plants have flattened oval pseudobulbs (swollen stems), each of which produces two or three oval or strap-shaped leaves.

Popular hybrids
x *Odontioda* 'Dalmar Lyoth Bacchus' has deep red petals with crimped, pink-red edges. The lip is

Odontoglossum
odontoglossum

x *Odontioda 'Renée'*

Odontoglossum grande

□ Height up to 90cm (3ft)
□ Temperature minimum 16°C (61°F)
□ Bright filtered light
□ Orchid compost
□ Epiphytic orchid

pink with deep red markings. The blooms are about 10cm (4in) across and appear at any time of year.

x *Odontioda* 'Renée' has white, flat-faced flowers with lightly crimped edges. They are speckled and blotched with deep red and the lip is yellow and red.

x *Odontioda* 'Trixon' is a cross between x *Odontioda* 'Lautrix' and *O.* 'Saxon'. It has red, mauve-edged flowers measuring up to 9cm (3½in) across. The blooms may appear at any time of year.

Cultivation
During active growth, odontiodas need a well-ventilated position in bright filtered light at day temperatures of 16-24°C (61-75°F). To maintain humidity, place the pots on moist pebbles and mist-spray regularly. Water moderately when the compost is dry and feed monthly.

In winter, odontiodas require full sun and temperatures not below 10°C (50°F). Give less water than in summer.

Propagation Divide the pseudobulbs in spring or autumn every three years. Each section should have at least three pseudobulbs with some new growth. Water sparingly at first.

Pests and diseases Brown or black spots on the leaves or bulbs are due to leaf spot. Aphids may make plants sticky and sooty. Red spider mites may occur if the atmosphere is too dry.

Excellent orchids for growing in the home, odontoglossums bear a profusion of long-lasting flowers, packed in upright spikes or arching sprays.

These evergreen orchids have flattened, oval pseudobulbs (swollen stems), each with two lance-shaped to oval or strap-shaped leaves.

The flowers, which appear in spring, autumn or winter, are sometimes scented and come in shades of yellow, brown, red, white and pink. Petals and lips are often marked or striped in contrasting shades.

Several species and varieties are suitable for growing in the home. Numerous hybrids have also been developed and are rapidly replaced by new ones. *Odontoglossum* species have also been crossed with *Cochlioda* to create a new group of orchids, x *Odontioda*.

Odontoglossums grow wild in tropical parts of the Andes in Central and South America, where they enjoy constantly moist air.

Popular species and hybrids
Odontoglossum bictoniense, a strong, vigorous plant, bears upright flower spikes, up to 90cm (3ft) high, from mid autumn to mid spring. Each spike has 15 or more blooms up to 5cm (2in) across, which open in succession over a period of several weeks. They are yellow-green with chestnut-brown blotches; the large, crimp-edged lip is white or pale pink. It is an ideal orchid for beginners.

Odontoglossum 'Colwell' bears deep red, crimp-edged flowers. The small lip has a splash of yellow-orange at the base.

Odontoglossum crispum, the parent of many hybrids, bears sprays of up to 20 flowers on arching stems up to 60cm (2ft) long, at any time of year. The 10cm (4in) wide, wavy-edged blooms are white or pale pink with red spots and a yellow crest.

Odontoglossum 'Gold Cup Lemon Drop' has bright yellow flowers up to 2.5cm (1in) across. The lip is marked with golden brown. The flowers are exceptionally long-lasting.

Odontoglossum grande (tiger orchid) bears upright spikes of four to seven flowers from late summer to mid autumn. Each yellow, chestnut-brown-striped bloom is up to 18cm (7in) across. The short lip is cream or pale yellow and brown-red at the base with an orange crest.

Odontoglossum pendulum, syn. *O. citrosmum*, bears drooping sprays of up to 30 flowers in late spring to early summer. The sprays are 30-60cm (1-2ft) long and the 4-5cm (1½-2in) wide

Odontoglossum 'Theralo'

Odontoglossum bictoniense

Odontoglossum 'Colwell'

Oncidium

dancing lady orchid

Oncidium 'Tiger Wyld Babe'

☐ Height 45cm-1.5m (1½-5ft)
☐ Temperature minimum 13°C (55°F)
☐ Bright light
☐ Orchid compost
☐ Epiphytic orchid

flowers are white, sometimes flushed with rose. The rose-red lip has a yellow, red-spotted crest.

Odontoglossum pescatorei, syn. *O. nobile*, bears branching flower spikes, up to 60cm (2ft) high, in spring. The profuse, crimp-edged flowers are white, spotted with rose or light brown. The lip has a yellow crest.

Odontoglossum pulchellum (lily-of-the-valley orchid) bears pendent flower sprays up to 30cm (1ft) long in winter and spring. The highly fragrant, white blooms are 12mm-2.5cm (½-1in) across.

Odontoglossum 'Theralo' bears arching spikes of white, frilly edged flowers. The lower two petals are flushed with lavender rose and maroon. The lip is yellow at the base and has a central maroon blotch.

Cultivation

During active growth in spring, summer and autumn, odontoglossums need a well-ventilated position in bright filtered light at normal room temperatures. To maintain humidity, place the pots on moist pebbles and mist-spray regularly. Water moderately when the compost is dry and feed monthly.

During the short rest period, maintain a temperature of 16°C (61°F). Give less water.

Propagation Divide the rhizomatous roots every three years when the plants are being repot-

ted. Each section should have at least three pseudobulbs with some new growth.

Pests and diseases Brown or black spots on the leaves or bulbs are due to leaf spot. Aphids may make plants sticky and sooty. Red spider mites may occur if the atmosphere is too dry.

OLD LADY CACTUS – see *Mammillaria*
OLD MAID – see *Catharanthus*
OLD MAN CACTUS – see *Cephalocereus*
OLEANDER – see *Nerium*

Dancing lady orchids are small but profuse-flowering plants suitable for growing in the home, conservatory or greenhouse.

The brightly coloured blooms appear singly or in profuse arching or drooping sprays. Colours include yellow – often with brownish stripes and marks – and shades of lilac, pink and red.

The petals are generally widespread, and some species have two long narrow tepals rising from the top of the flowers, giving them the distinctive and graceful form that is described by the common name.

The mid to dark green leaves are strap- or lance-shaped and appear in pairs from the top of the oval pseudobulbs.

Popular species and hybrids

Oncidium flexuosum (dancing doll orchid) is a climbing species with slender, arching flower stems up to 90cm (3ft) long. The profuse bright yellow, 2.5cm (1in) wide flowers are streaked with cinnamon-brown.

Oncidium ornithorhynchum (dove orchid) has arching sprays of profuse, sweetly scented flowers on stems up to 60cm (2ft) long. The blooms are up to 2.5cm (1in) across with soft rose-lilac petals and a darker rose-lilac, yellow-crested lip. The blooms appear from mid autumn to early winter. The variety 'Album' is white.

Oncidium papilio (butterfly orchid) usually produces one flower

Oplismenus

ribbon or basket grass

Oncidium papilio

at a time on slender, swaying stems up to 1.2m (4ft) long. The blooms, which appear at any time of year, are yellow with chestnut-brown stripes and have two long, narrow, backward-pointing tepals. They measure up to 13cm (5in) across.

Oncidium 'Tiger Wyld Babe' has arching, sometimes upright sprays of small yellow, fragrant flowers with brown markings, usually borne in autumn and winter.

Oncidium varicosum bears a branching flower spike up to 1.5m (5ft) long, with up to 90 flowers. They are yellow-green with pale red-brown bars and large golden-yellow, red-blotched and yellow-crested lips. The flowers appear in autumn.

Cultivation

Dancing lady orchids need full sun, except around noon, though *O. varicosum* prefers filtered light. Temperatures around 18°C (64°F) are ideal. At higher temperatures, good humidity is essential: stand the pots on moist pebbles and mist-spray regularly.

During active growth, water sparingly, enough to moisten the compost thoroughly; feed at every third or fourth watering. During the rest period, move to a cooler position with temperatures of 13°C (55°F) and keep just moist.

Propagation Divide and replant large clumps in spring.

Pests and diseases Thrips may infest leaves and flowers, causing mottling and discolouring. Red spider mites cause similar symptoms.

Oplismenus hirtellus 'Variegatus'

- ☐ Height up to 60cm (2ft)
- ☐ Temperature minimum 13°C (55°F)
- ☐ Bright light
- ☐ Soil-based compost
- ☐ Foliage plant

Ribbon grass (*Oplismenus hirtellus*) is a showy foliage plant, ideal for hanging baskets with its trailing branching stems and striped foliage. The narrow oval, stalkless leaves are about 5cm (2in) long and mid green, tinged with pink or purple in bright light.

The form 'Variegatus' is the most colourful, with leaves striped white and green.

The plant grows upright at first, but soon develops a trailing habit.

Mature plants bear insignificant sprays of green flowers which are usually removed as soon as they appear.

Although ribbon grass is a perennial it begins to look shabby after its first year and is best dis-carded. However, new plants are easily propagated.

Cultivation

Ribbon grass thrives in bright light, including direct sunlight, in normal room temperatures. During active growth, water plentifully, keeping the compost thoroughly moist, and feed monthly.

During the winter rest, maintain temperatures around 13°C (55°F) and give only enough water to prevent the compost from drying out completely. Repotting is unnecessary as the plants are generally discarded after one year.

Propagation Take tip cuttings in spring or summer.

Pests and diseases Trouble free.

Opuntia
prickly pear

Opuntia verschaffeltii

Opuntia rufida

- ☐ Height 15-45cm (6-18in)
- ☐ Temperature minimum 7°C (45°F)
- ☐ Bright light
- ☐ Cactus compost
- ☐ Cactus

The prickly pears, from North and South America, belong to a large distinctive group of cacti, characterized by flattened jointed pads (stem sections) or cylindrical stems.

Areoles (cushion-like pads), dotted at regular intervals over the surface, bear often fierce spines as well as fine barbed bristles known as glochids. They are almost invisible, but penetrate the skin easily, causing irritation.

The common name refers to the spiny pear-shaped fruits produced on plants in the wild. Pot-grown opuntias rarely if ever flower indoors and never set fruit.

Popular species
Opuntia basilaris, a branching species up to 30cm (1ft) high, has blue-green oval pads and reddish brown glochids, usually without spines. Mature specimens sometimes bear carmine-pink flowers up to 7.5cm (3in) across in early summer.
Opuntia leucotricha, up to 45cm (1½ft) high, has cylindrical stems at first which later become flattened. They are dark green with white spines.
Opuntia microdasys (bunny ears), a slow-growing species but eventually up to 45cm (1½ft) high, is one of the most familiar cacti. It

has oval, pale green pads and deep yellow glochids. The variety *albispina* is particularly slow-growing and has white glochids.
Opuntia ovata, up to 15cm (6in) high, forms a clump of thick pale green, oval pads. The glochids are pale yellow; grey spines sometimes appear.
Opuntia robusta, up to 30cm (1ft) high, has almost circular blue-green pads with brown glochids. Yellow spines sometimes appear.
Opuntia rufida (cinnamon cactus), about 20cm (8in) high, has thick grey-green pads and dark red-brown glochids.
Opuntia scheerii, up to 30cm (1ft) high, has oblong, blue-green pads covered with a network of golden spines and hairs. The glochids are yellow-brown.

Opuntia verschaffeltii is a slow-growing, spreading species up to 30cm (12in) high. It has cylindrical, jointed stems up to 18mm (¾in) thick. They are dull green with long slender, white spines. Striking red flowers appear in summer.

Cultivation
Prickly pears thrive in bright direct sun in normal room temperatures. During active growth, water moderately when the compost is dry; feed fortnightly.

During the winter rest, maintain an ideal temperature of 7°C (45°F) and give only enough water to prevent the compost from drying out completely. When watering, do not splash the stems.
Propagation Detach stem sections in summer and allow to dry for two days before potting up. Alternatively, grow from seed.
Pests and diseases Root mealy bugs infest roots. Corky scab may cause spots on the stems.

Opuntia leucotricha

ORANGE – see *Citrus*
ORCHID CACTUS – see *Epiphyllum*

Oxalis

oxalis

Oxalis succulenta

☐ Height 10-25cm (4-10in)
☐ Temperature minimum 7°C (45°F)
☐ Bright light
☐ Soil-based compost
☐ Flowering perennials

Members of the wood sorrel family, oxalis species bear clover-like leaves and dainty, funnel-shaped flowers.

Popular species

Oxalis deppei, a bulbous perennial up to 25cm (10in) high, has pale green leaves marked with maroon, and profuse carmine-pink to red flowers in early summer.

Oxalis succulenta, a shrubby species trailing to 60cm (2ft) or more, has fleshy, bright green leaves, and yellow flowers from spring to autumn.

Cultivation

Oxalis need full sun and temperatures not exceeding 21°C (70°F). During active growth, water moderately when the compost is dry on top, and feed fortnightly. During the winter, rest the plants at 7-10°C (45-50°F) and water less.

Propagation Divide and repot in spring.

Pests and diseases Trouble free.

Pachyphytum

moonstones

Pachyphytum oviferum

☐ Height up to 30cm (1ft)
☐ Temperature minimum 10°C (50°F)
☐ Bright light
☐ Cactus compost
☐ Succulent

Moonstones are Mexican plants valued for their attractive rosettes of plump leaves in shades of grey, green and blue.

The leaves are egg- or spoon-shaped and borne on sparsely branching stems. Some species have bell-shaped flowers.

Popular species

Pachyphytum bracteosum, up to 30cm (1ft) high, has spoon-shaped greyish leaves covered with a white bloom. Each leaf is about 7.5cm (3in) long.

Pachyphytum oviferum, also known as sugar almond plant, is up to 15cm (6in) high. The egg-shaped leaves are grey with a pink tinge and are covered with a white bloom. They are 2.5cm (1in) long. Bright red flowers appear in late winter and spring.

Cultivation

Moonstones thrive in direct sun and normal room temperatures. During active growth, water moderately when the top of the compost is dry, but do not feed at any time.

During the winter rest, move to a position with temperatures of 10-16°C (50-61°F) and water less frequently.

Propagation Take leaf or stem cuttings in spring. Allow to dry for three days before potting up.

Pests and diseases Trouble free.

Pachystachys

lollipop plant

Pachystachys lutea

☐ Height 45-90cm (1½-3ft)
☐ Temperature minimum 16°C (61°F)
☐ Bright filtered light
☐ Soil-based compost
☐ Flowering shrub

Lollipop plant (*Pachystachys lutea*) is an evergreen shrub with long-lasting, upright spikes of golden yellow flower bracts throughout summer. Slender white flowers protrude from the bracts.

The upright stems bear glossy dark green, lance-shaped leaves. They are puckered, deeply veined and about 15cm (6in) long.

Cultivation

Lollipop plant thrives in bright filtered light and normal room temperatures, which should not fall below 16°C (61°F). During active growth, water moderately when the top of the compost is dry and feed fortnightly. The plant does not need a winter rest.

Propagation Take tip cuttings.

Pests and diseases Whiteflies and red spider mites may occur.

PAINTED DROP TONGUE – see *Aglaeonema*
PAINTED FINGERNAIL – see *Neoregelia*
PAINTED LADY – see *Echeveria*
PAINTED NET LEAF – see *Fittonia*
PAINTER'S PALETTE – see *Anthurium*

Pandanus

screw pine

Pandanus sanderi

☐ Height 90cm (3ft) or more
☐ Temperature minimum 13°C (55°F)
☐ Bright indirect light
☐ Soil-based compost
☐ Shrub

Prized for its long, narrow leaves arranged spirally on a woody trunk, screw pine (*Pandanus sanderi*) is an ornamental evergreen shrub. The leathery, glossy leaves are mid green with narrow golden stripes. About 7.5cm (3in) wide and up to 90cm (3ft) long, they have finely toothed edges.

P. baptistii has smooth-edged, blue-green leaves striped with white or yellow.

Cultivation

Screw pine likes bright but filtered light and normal room temperatures. During active growth, keep the compost moist and feed fortnightly. During the winter rest, maintain a temperature around 13°C (55°F) and keep just moist.

Propagation Detach rooted offshoots from the base in spring and pot up.

Pests and diseases Trouble free.

PANDA PLANT – see *Kalanchoë*
PANSY ORCHID – see *Miltonia*

Paphiopedilum

slipper orchid

Paphiopedilum 'Maudiae'

☐ Height up to 45cm (1½ft)
☐ Temperature minimum 16°C (61°F)
☐ Filtered light
☐ Orchid compost
☐ Terrestrial orchid

The graceful slipper orchids are easily distinguished from other orchids by their pouch-like lips. Above the lip are two petals, held horizontally or slightly drooping, with a third often broader erect petal at the top. The flowering season is usually autumn to spring.

Flower colours include green, white, maroon, golden yellow and deep red. The blooms may be suffused with purple or pink.

The slender stems, each bearing a single flower, rise from a low tuft of lance-shaped, fleshy leaves. They are light to dark green and often attractively mottled in shades of brown or purple.

Popular species and hybrids
Paphiopedilum 'Maudiae' has downward-curving lower petals, which, like the upper petal, are streaked green and white. The lip is pale yellow.
Paphiopedilum purpuratum bears 7.5cm (3in) wide flowers in summer and autumn. They are crimson-purple with a white striped upper petal.
Paphiopedilum 'Supersuk' has the upper petal striped white, plum and green. The side petals are green spotted brown-black, the lip is pale green and plum.

Cultivation
Slipper orchids need a well-ventilated position in medium light, out of direct sun, and temperatures of 16-24°C (61-75°F). To maintain humidity, stand the pots on moist pebbles and mist-spray daily in warm weather.

During active growth, water moderately when the top of the compost is dry; feed fortnightly.
Propagation Divide and replant the rhizomes after flowering.
Pests and diseases Trouble free.

Parodia

parodia

Parodia chrysacanthion

☐ Height up to 12.5cm (5in)
☐ Temperature minimum 10°C (50°F)
☐ Bright light
☐ Cactus compost
☐ Desert cactus

The slow-growing parodias are popular indoor cacti as they flower readily when only two or three years old. They have globular or cylindrical bodies with a spiral network of small bumps or tubercles, with areoles at the tips and long bristly spines.

The globular *Parodia chrysacanthion*, which takes several years to reach a height of 12.5cm (5in), bears yellow spines and, in summer, several funnel-shaped, golden yellow flowers.

Cultivation
Parodias thrive in strong light, including direct sun, and in normal room temperatures. During the growing season, water moderately, allowing the compost to dry out between waterings. Feed once a month. The best flowering display occurs after a winter rest, at 10°C (50°F), when the plants should be watered only to prevent shrivelling.
Propagation Mature plants may produce offsets which can be removed and potted up in spring. Otherwise grow from seed.
Pests and diseases Trouble free.

Pelargonium

pelargonium, geranium

Pelargonium graveolens 'Variegatum'

Zonal pelargonium 'Cabaret'

Pelargonium crispum 'Variegatum'

☐ Height 15-60cm (6in-2ft)
☐ Temperature minimum 10°C (50°F)
☐ Bright light
☐ Soil-based compost
☐ Flowering perennial

Pelargoniums – popularly and erroneously known as geraniums – make spectacular plants for indoor display with their brightly coloured flower clusters and decorative foliage. They are not closely related to *Geranium* species.

These easy-to-care-for plants make a fine display in pots as specimen plants or mixed with other plants in a trough; some types are ideal for trailing in hanging baskets.

The five-petalled flowers are usually borne throughout the summer and autumn. They come in shades of pink, red, purple, orange and salmon, or white. The petal veins are often suffused with a deeper colour and many types are bicoloured. Petal edges may also be frilled or wavy. Most pelargoniums are hybrids, and varieties come with single, double or semi-double flowers.

Although pelargoniums are prized for their flowers, several types are grown primarily for their foliage. Known as scented-leaved geraniums, their felted, lobed leaves give off enticing scents when touched or crushed, ranging from peppermint to chocolate and nutmeg.

Other pelargoniums, such as ivy-leaved, zonal or fancy-leaved types, have, in addition to their flowers, ornamental leaves with striking colour variegations or decorative margins.

Popular species and varieties

IVY-LEAVED types are derived from *Pelargonium peltatum* and have trailing stems up to 90cm (3ft) long. They have ivy-shaped fleshy leaves and flower from late spring to mid autumn. The species has mid green leaves and clusters of carmine-pink flowers. New varieties are constantly being introduced and include:

'Crocodile' with leaf veins marked in white; pink flowers.

'L'Elegante' has cream-and-pink-edged leaves and bears white and mauve flowers.

'Mrs W.A.R. Clifton' has double scarlet flowers.

'Snow Queen' bears double, lilac-tinged white flowers.

REGAL pelargoniums, up to 60cm (2ft) high, have lobed and toothed leaves on erect stems; they bear clusters of showy flowers, up to 5cm (2in) across. The blooms come in vivid shades of pink, red and purple or white and are often bicoloured and/or frilled. Named varieties include:

'Applause' has pink flowers with frilled edges.

'Aztec' has pink-red flowers with red-purple veins and white, frilled edges.

'Grand Slam' has rose-red flowers shading to violet-red.

'Lavender Grand Slam' has silvery mauve flowers with lighter maroon blotches.

SCENTED-LEAVED pelargoniums, 30-60cm (1-2ft) high, are chiefly grown for their scented, often felted leaves. The flowers are smaller than in other types of pelargoniums and generally insignificant. They include:

Pelargonium capitatum, up to 30cm (1ft) high, has straggling stems and lobed and toothed leaves with a scent of mint and roses.

Pelargonium 'Chocolate Peppermint' is a trailing plant with chocolate peppermint-scented felted leaves that are lobed and with brown stains.

Pelargonium crispum, syn. *P.* x *citrosum* (lemon geranium), up to 60cm (2ft) high, has small, lemon-scented mid green leaves which are lobed with toothed and crimped edges. Small clusters of narrow-petalled, pink flowers appear throughout summer. 'Variegatum' has white-edged leaves.

Pelargonium x *fragrans* (nutmeg geranium) has nutmeg-scented, three-lobed leaves.

Pelargonium graveolens (rose-scented geranium), up to 60cm (2ft) high, is a spreading species with three-lobed, deeply divided and toothed leaves. They are greyish green and smell of roses. Rose-pink flowers with a dark purple spot in the centre appear in clusters in summer and autumn. 'Variegatum' has creamy white leaf markings.

Regal pelargonium 'Aztec'

Ivy pelargonium 'Mrs W.A.R. Clifton'

Ivy-leaved pelargonium 'Crocodile'

Pelargonium 'Lady Plymouth' has hairy stems with rose-scented, lobed and toothed leaves with cream margins. It grows about 60cm (2ft) tall.

Pelargonium quercifolium (oak-leaved pelargonium), up to 60cm (2ft) high, has aromatic, deeply lobed and toothed mid green leaves with wavy edges. The pink flowers have purple veins and deep purple blotches. They appear in small clusters in late spring and summer.

Pelargonium tomentosum (peppermint geranium) trails naturally and can also be trained as a climber, reaching a height of 1.2m (4ft). It has shallowly lobed, velvety, pale green leaves with a profound peppermint scent; it bears inconspicuous white flowers throughout summer. 'Variegatum' has cream-white edged leaves.

ZONAL pelargoniums are among the most popular types. They grow 30-60cm (1-2ft) high; miniature types up to 15cm (6in) high are also available. Zonal pelargoniums are distinguished by their rounded, pale to mid green leaves which have a conspicuous brown or maroon zone. The leaf edges are often scalloped or wavy.

From late spring to mid autumn they bear dense, rounded heads of flowers in shades of pink, red and orange, or white. The blooms may be bicoloured with wavy or frilled edges. This group of pelargoniums also includes fancy-leaved types which have more colourful leaves with the zones picked out in shades of red-brown, yellow, green and copper. Varieties include:

'A Happy Thought', a fancy-leaved type with green leaves with yellow markings, and red flowers.

'Cabaret' has rounded heads of bright red flowers.

'Carefree' is a seed strain offering a range of varieties with white, pink, salmon-pink and scarlet flowers.

'Electra' has crimson semi-double flowers.

'Masquerade' bears bicoloured scarlet, pink or cerise flowers with white centres.

'Michelle' is a miniature zonal type, with pale salmon-pink flowers.

'Mrs Henry Cox' has leaves splashed with maroon, red, green and cream, and salmon flowers.

'Mrs Quilter' has golden bronze leaves.

'Red Black Vesuvius' is a miniature fancy-leaved variety with foliage heavily flushed with black-purple, and bright scarlet flowers.

Cultivation

Pelargoniums thrive in direct sunlight and ordinary room temperatures. During active growth, water thoroughly when the compost is dry and feed fortnightly.

During the winter rest, move to a position with temperatures around 10°C (50°F) and water sparingly.

To encourage bushy growth, cut back all stems by half in spring. Repot mature plants annually in spring.

Propagation Take stem cuttings in spring or grow from seed. Pinch out the tips of young plants to encourage side-shoots.

Pests and diseases Aphids may make plants sticky and sooty. Whiteflies form colonies on the undersides of leaves (especially on regal types).

Blackening of stem bases is caused by black leg disease. Often due to wet potting mixture, cuttings and whole plants collapse.

Pellaea

pellaea

Pellaea rotundifolia

- ☐ Height 30-60cm (1-2ft)
- ☐ Temperature minimum 10°C (50°F)
- ☐ Indirect light
- ☐ Peat-based compost
- ☐ Fern

Although the two species of pellaea grown as house plants are quite different, both have long, wiry and furry, dark brown leaf stalks rising from a branching rhizome. They bear attractive leaf fronds, which are divided into numerous pinnae.

Popular species
Pellaea rotundifolia (button fern) is the most popular indoor species. The stalks grow up to 30cm (1ft) long and arch downwards, trailing as they reach maximum length. The fronds bear pairs of button-like, round, leathery pinnae on black stalks.
Pellaea viridis (green cliffbrake fern) looks more like a typical fern, with upright, bright green deeply divided fronds supported on 15cm (6in) stalks. The fronds can grow up to 60m (2ft) long.

Cultivation
Pellaeas like medium light, out of direct sun, in normal room temperatures. During active growth, keep the compost constantly moist but not wet, and feed fortnightly. Give less water during the short winter rest period when the ferns will tolerate a temperature of 10°C (50°F).
Propagation Divide and repot the rhizomes in spring.
Pests and diseases Trouble free.

Pentas

Egyptian star cluster

Pentas lanceolata

- ☐ Height 30-45cm (1-1½ft)
- ☐ Temperature minimum 10°C (50°F)
- ☐ Bright light
- ☐ Soil-based compost
- ☐ Flowering shrub

A small evergreen shrub, Egyptian star cluster (*Pentas lanceolata*, syn. *P. carnea*) is prized for its showy clusters of flowers which appear in winter. It is not a difficult plant, but needs plenty of sun as it comes from tropical East Africa and the Middle East.

A soft-wooded branching shrub, Egyptian star cluster can grow up to 90cm (3ft) tall, but as a pot plant rarely exceeds 30-45cm (1-1½ft). The dense flower heads are pink, red, lilac, magenta or white.

The plant's common name aptly describes the blooms, with tiny star-like flowers borne in clusters up to 10cm (4in) across. The leaves are bright green, lance-shaped and hairy.

Cultivation
Egyptian star cluster needs bright light, with at least four hours a day of direct sun. The ideal temperature range is 18-27°C (64-80°F), with a night minimum of 10°C (50°F).

During active growth, water moderately when the top of the compost is dry, and feed fortnightly. When the flowers fade, let the plant rest for two months, giving less water and no feed.
Propagation Take tip cuttings in spring and summer.
Pests and diseases Aphids and whiteflies may infest the leaves.

Peperomia

peperomia

Peperomia magnoliifolia

- ☐ Height 10cm-1.5m (4in-5ft)
- ☐ Temperature minimum 13°C (55°F)
- ☐ Bright filtered light
- ☐ Soil- or peat-based compost
- ☐ Foliage plants

Peperomias belong to a large genus that includes more than 1,000 species. The outstanding feature is the great variety of leaf forms and textures: blotched, spotted, striped or marbled; crinkly or veined, glossy or hairy. The florets are unusual rather than attractive – minute cream or white flowers borne in upright to arching rat-tail spikes are characteristic.

Of the dozen or so readily available as house plants, most peperomias are fairly small and bushy. Because they grow slowly, the smaller peperomias are popular in bottle gardens, where they flourish in the humid environment.

Peperomias are not difficult to grow, given the right conditions of warmth and high humidity. They dislike being too wet, and over-watering is the main cause of failure.

Popular species
Peperomia argyreia (water-melon peperomia), syn. *P. sandersii*, up to 30cm (1ft) high, has green and silver-striped shiny, near-round leaves tapering to a point. They are carried on red stalks.
Peperomia caperata has heart-shaped, deeply corrugated leaves on pink stalks and grows up to 25cm (10in) high. White flower spikes, on pink stalks, rise up above the leaves in summer and autumn. Varieties include

Peperomia fraseri

Peperomia caperata 'Variegata'

'Emerald Ripple' (more compact than the species); 'Little Fantasy' (dwarf); 'Luna Red' (grey-green leaves and red flower stalks); and 'Variegata' (syn. 'Tricolor', smaller leaves than the species, with wide white borders).

Peperomia fraseri, syn. *P. resediflora* (flowering mignonette), is up to 60cm (2ft) high and bears scented white flowers in cone-shaped fluffy clusters on long stalks. The leaves are small and heart-shaped with red undersides.

Peperomia glabella (wax privet) is a sprawling plant only 15cm (6in) high. The leaves are fleshy and bright green; those of 'Variegata' have cream-coloured edges.

Peperomia griseo-argentea, syn. *P. hederifolia* (ivy or silverleaf peperomia), is similar to *P. caperata* but only about 15cm (6in) high. The olive-green leaves have deeply channelled dark green veins giving them a quilted look.

Peperomia magnoliifolia (desert privet) grows upright to 30cm (1ft), then may begin to trail. It has densely packed glossy green leaves, but is usually seen in variegated forms. 'Jeli' has more slender grey-green leaves edged with cream and pink. 'Variegata' has cream-edged green leaves on red-spotted stems.

Peperomia argyreia

Peperomia obtusifolia, up to 30cm (1ft) high, has large, broadly oval, dark green glossy leaves with purple margins and stems. Profuse white flower spikes, up to 5cm (2in) long, appear during summer. Variegated forms include 'Alba' (lemon-yellow leaves); 'Albo-marginata' (grey-green leaves with silver borders); and 'Greengold' (leaves with pale yellow patches on a grey-green background).

Peperomia scandens, syn. *P. serpens*, is only available in its variegated form. Unlike other species, it is a climbing or trailing plant with shoots up to 1.5m (5ft) long. They can be trained upwards or allowed to trail. The leaves are heart-shaped, cream when young, maturing to pale green with a cream border. They contrast with pale pink leaf stalks.

Peperomia verticillata grows up to 30cm (1ft) high. It has 5cm (2in)

Peperomia griseo-argentea

long sharp-pointed, glossy leaves set in whorls along the stems.

Cultivation
Peperomias prefer bright light but out of direct sun. They tolerate moderate shade in spring and summer, but need as much light as possible in winter, particularly the variegated species.

Keep at normal room temperatures. They need high humidity, especially in warm rooms; stand the pots on moist pebbles or surround with damp coir, otherwise leaf drop will occur. Water sparingly when the compost feels quite dry. During active growth, give a weak feed monthly. Use tepid water for watering.

During the winter rest, the temperature should not fall below 13°C (55°F). Repot mature peperomias every year in mid spring.

Propagation All species can be increased from tip cuttings in spring. *P. argyreia*, *P. caperata* and *P. griseo-argentea* can also be grown from leaf cuttings.

Pests and diseases Trouble free.

PEPPER – see *Capsicum*, *Piper*
PERSIAN IVY – see *Hedera*
PERUVIAN APPLE CACTUS – see *Cereus*
PETTICOAT PALM – see *Washingtonia*

Philodendron
philodendron

Philodendron 'Burgundy'

☐ Height 60cm-3m (2-10ft)
☐ Temperature minimum 13°C (55°F)
☐ Bright, filtered light
☐ Soil- and/or peat-based compost
☐ Foliage plants

Philodendrons are evergreen shrubby or climbing plants, prized for their handsome glossy leaves. They may be heart-shaped, spear-like, arrow-shaped or palm-like, and are often deeply indented or perforated. Young leaves often vary considerably from mature foliage.

In the wild, philodendrons grow up tree trunks, clinging with aerial roots; they can climb as high as 18m (60ft), though a few species remain shrubby. As house plants, the climbers can reach 2-3m (6-10ft) if their aerial roots are allowed to attach themselves to moss-covered support poles. Keep the moss moist with frequent mist-sprays. Pot plants do not flower.

Popular species and hybrids
Philodendron bipennifolium (fiddle-leaf philodendron) is a rapid climber up to 1.8m (6ft) high. The large leathery, pale olive green leaves are heart-shaped when young but become fiddle-shaped as they mature. The plant needs strong support.

Philodendron bipinnatifidum does not climb. It has roughly arrow-shaped leaves and makes a shrubby plant up to 1.2m (4ft) high. As it matures the leaves become indented and very large, up to 60cm (2ft) long and 45cm (1½ft) across.

Philodendron domesticum, syn. *P. hastatum* (elephant's ear), has fleshy leaves over 60cm (2ft) long, resembling elephants' ears. It is one of the smaller species and

Philodendron scandens

Philodendron selloum

Philodendron melanochrysum

Philodendron 'Panache'

climbs to a height of 1.2m (4ft).

Philodendron elegans is a robust plant, to 1.2m (4ft) high. The dark green, glossy leaves are up to 38cm (15in) wide and slightly longer, deeply incised into palm-like fronds.

Philodendron erubescens has narrow heart-shaped leaves 25cm (10in) long, with a purple sheen and red edge, set on red stalks.

Philodendron hybrids include 'Burgundy' (red new growth and magenta undersides to the leaves) and 'Panache' (grey-green leaves marbled with white).

Philodendron imbe, a fast-growing species, can reach 2m (7ft) in

two to three years. The arrow-shaped leaves are 30cm (1ft) long. *Philodendron melanochrysum*, syn. *P. andreanum*, has heart-shaped leaves with a deep coppery sheen. They have white midribs and veins and droop vertically from the stems. It grows 1.8m (6ft) high.

Philodendron scandens (sweetheart plant) is one of the most popular and easiest-grown indoor plants. It has 7.5-10cm (3-4in) long, heart-shaped glossy leaves, and can be grown as a climber or trailer, or as a shrub if the tips are pinched out.

Philodendron selloum does not climb; the 30-45cm (1-1½ft) long leaves grow in a rosette from a short thick stem. The leaves are deeply incised to give a lacy look.

Cultivation

Grow climbing philodendrons on moss-covered poles. Bushy types need no support.

All thrive in bright filtered light, out of direct sun in normal room temperatures. In poor light, stems become elongated and ungainly. Keep moist all year and water freely from spring to

autumn, sparingly for the rest of the year. Feed fortnightly during active growth. Stand the pots on moist pebbles and mist-spray regularly, including the moss-covered poles.

Propagation Take stem or tip cuttings of climbing species in spring. Grow shrubby types from seed.

Pests and diseases Mealy bugs may infest the sheath-like bases of leaf stalks.

Phoenix

date palm

Pilea

pilea

Phoenix roebelenii

Pilea involucrata 'Silver Tree'

☐ Height 1.2-3m (4-10ft)
☐ Temperature minimum 10°C (50°F)
☐ Bright or filtered light
☐ Soil-based compost
☐ Palm

Date palms are slow-growing decorative foliage plants suitable for growing as specimen plants in large sunny rooms. The long leaf fronds are divided into numerous slender leaflets, giving them an almost feathery appearance. They will eventually grow too large for the average room, but take many years to do so.

Date palms come from the tropical and sub-tropical regions of Africa and Asia.

Popular species
Phoenix canariensis (Canary date palm), up to 1.8m (6ft) tall, has stiff, erect fronds up to 90cm (3ft) long, growing from a short husk-like trunk. Each frond is divided into many pairs of long narrow leaflets in a herringbone pattern; they are shorter at the base and tip of the leaf than in the middle.
Phoenix dactylifera (edible date palm) grows quickly and can reach 3m (10ft) high with a spread of 1.8m (6ft). The fronds are blue-green with long, slightly prickly leaflets arching gracefully from the midribs.
Phoenix roebelenii (miniature or pygmy date palm) rarely grows more than 90cm (3ft) high, but can spread up to 1.2m (4ft). The dark green fronds arch down-

wards and the leaflets, finer than those of other types, carry white scales.

Cultivation
Phoenix canariensis and *P. dactylifera* like direct sunlight; *Phoenix roebelenii* tolerates some sun but prefers filtered light.

Keep all date palms at normal room temperatures during the growing season. They benefit from a winter rest in a cooler place at 10-13°C (50-55°F). Feed every two weeks during active growth, and water plentifully. Water sparingly during the winter rest.

Suckering shoots sometimes produced by *P. roebelenii* spoil its shape – remove them while young.
Propagation Buy new plants or try germinating date stones. Rooted suckers can be detached from the base of *P. roebelenii* and potted up.
Pests and diseases Generally trouble free.

PIGGY-BACK PLANT – see *Tolmiea*
PIG'S EARS – see *Cotyledon*

☐ Height 10-30cm (4-12in)
☐ Temperature minimum 13°C (55°F)
☐ Low light
☐ Peat-based compost
☐ Foliage plant

Pileas are easy-to-grow foliage plants, offering a fascinating variety of differently coloured and textured leaves. Most are small and bushy, though some species creep to form low mounds or clumps. They deteriorate with age and should be replaced every few years.

Popular species
Pilea cadierei (aluminium plant) grows up to 30cm (1ft) high. Its oval 7.5cm (3in) long leaves are quilted, with silvery patches between criss-cross green veins. The variety *P. cadierei* 'Minima' grows only 15cm (6in) high.
Pilea involucrata, syn. *P. pubescens*, has 15cm (6in) long stems bearing small almost round but pointed leaves with serrated edges. It is usually seen as the hybrid 'Moon Valley'. This bears tight rosettes of bright green leaves quilted with bronze veins. Other hybrids include 'Silver Tree' (syn. 'Bronze'), a shrubby plant growing up to 15cm (6in) high, with 7.5cm (3in) long oval leaves that are bronze-green with a splash of silver down the centre; and 'Norfolk', a creeper with almost round bronze-green leaves, 4-7.5cm (1½-3in) across; they are borne in crosswise pairs.

Pilea involucrata 'Moon Valley'

Piper
ornamental pepper

Piper crocatum

☐ Trails to 2-3m (7-10ft)
☐ Temperature minimum 16°C (61°F)
☐ Bright filtered light
☐ Soil-based compost
☐ Trailing or climbing foliage plant

Pilea microphylla, syn. *P. muscosa* (artillery plant), is 25cm (10in) high, and has feathery sprays of foliage bearing tiny mid green leaves. Its inconspicuous green-yellow flowers expel clouds of pollen up to 90cm (3ft) away, hence the common name.

Pilea nummulariifolia (creeping Charley) is a quick-growing creeping or trailing plant spreading to 30cm (1ft) across. It bears pale green quilted, almost round leaves, only 2cm (¾in) across. The form 'Variegata' has white and pink leaf markings.

Pilea repens is a spreading species up to 20cm (8in) high. The 2.5cm (1in) long quilted leaves are dark coppery green on top, purple on the undersides.

Cultivation
Although pileas thrive at low light levels, species with bronze tints need filtered sun to bring out the colour. Provide normal room temperatures at all times, never below 13°C (55°F). High humidity is essential; stand the pots on moist pebbles.

Water sparingly when the top two-thirds of the compost has dried out. Feed every two weeks

Pilea cadierei

from mid spring to late summer. Pinch out growing tips to encourage side-shoots and dense growth.
Propagation Take tip cuttings in late spring.
Pests and diseases Trouble free.

PINEAPPLE – see *Ananas*
PIN WHEEL – see *Aeonium*

Ornamental pepper (*Piper*) is an evergreen climbing or trailing plant with heart-shaped leaves marbled in silver and pink and usually red underneath. It makes a striking display tumbling from a hanging basket.

Popular species
Piper crocatum trails for 2m (7ft) or more if given space. The leaves, up to 13cm (5in) long, are olive-green with silver-pink markings and a puckered surface. The undersides and stems are red.

Piper ornatum is almost identical but has silvery pink marbling and light green undersides to the leaves.

Cultivation
Ornamental peppers must have constant warmth (minimum 16°C/61°F), bright filtered light and a humid atmosphere. Stand pots on moist pebbles and mist-spray every week. Water moderately throughout the year when the compost is dry on top; feed fortnightly except in winter.
Propagation Take stem cuttings in late spring or early summer.
Pests and diseases Trouble free.

Pisonia

pisonia, birdcatcher tree

Pisonia umbellifera 'Variegata'

☐ Height 90-120cm (3-4ft)
☐ Temperature minimum 10°C (50°F)
☐ Bright light
☐ Soil-based compost
☐ Foliage plant

The birdcatcher tree, *Pisonia umbellifera* 'Variegata', syn. *Heimerliodendron brunonianum*, is an evergreen, much-branched shrub notable for its large oblong leaves marbled with creamy yellow and edged with white, sometimes shot with pink. The leaves can grow up to 38cm (15in) long and 13cm (5in) wide. The mid ribs are coated in a sticky gum, which explains the plant's common name, birdcatcher tree.

Pisonia is tree-like in the wild, but remains shrub-like as a pot plant, rarely exceeding 1.2m (4ft) in height.

Cultivation
Pisonia needs bright light, with three to four hours a day of direct sun if it is to retain its bright colouring. The temperature should average 18-24°C (64-75°F) and never drop below 10°C (50°F).

During active growth, water moderately when the top layer of compost has dried out, and feed fortnightly. Water sparingly during the winter rest.

Propagation Take tip cuttings in the spring.

Pests and diseases Generally trouble free.

PITCHER PLANT – see
Sarracenia

Pittosporum

pittosporum

Pittosporum eugenioides 'Variegatum'

☐ Height 1.2-3m (4-10ft)
☐ Temperature minimum 10°C (50°F)
☐ Bright light
☐ Soil-based compost
☐ Flowering shrub

Pittosporums are large evergreen shrubs, grown for their shiny leathery leaves and fragrant, usually cream-coloured flowers borne in clusters from the centre of a whorl of leaves. They thrive outdoors in frost-free sheltered gardens where they are popular as hedging plants. Indoors, pittosporums thrive in cool rooms. Some species attain the size of small trees, and although the species grown indoors are more shrubby and branching, they still make large specimen plants ideal for growing in tubs. *P. tobira* is particularly good as a house plant.

Popular species
Pittosporum crassifolium is an upright shrub growing to 3m (10ft) in a tub. The pointed oval, leathery leaves, 5-7cm (2-2¾in) long, are glossy green on top, downy white underneath. Young leaves and twigs are also downy. The dull red flowers are borne in spring.

Pittosporum eugenioides is an upright to spreading shrub, reaching 3m (10ft) high in a tub. In the wild it becomes a tree up to 12m (40ft) high. The leaves, 5-10cm (2-4in) long, are glossy green and oval with wavy edges. The tiny yellow flowers are honey-scented. *P. e.* 'Variegatum' has creamy white leaf margins.

Pittosporum tobira rarely exceeds 1.2-1.5m (4-5ft) in height when confined to a pot, and is slow-growing. The glossy oval leaves

Platycerium

platycerium

Pittosporum tobira 'Variegata'

are pointed at the stalk end and rounded at the tip. They grow up to 10cm (4in) long and 2.5cm (1in) across, with downward-curving edges, and are set in whorls on the woody stems. In late spring and early summer the whorls of leaves are crowned with 5cm (2in) wide flat-headed clusters of white or pale yellow flowers. The tiny individual flowers are tubular and star-like, with a heavy scent reminiscent of orange blossom. *P. t.* 'Variegata' has leaves variegated with white or cream markings along their edges.

Pittosporum undulatum (Victorian box) grows up to 3m (10ft) in a pot, with oval leaves up to 13cm (5in) long. The flowers are white and fragrant.

Cultivation

Pittosporums grow best in bright light and at least three hours of direct sun each day, in normal room temperatures. In winter they benefit from a rest at about 10°C (50°F).

During active growth, water plentifully, keeping the compost moist, and feed fortnightly. Water sparingly when the plants are resting. Prune back overlong and twiggy shoots in spring, making each cut immediately above a whorl of leaves.

Propagation Take tip cuttings in late spring.

Pests and diseases Trouble free.

Platycerium bifurcatum

☐ Height 30cm-1.5m (1-5ft)
☐ Temperature minimum 13°C (55°F)
☐ Bright filtered light
☐ Peat-based compost
☐ Epiphytic fern

Platyceriums are spectacular and dramatic plants, almost like living pieces of sculpture. The huge green fronds bear little resemblance to ferns, being solid and multi-branched like the antlers of a stag. To simulate their natural habitat – tropical rainforest – they are often grown on pieces of bark rather than in pots.

Popular species

Platycerium bifurcatum, syn. *P. alcicorne* (stag's horn fern), is the easiest species to grow. The long decorative fronds are fertile and grow from a single shield-shaped sterile frond that holds the plant to its support. This is green when young, becomes brown with age and is continually being replaced. The antler-shaped fronds, fleshy and deep green, are covered with a thin layer of white powdery scales, giving them a silvery look.

They can be up to 90cm (3ft) long, forking into spikes or 'antlers' up to 23cm (9in) long at the tips, and semi-erect or downward drooping. *Platycerium grande* grows up to 1.5m (5ft) high and nearly as broad. Sterile fronds, up to 60cm (2ft) wide, grow upwards to form a large fan. The fertile fronds are also fan-shaped, but more deeply divided, and often droop downwards.

Cultivation

Platycerium needs bright but filtered light, in temperatures up to 24°C (75°F), with a winter minimum of 13°C (55°F), and high humidity – mist-spray every day. Water well in spring and summer when the compost is almost completely dried out. Water sparingly during the rest period. Grow the plants in sphagnum moss or coir tied to pieces of bark, or set them in slatted orchid baskets.

Propagation Buy new plants.

Pests and diseases Scale insects may infest the fronds.

Plectranthus

plectranthus

Plectranthus coleoides 'Marginatus'

- ☐ Trails to 90cm (3ft)
- ☐ Temperature minimum 13°C (55°F)
- ☐ Bright light
- ☐ Soil-based compost
- ☐ Foliage plant

Most plectranthus are trailing plants, useful for hanging baskets in sunny spots. The long stems bear an abundance of almost round, furry and aromatic leaves, sometimes purple-backed, with scalloped edges.

Popular species

Plectranthus coleoides (candle plant) is usually seen in the variegated form 'Marginatus'. This grows upright at first but trails later, up to 30cm (1ft) or more. The 6cm (2½in) long leaves, heart-shaped and hairy, have a broad band of white around the edge. *Plectranthus oertendahlii* (Swedish ivy) has almost round, 2.5cm (1in) wide leaves which are furry and veined in white, with purple edging and undersides.

Cultivation

Plectranthus need three to four hours direct sun daily. They grow well in normal room temperatures with good humidity. Rest in winter at about 13°C (55°F).

Keep the compost moist during active growth; feed fortnightly.
Propagation Take tip cuttings.
Pests and diseases Trouble free.

Pleione

pleione

Pleione bulbocodioides 'Oriental Splendour'

- ☐ Height 15-20cm (6-8in)
- ☐ Temperature minimum 10°C (50°F)
- ☐ Bright filtered light
- ☐ Orchid compost
- ☐ Epiphytic orchid

Pleiones produce flowers that are large in relation to their height. They may be white, yellow, pink or lilac, often heavily marked with a contrasting colour. Although they are epiphytic orchids, in nature they tend to grow on mossy rocks and logs rather than on trees. They are easy to grow, but must be given a cool resting period in winter.

Pleione bulbocodioides, syn. *P. limprichtii*, is the most commonly grown species. Each rounded pseudobulb, 2.5cm (1in) high, carries one or two bright green and heavily veined folded leaves and a 5-15cm (2-6in) flower stalk with blooms up to 10cm (4in) wide, singly or in pairs. They have long narrow petals and sepals and range from pure white to pale or deep lilac, with a paler, trumpet-shaped, fringed lip usually spotted with red or yellow.

Popular hybrids of *P. bulbocodioides* include: 'Blush of Dawn' (pale lilac petals and a white lip tinged with pale mauve); 'Limprichtii' (magenta-purple petals with a paler lip spotted and streaked with red); 'Oriental Splendour' (pale violet petals and a white lip finely lined with orange); and 'Polar Sun' (pure white).

Cultivation

Pleiones need full but filtered sun, and tolerate normal room temperatures in summer, but must be kept cool during the dormant winter rest – at less than 13°C (55°F). Good humidity is important – place the pots on moist pebbles and mist-spray regularly. Water generously and feed fortnightly when in active growth. Reduce the water supply as the leaves yellow and die away.

For a good display of flowers plant three to five pseudobulbs in a 10-15cm (4-6in) half-pot. Replant every year in spring as new growth begins.
Propagation Divide the clumps in spring or detach offsets formed at the base of the pseudobulbs.
Pests and diseases Red spider mites may infest leaves, causing mottling and yellowing.

Plumbago
leadwort

Plumbago capensis

☐ Height up to 3m (10ft)
☐ Temperature minimum 7°C (45°F)
☐ Bright light
☐ Soil-based compost
☐ Flowering shrub

Leadwort bears a profusion of small flowers, usually blue or white, for many months from spring to autumn.

Popular species

Plumbago capensis, syn. *P. auriculata* (Cape leadwort), has stems up to 3m (10ft) long; they are weak and trailing unless tied to supports or wire frames. The mid green leaves are 5cm (2in) long and curl downwards. Numerous clusters of small pale blue tubular flowers, with a darker blue line down the centre of each petal, are produced from the leaf axils.
Plumbago indica, syn. *P. rosea* (scarlet leadwort), is a shrubby species growing up to 60cm (2ft) high. The pink to red flowers are carried in 15-23cm (6-9in) spikes.

Cultivation

Leadworts thrive in full sun, in normal room temperatures. They require a rest around 10°C (50°F)

Plumbago indica

in winter. Water plentifully when in active growth and feed fortnightly. Water sparingly when resting. Prune hard in spring to ensure new flowering shoots.
Propagation Take soft cuttings in spring or summer.
Pests and diseases Trouble free.

POINSETTIA – see *Euphorbia*

Polianthes
tuberose

Polianthes tuberosa

☐ Height 60-90cm (2-3ft)
☐ Temperature minimum 18°C (64°F)
☐ Bright filtered light
☐ Soil-based compost
☐ Flowering perennial

The tuberose – *Polianthes tuberosa* – is a greenhouse plant, which can be brought into a sunny living room during its long flowering period in summer and early autumn. The beautiful sprays of creamy white, deeply fragrant flowers, up to 7cm (2¾in) long, are borne on erect, pale green unbranching stems up to 1m (3ft) high. Each flower has six open petals that open flat from a funnel-shaped tube. The strap-shaped rather fleshy leaves appear at the base of the stems. 'The Pearl' is a double-flowered variety and the one most commonly available.

Cultivation

Tuberose thrives in bright light out of direct sun, at temperatures around 18°C (64°F). Plant the rhizomes in moist compost, and do not water until the first leaves appear. Then water lightly when the compost feels dry. Liquid feed fortnightly when in flower. Discard after flowering.
Propagation Buy new rhizomes annually.
Pests and diseases Trouble free.

POLKA DOT PLANT – see *Hypoestes*

139

Polypodium
hare's foot fern

Polypodium aureum

- ☐ Height up to 1m (3ft)
- ☐ Temperature minimum 10°C (50°F)
- ☐ Medium light
- ☐ Peat-based compost
- ☐ Fern

Hare's foot fern (*Polypodium aureum*, syn. *Phlebodium aureum*) is a striking foliage plant, with deeply divided wavy fronds.

This is a plant that needs plenty of space – each triangular arching frond can reach a length of over 1m (3ft), and is up to 45cm (1½ft) across at the base. The 5cm (2in) wide pinnae grow in pairs and when mature are marked underneath with a double row of golden brown spots which contain the spores.

The fronds grow from a branching rhizome which should be set partly above the surface of the compost; it is covered in brown or white furry scales resembling a hare's foot. The variety 'Mandaianum' has silvery blue-green fronds with wavy, ruffled edges to the pinnae.

Cultivation
Hare's foot fern needs medium light and normal room temperatures at all times. Water plentifully, keeping the compost moist, and feed weekly during active growth. In temperatures above 21°C (70°F) increase humidity by placing the pot on moist pebbles and mist-spraying frequently. Plant in wide shallow containers to give the rhizomes plenty of space to spread. Repot when the rhizomes have covered the surface.
Propagation Divide and repot the rhizomes in spring.
Pests and diseases Trouble free.

Polystichum
polystichum

Polystichum tsus-simense

- ☐ Height 30-90cm (1-3ft)
- ☐ Temperature minimum 13°C (55°F)
- ☐ Medium to bright light
- ☐ Peat-based compost
- ☐ Fern

Polystichums are mainly hardy garden ferns, but one species, *Polystichum tsus-simense* (Tsusina holly fern), is compact enough to be grown as a house plant. It has fronds divided into many smaller sections and subsections (pinnae and pinnules), giving it an attractive lacy effect. Under the right conditions this fern grows actively all year round. Another species – *P. acrostichoides* – is sometimes available, but needs plenty of space.

Popular species
Polystichum acrostichoides (Christmas fern) grows up to 90cm (3ft) high, with upright, pointed fronds bearing strap-like pinnae arranged in a single herringbone pattern. It comes from north-eastern America, where it is popular for indoor Christmas decoration.
Polystichum tsus-simense (Tsusina holly fern) has arching triangular fronds up to 30cm (1ft) long and 13cm (5in) across at the base and divided into numerous pinnae arranged in a double herringbone pattern. The pinnae are subdivided into pinnules with sharply pointed tips, giving them an appearance of miniature holly leaves. The plant grows from branching rhizomes covered with black scales and forms a neat clump.

Cultivation
Tsusina holly fern thrives in medium to bright light (direct sun will scorch ferns) and ordinary room temperatures. Above 18°C (64°F), increase humidity by placing the pots on moist pebbles and mist-spraying daily with tepid water. Water plentifully, keeping the compost moist, and feed every two to four weeks during active growth. In winter, the temperature should not fall below 13°C (55°F). The Christmas fern thrives in similar conditions, but will tolerate winter temperatures down to 7°C (45°F).
Propagation Divide the rhizomes in early spring and pot sections half-buried in the compost.
Pests and diseases Trouble free.

POMEGRANATE – see *Punica*
POOR MAN'S ORCHID – see *Schizanthus*
POWDER PUFF CACTUS – see *Mammillaria*
PRAYER PLANT – see *Maranta*
PRICKLY PEAR – see *Opuntia*
PRIMROSE – see *Primula*

Primula

primula, primrose

Primula x *kewensis*

☐ Height 10-45cm (4-18in)
☐ Temperature minimum 4-7°C
  (40-45°F)
☐ Bright light
☐ Soil- or peat-based compost
☐ Flowering plant

Primulas provide a colourful
display when flowers are in short
supply, blooming freely from late
winter to late spring; many are
also fragrant. Modern hybrids
provide a wide choice of colourful
flowers, usually with a strongly
contrasting central eye. Their
compact growth habit makes
them ideal for sunny window-
sills. Most indoor primulas are
grown as short-term plants and
discarded after flowering, though
P. vulgaris and the colourful
polyanthus hybrids are fully
hardy and can be planted out in
the garden in spring.

Popular species

Primula x *kewensis* grows up to
38cm (15in) tall, with bright
yellow fragrant flowers. They are
2cm (¾in) across and are borne in
whorls one above the other. The
leaves are elongated ovals with
serrated wavy edges, covered with
a fine white powder.

Primula malacoides (fairy primrose) has small fragrant flowers.
It grows up to 45cm (1½ft) tall
and bears tiers of 20-30 white,
pink or red flowers with yellow
eyes, rising on slender stems from
the centre of hairy light green,
lobed and toothed leaves. Popular
varieties include: 'Carmine Pearl'
(dwarf, carmine-red); 'Fire Chief'
(brick-red); 'Juleia' (cerise); 'Lilac
Queen' (pale lilac, double); 'Mars'
(mauve); and 'White Pearl'
(dwarf, pure white).

Primula obconica bears large

Primula malacoides 'Juleia'

Pteris
pteris, brake ferns

Primula vulgaris varieties

Pteris cretica 'Albo-lineata'

☐ Height 15-60cm (6in-2ft)
☐ Temperature minimum 13°C (55°F)
☐ Bright filtered light
☐ Peat-based compost
☐ Fern

Pteris or brake ferns make ideal specimen plants for cooler rooms. The fronds are borne in a variety of different herringbone patterns and are often attractively variegated. Some species bear separate fertile fronds as well as shorter sterile ones, others have only one type of frond, fertile or sterile.

Popular species and varieties
Pteris cretica (Cretan brake, table or ribbon fern) has only one type of frond, about 30cm (1ft) long and 20cm (8in) wide. It is pale green and arches at the tip as it matures. The frond stalk is about 15cm (6in) long and black. Each frond blade has up to four pairs of strap-shaped, tapering, sometimes serrated pinnae, with a single one at the tip. Varieties include 'Albo-lineata' which has a creamy white stripe running along the mid rib; 'Alexandrae' (cristate table fern) has spiky-looking pinnae tipped with cockscomb crests. 'Rivertoniana', another variety, has feathery pinnae with lobes that are elongated and pointed.
Pteris ensiformis (sword brake) has two types of frond. The fertile ones have triangular blades up to 35cm (14in) long and 20cm (8in) wide, borne on 15cm (6in) stalks.

showy flowers 2.5cm (1in) across, in shades of pink, lilac, red and white, all with a large pale green eye. Fragrant and long-lasting, they bloom from mid winter through to early summer. They are carried in upright clusters at the top of a 30cm (1ft) flower spike. The hairy leaves are almost round with crinkled edges. Popular varieties include: 'Apricot Brandy' (syn. 'Apple-Blossom', cream opening to apricot); 'Coerulea' (blue); 'Snowstorm' (white); and 'Wyaston Wonder' (bright crimson).
Primula sinensis (Chinese primrose) produces flower spikes up to 30cm (1ft) high. The blooms are pink, red, orange, purple or white with frilly-edged petals and yellow eyes. The leaves are hairy and lobed, with deeply serrated edges.
Primula vulgaris, syn. *P. acaulis* (common primrose), is the familiar wild or garden species with pale yellow flowers. Cultivated varieties come in a range of pinks, reds and purples, all with a pronounced yellow eye. Plants are 10-15cm (4-6in) high, and the flowers, 2.5-4cm (1-1½in) across, are borne on 7.5cm (3in) stalks from the centre of a rosette of oblong wrinkled bright green leaves. Polyanthus primroses are in part derived from this species and bear large, brightly coloured flower trusses.

Cultivation
Primulas thrive in bright light, including some direct sun. When

Primula obconica

bought already in flower, keep them at temperatures of no more than 13-16°C (55-61°F) to prolong the flowering period. If the temperature is higher, increase humidity by placing the pots on moist pebbles, and mist-spraying frequently. Water plentifully, keeping the compost moist; feed fortnightly during flowering.
Propagation Buy new plants or raise from seed every year.
Pests and diseases *P. sinensis* is susceptible to root rot.

PRINCE OF WALES FEATHERS – see *Celosia*

Pteris ensiformis 'Victoriae'

The blades have up to eight pairs of narrow pinnae, each up to 10cm (4in) long. Sterile frond blades are similarly shaped but smaller, with broader pinnae. Both types are sometimes divided into small pinnules. Varieties include 'Victoriae', which has silvery stripes along the centre of the pinnae.

Pteris quadriaurita has leathery fronds up to 60cm (2ft) long and finely divided into many pinnae and pinnules. The variety usually grown is 'Argyraea', with pinnae bearing a white stripe down the centre.

Pteris tremula (Australian brake) is large and fast-growing. The triangular fronds can reach 60cm (2ft) long and 30cm (1ft) wide, on stalks up to 38cm (15in) long. The lance-shaped pinnae are divided into pinnules, giving the fronds an attractive feathery look.

Cultivation
Brake ferns enjoy bright light out of direct sunlight, at normal room temperatures, throughout the year. In warm rooms, increase humidity by placing the pots on moist pebbles and mist-spraying daily. The plants cannot tolerate

Pteris cretica 'Albo-lineata'

dry roots, so water plentifully and keep the compost moist at all times. Feed every two or four weeks during active growth. Cut away old outer fronds when they begin to fade and shrivel; new ones will unfurl to take their place.
Propagation Divide and repot the rhizomes of large plants in spring.
Pests and diseases Trouble free.

Punica
pomegranate

Punica granatum 'Nana'

☐ Height up to 1.2m (4ft)
☐ Temperature minimum 13°C (55°F)
☐ Bright light
☐ Soil-based compost
☐ Flowering shrub

A dwarf form of the commercial pomegranate (*Punica granatum* 'Nana') is popular as a house plant. It makes a handsome specimen for a sunny window.

It is a compact shrub, slowly reaching a height of 1-1.2m (3-4ft). The lance-shaped glossy leaves, 2.5cm (1in) long, are borne on twiggy branches on short leafstalks. The orange-red bell-shaped flowers, 2.5cm (1in) long, usually appear singly at the tips of side-shoots in summer and early autumn. The round fruits, up to 5cm (2in) across, with a well-developed calyx, are edible.

Cultivation
In active growth dwarf pomegranate needs bright light, with three or four hours of direct sun every day, in normal room temperatures. Water plentifully, keeping the compost constantly moist, and feed fortnightly. In late autumn, when the leaves drop, move the plant to a position at about 13°C (55°F), in medium light.
Propagation Take heel cuttings from side-shoots in mid summer.
Pests and diseases Trouble free.

PURPLE HEART – see
Setcreasea
QUEEN'S TEARS – see
Billbergia

Radermachera

radermachera

Radermachera sinica

☐ Height up to 1.2m (4ft)
☐ Temperature minimum 10°C (50°F)
☐ Bright filtered light
☐ Soil-based compost
☐ Foliage plant

Radermachera belongs to a genus of evergreen trees and shrubs, one of which has recently been introduced as a house plant. This is *Radermachera sinica*, syn. *Stereospermum sinicum* or *S. chelonoides*. It is a vigorous plant which can be kept at 1.2m (4ft) by regular pruning – it then makes a striking foliage plant. The sharply pointed oval leaves, up to 6cm (2½in) long, are a rich shining green with prominent veins.

Cultivation
Radermachera flourishes in bright light, out of direct sun, at normal room temperatures. Water plentifully when in active growth, but allow the compost to dry out before each watering. Increase humidity by standing the pot on moist pebbles. Water moderately during the winter rest, at about 10°C (50°F).
Propagation Take tip cuttings in spring and root in a heated propagator.
Pests and diseases Aphids, scale insects and red spider mites may infest the leaves.

RAT'S TAIL CACTUS – see
Aporocactus
RAT-TAIL PLANT – see
Crassula
RATTLESNAKE PLANT – see
Calathea

Rebutia

rebutia

Rebutia senilis kesselringiana

☐ Height up to 15cm (6in)
☐ Temperature minimum 4-7°C (40-45°F)
☐ Bright light
☐ Cactus compost
☐ Cactus

Rebutias are popular cacti because they are small, fast-growing and start to bear large, colourful flowers when still young – some when only 2.5cm (1in) in diameter.

The flowers, usually red, but sometimes yellow or violet, are funnel-shaped and produced in abundance from late spring to mid summer. The plant bodies are globular or cylindrical and covered in closely set small swellings or tubercles, with central areoles (cushion-like pads) carrying clusters of short rather soft brown or white spines. Most rebutias are clump-forming, but some produce just a single rather elongated stem.

Unlike many cacti, rebutias are short-lived – after about five years they have exhausted themselves through prolific flowering; they then shrivel and die, but offsets replace the parent plant.

Popular species
Rebutia chrysacantha has globular or short cylindrical stems 5-7cm (2-2½in) high. The flowers, blood-red and orange-yellow, are about 4cm (1½in) long.
Rebutia deminuta has 7.5-10cm (3-4in) high globular stems. The flowers are up to 3cm (1¼in) long and deep orange-red.
Rebutia kupperiana has dark green stems up to 10cm (4in) high and 5cm (2in) wide covered with brown, needle-like spines. The flowers are deep red, more than 2.5cm (1in) long, and are borne higher up the stem than those of other rebutias.
Rebutia minuscula (red crown cactus, Mexican sunball) has globular pale green stems only 5cm (2in) across which may be solitary or form clumps; they are covered with bristle-like white spines. The flowers are light red or pink and about 4cm (1½in) long. The variety *R. minuscula violaciflora* has purple-pink flowers.
Rebutia pygmaea grows only 2.5-5cm (1-2in) high; the stems are finger-shaped with the tubercles arranged in vertical rows. The

Rhipsalidopsis

rhipsalidopsis

Rebutia minuscula

2.5cm (1in) long flowers are rose-purple.

Rebutia senilis (fire crown cactus) has pale green globular stems up to 7.5cm (3in) across. Clusters of 35-40 white spines, each 2.5cm (1in) long and growing from every areole, give it a silvery bearded look. The flowers are pale red and 4cm (1½in) long. The variety *R. s. kesselringiana* has golden flowers.

Rebutia xanthocarpa has pale green stems up to 7.5cm (3in) high. The pale pink flowers are 2cm (¾in) long. The variety *salmonicolor* is salmon-pink.

Cultivation

Rebutias flourish in direct sun, which should be filtered in high summer, at ordinary room temperatures. Water moderately when the top of the compost has dried out and feed every two to four weeks while the plants are in active growth. To ensure plenty of flowers, give a winter rest at 5-10°C (41-50°F), watering just enough to prevent the compost from drying out.

Propagation Detach and pot up offsets when they are large enough to handle or grow from seed.

Pests and diseases Mealy bugs may show as tufts of white wool.

RED-HOT-CATTAIL – see *Acalypha*
REED PALM – see *Chamaedorea*

Rhipsalidopsis gaertneri

☐ Height 30cm (1ft)
☐ Temperature minimum 10°C (50°F)
☐ Medium light
☐ Cactus compost
☐ Cactus

Rhipsalidopsis, a jungle cactus from Brazil, is popular for its profusion of scarlet flowers borne in early spring on arching stems.

Popular species

Rhipsalidopsis gaertneri, syn. *Schlumbergera gaertneri* (Easter cactus), has branching and arching stems, up to 30cm (1ft) long, made up of thin, flat stem segments 5cm (2in) long and 2.5cm (1in) wide. Their edges are notched, with a tiny areole in each depression. The scarlet flowers, open-bell shaped with sharply pointed petals, are 4cm (1½in) across.

Rhipsalidopsis rosea has smaller stem segments which may be flat or three- or four-angled. The flowers are rose-pink, flatter and more star-like than Easter cactus.

Hybrids of the two species have flat stem segments and flowers

Rhipsalidopsis rosea

ranging from pink to crimson.

Cultivation

Rhipsalidopsis thrives in medium light at normal room temperatures. Water plentifully, keeping the compost moist, and feed every two to four weeks. Mist-spray daily. After flowering, reduce watering.

Propagation Detach and pot up stem segments.

Pests and diseases Trouble free.

Rhipsalis

rhipsalis

Rhipsalis pilocarpa

☐ Trails to 90cm-2m (3-7ft)
☐ Temperature 16-24°C (61-75°F)
☐ Medium light
☐ Cactus compost
☐ Epiphytic cactus

Rhipsalis, unusual trailing cacti ideal for growing in hanging baskets, have multi-branching stems, and small star-shaped flowers in spring, followed by berry-like fruits.

Popular species

Rhipsalis cassutha (mistletoe cactus) has slender rounded stems trailing up to 2m (7ft). Creamy white flowers are followed by round white fruits.

Rhipsalis pilocarpa has thin rounded stems up to 90cm (3ft) long, which are erect when young but become pendent with age. Greyish bristles grow from the joints. Pink or white flowers are followed by purple-red fruits.

Cultivation

Rhipsalis thrive in medium light out of direct sun, at normal room temperatures, throughout the year. In summer move the plants to a shady place outdoors, or increase humidity by standing the pots on moist pebbles and mist-spraying daily. Water plentifully when in active growth, moderately in winter. Feed fortnightly when in flower.

Propagation Take stem segment cuttings in spring or summer.

Pests and diseases Trouble free.

Rhododendron

azalea

Rhododendron simsii

☐ Height up to 45cm (1½ft)
☐ Temperature maximum 16°C (61°F)
☐ Bright filtered light
☐ Peat-based compost
☐ Flowering shrub

The profusely flowering plants commonly known as azaleas or Indian azaleas are mainly hybrids of *Rhododendron simsii*. Another species, *R. obtusum* (one of the parents of Kurume azaleas), is less popular as it has smaller and fewer blooms, but it has the advantage that it can be planted outdoors after flowering. The more showy hybrid pot plants rarely survive for a second year indoors unless kept continually cool and moist. Move them outdoors when all danger of frost has passed and keep in a shady spot until early autumn.

Azaleas bloom for many weeks, especially if kept in a cool room, and can be bought in bud from early winter well into spring.

Popular hybrids

Rhododendron obtusum hybrids make shrubby plants no more than 45cm (1½ft) tall. The funnel-shaped flowers, 2.5cm (1in) across, are produced singly, in pairs or threes, in shades of pink, white, magenta and red.

Rhododendron simsii hybrids (Indian azaleas) are similar to *R. obtusum* but have larger, more profuse flowers. They are borne in clusters of two to five, each flower being 4-5cm (1½-2in) across, either single or double, and sometimes with ruffled petals. Colours

Rhododendron simsii hybrid

are red, pink, white and orange, with some bicoloured forms.

Cultivation

Azaleas in flower enjoy bright light, but out of direct sun, at temperatures between 7-16°C (45-61°F). The cooler the temperature, the longer the flowers will last. Water plentifully with soft, lime-free water or water containing a sequestrene compound. Increase humidity by standing the pots on moist pebbles. Feed once a fortnight with lime-free liquid fertilizer.

Propagation Buy new plants.

Pests and diseases Trouble free.

Rhodohypoxis
rhodohypoxis

Rhodohypoxis baurii 'Susan'

- ☐ Height 7.5cm (3in)
- ☐ Temperature minimum 4-7°C (40-45°F)
- ☐ Bright light
- ☐ Peat-based compost
- ☐ Flowering perennial

Rhodohypoxis baurii, a small compact perennial with colourful flowers, makes an attractive display on a sunny window-sill or in a conservatory.

The plant forms a clump, reaching no more than 7.5cm (3in) high, with 5cm (2in) long leaves rising from the base; they are pale green, narrowly strap-shaped and pointed, with whitish hairs. The 2cm (¾in) wide six-petalled flowers, in shades of pink to red and also in white, are borne from mid spring to early autumn.

Popular varieties include: 'Allbrighton Red' (deep red); 'Fred Broome' (creamy pink); 'Margaret Rose' (bright pink); and 'Susan' (deep pink).

Cultivation
Rhodohypoxis thrive in full sun. They are near-hardy garden plants and need cool temperatures as house plants. Water moderately when the surface of the compost feels dry and feed fortnightly. Repot annually in spring.
Propagation Divide the rhizomes or remove and replant offsets after flowering.
Pests and diseases Generally trouble free.

Rhoicissus
rhoicissus

Rhoicissus rhomboidea 'Ellen Danica'

- ☐ Height 1.8-3m (6-10ft)
- ☐ Temperature minimum 10°C (50°F)
- ☐ Medium or bright filtered light
- ☐ Soil-based compost
- ☐ Foliage plant

Rhoicissus have large, vine-like, glossy leaves. They are quick-growing evergreen climbers, clinging to supports by tendrils and twining stems.

Popular species
Rhoicissus capensis, syn. *Cissus capensis* (Cape grape), grows up to 1.8m (6ft) tall and bears 20cm (8in) wide, deeply veined, round or heart-shaped toothed leaves, glossy emerald green in colour.
Rhoicissus rhomboidea, syn. *Cissus rhombifolia* (grape ivy), has glossy leaves 10cm (4in) across, divided into three leaflets each 5cm (2in) long. New growth bears fine hairs that give a silvery look. It can reach more than 3m (10ft) in four years. 'Ellen Danica' (mermaid vine) has larger, more deeply lobed leaflets.

Cultivation
Rhoicissus thrive in bright light, out of direct sun, and will also tolerate shade, in ordinary room temperatures. Water plentifully when in active growth, keeping the compost permanently moist, and feed fortnightly. Water sparingly in winter when the plants should rest at 10-13°C (50-55°F).

Pinch out stem tips to encourage bushy growth and tie shoots to supports as required. Overgrown plants can be cut back hard in spring.
Propagation Take tip cuttings in spring.
Pests and diseases Red spider mite infestations occur in dry air.

RIBBON GRASS – see
Oplismenus
RIBBON PLANT – see *Dracaena*

Rochea

rochea

Rochea coccinea

☐ Height up to 45cm (1½ft)
☐ Temperature minimum 10°C (50°F)
☐ Bright light
☐ Cactus compost
☐ Succulent

Rocheas are small evergreen succulent shrubs with attractive fleshy leaves and clusters of often fragrant flowers in spring and summer. They thrive on sunny window-sills.

Popular species
Rochea coccinea has bright red, tubular flowers, borne in clusters 5-7.5cm (2-3in) across at the tips of the stems. These rarely grow more than 45cm (1½ft) high. The 2.5cm (1in) long fleshy leaves grow close together in vertical rows.
Rochea versicolor has narrower, more lance-shaped leaves, and the flowers are pink, yellow or white, sometimes speckled with tiny red dots.

Cultivation
Rocheas need bright light, including direct sun, in normal room temperatures. Water moderately during active growth when the top of the compost is dry and feed fortnightly with tomato fertilizer. During the winter rest, at 10-16°C (50-61°F), give only enough water to moisten the compost when the top two-thirds have dried out.
Propagation Take stem cuttings in spring or summer.
Pests and diseases Generally trouble free.

Rosa

miniature rose

Rosa chinensis 'Minima'

☐ Height 23-30cm (9-12in)
☐ Temperature minimum 7°C (45°F) and below
☐ Bright light
☐ Soil-based compost
☐ Flowering shrub

Miniature roses grown as house plants are almost all hybrids of the dwarf China rose, *Rosa chinensis* 'Minima', syn. *R. c.* 'Roulettii'. They are as varied as the garden species, and can be shrubby, climbing or standard, with usually fragrant single, semi-double or double flowers in many colours. The leaves are oval and glossy, and there are few thorns.

Miniature roses are often grown as temporary house plants, but if put outdoors for a cool rest in late autumn and brought back indoors in late winter they often flower again.

Choose roses which do not exceed 30cm (1ft) in height. They are grown from micro-cuttings and, unlike garden roses, are not grafted. Some of the more widely available varieties include: 'Colibri' (double, orange-yellow, tinted red); 'Rosina' (bright yellow); 'Starina' (bicoloured scarlet and gold); and 'Sweet Fairy' (double, lilac-pink).

Cultivation
Miniature roses need 14-16 hours of bright light every day if they are to flower freely; they may need supplementary fluorescent lighting when the days are short. Temperatures of 16-21°C (61-70°F) are suitable during active growth. After flowering, move outdoors for two months and bring back indoors in late winter; cut back by up to half. During active growth, water moderately and feed fortnightly.
Propagation Take stem cuttings in early spring.
Pests and diseases Common problems are greenfly, black spot and mildew.

ROSARY VINE – see *Ceropegia* and *Crassula*
ROSE BAY – see *Nerium*
ROSE PINCUSHION – see *Mammillaria*
RUBBER PLANT – see *Ficus*

Saxifraga

mother-of-thousands

Saxifraga stolonifera

☐ Trails to 90cm (3ft)
☐ Temperature minimum 4°C (40°F)
☐ Bright light
☐ Soil-based compost
☐ Foliage and flowering plant

Mother-of-thousands (*Saxifraga stolonifera*, syn. *S. sarmentosa*) produces numerous pendent plantlets, making it ideal for a hanging basket.

The plant grows no more than 23cm (9in) high, but the red stolons can trail for 90cm (3ft). The almost round, slightly hairy leaves, up to 10cm (4in) across, are olive-green with silver veins and red-purple undersides. Flower spikes, up to 45cm (1½ft) high, bear clusters of star-shaped white flowers in late summer.

The variety 'Tricolor' is smaller and less vigorous, with pink, cream and green leaves.

Cultivation
Mother-of-thousands enjoys bright light, ideally at temperatures of 10-16°C (50-61°F), although higher temperatures are tolerated during active growth. 'Tricolor' needs at least three hours direct sun every day to maintain its leaf colour. When temperatures rise above 18°C (64°F) increase humidity – stand pots on moist pebbles, or hang saucers of water below baskets. Water plentifully during active growth and feed monthly.
Propagation Detach and pot up plantlets.
Pests and diseases Aphids and whiteflies infest leaves and stems.

Schefflera

umbrella tree

Schefflera actinophylla

☐ Height 1.8-2.4m (6-8ft)
☐ Temperature minimum 13°C (55°F)
☐ Bright filtered light
☐ Soil-based compost
☐ Foliage shrub

Umbrella tree (*Schefflera actinophylla*) is an evergreen shrub with glossy green leaves which radiate from a central point on slender stalks like the spokes of an umbrella. It makes a handsome specimen plant but needs plenty of space.

Cultivation
Umbrella tree needs bright light but out of direct sun, in normal room temperatures. Water plentifully in spring and summer; feeding is unnecessary for plants repotted annually. Water sparingly in winter.

Left to itself the umbrella tree will grow a single upright stem, but it can be induced to form a bushy and branching habit by pinching out the growing tip when the plant has reached the desired height.

Sponge the leaves with lukewarm water at regular intervals to keep their glossy appearance.
Propagation Take stem cuttings in spring.
Pests and diseases Aphids and scale insects may infest leaves and leaf stalks.

Schizanthus

poor man's orchid

Schizanthus 'Monarch'

☐ Height 30-45cm (1-1½ft)
☐ Temperature 10-16°C (50-61°F)
☐ Bright light
☐ Soil- or peat-based compost
☐ Flowering plant

Poor man's orchid or butterfly flower (*Schizanthus*) is a half-hardy annual grown in cool conservatories for its colourful flowers, which are borne so profusely that the leaves are scarcely visible. The blooms resemble orchids and have unevenly lobed petals with yellow centres and spotted or streaked in a contrasting colour.

The single flowers are 2.5-4cm (1-1½in) across, in shades of pink, red, lilac, purple and white. Fern-like 5cm (2in) long, mid green leaves are borne in low rosettes.

In the garden, plants can grow 60cm-1.2m (2-4ft) tall, but dwarf strains grown as pot plants reach only 30-45cm (1-1½ft). Some of these are sold as *Schizanthus* x *wisetonensis* but are identical to *S. pinnatus* hybrids.

Popular hybrids include: 'Dwarf Bouquet' (30-45cm/1-1½ft); 'Royal Pierrot Mixed' (38-45cm/15-18in); and 'Star Parade' (15-23cm/6-9in). These come in the full range of poor man's orchid colours. Another variety – 'Monarch' – is white with broad deep pink edging and yellow centre strongly marked with red streaks; it reaches 45cm (18in) high.

Hybrids listed in catalogues as suitable for outdoors do equally well indoors. 'Disco', an F2 hybrid with a neat, compact habit, comes in a range of colours and is vigorous and robust; the 'Butterfly' mixture grows 45cm (18in) high and bears flowers in white, pink,

Schizanthus hybrid

carmine, crimson and purple. 'Sweet Lips', about 30cm (12in) high, has flowers with a picotee edging and comes in deep rich carmines, reds and pinks.

Cultivation
Poor man's orchids thrive in bright light in temperatures of 10-16°C (50-61°F). Water moderately when the top of the compost is dry, and feed fortnightly.

Propagation Buy new plants or grow from seed.

Pests and diseases Aphids may infest the leaves. Crown, foot and root rot, due to different fungi, can cause plants to collapse, particularly if they have been overwatered.

Schizanthus hybrid

Schlumbergera
schlumbergera

Schlumbergera 'Bridgesii'

☐ Height about 30cm (12in)
☐ Temperature minimum 16°C (61°F)
☐ Medium light
☐ Cactus compost
☐ Epiphytic flowering cactus

Schlumbergeras are easily grown jungle cacti, prized for their profusion of mainly red flowers in winter. They are distinguished by pendent stems composed of flattened stem segments and look attractive in hanging baskets.

Popular species and hybrids
Schlumbergera 'Bridgesii', syn. 'Buckleyi' (Christmas cactus), is a hybrid between *S. truncata* and *S. russelliana*. It differs from the claw cactus in having stem segments with rounded notches and rounded ends, and bears deep pink flowers in early winter or later.
Schlumbergera truncata, syn. *Zygocactus truncatus* (claw or crab cactus), has toothed flattened stem segments with claw-like projections at the tips. The branching semi-pendent stems grow 30cm (1ft) long. The 4-7.5cm (1½-3in) long pink to deep red flowers with swept-back petals appear from early winter. Numerous hybrids have been bred from the species.

Cultivation
Schlumbergeras thrive in medium light at normal room tempera-

Schlumbergera truncata

tures throughout the year. To initiate flowering, keep the plants in unlit rooms from late autumn so as to simulate short days and long nights. Water plentifully and feed fortnightly with high-potassium fertilizer. Water moderately after flowering and before new stem growth begins. Do not alter the plant's position once buds appear as this may cause them to drop. Stand the plants in a shady outdoor spot in summer.

Propagation Take stem cuttings in spring.

Pests and diseases Trouble free.

Scindapsus

scindapsus

Scindapsus aureus

- ☐ Height 1.2-1.8m (4-6ft)
- ☐ Temperature minimum 10°C (50°F)
- ☐ Bright filtered light
- ☐ Soil-based compost
- ☐ Foliage plant

Scindapsus is a striking climbing plant with large heart-shaped variegated leaves. Although it is capable of quickly reaching 1.8m (6ft) in height, it can be kept within bounds by annual pruning. It makes a imposing specimen plant, trained up supports or moss-covered poles, or allowed to trail from a hanging basket or a pot raised on a pedestal.

Popular species
Scindapsus aureus, syn. *Rhaphidophora aurea* (devil's ivy), has angular stems up to 1.8m (6ft) high and clings to its support by aerial roots. The leathery, shiny, heart-shaped leaves are green marbled with yellow. They are usually 10-15cm (4-6in) long, but can be twice that on well-established plants.

Popular varieties include: 'Golden Queen' (golden hunter's robe, yellow leaves marbled with green); 'Marble Queen' (white leaves marbled with green); and 'Wilcoxii' (leaves with sharply defined green and yellow areas).
Scindapsus pictus 'Argyraeus', syn. *Pothos argyraeus* (silver vine), is a smaller plant with rounded stems. The matt-surfaced, 5-7.5cm (2-3in) long leaves

Scindapsus pictus 'Argyraeus'

Scindapsus aureus 'Marble Queen'

are green with silver spots and a white line round the edges.

Cultivation
Scindapsus thrive in bright filtered light at normal room temperatures. Water moderately when the top of the compost is dry and feed fortnightly during active growth. In warm rooms, increase humidity by standing the pots on moist pebbles. Water sparingly during the winter rest period at a temperature of 10-16°C (50-61°F).

Move the plants to larger pots every spring, using a soil-based compost. Cut the stems of large plants back just above a healthy leaf in spring.
Propagation Take tip cuttings in mid spring.
Pests and diseases Trouble free.

SCREW PINE – see *Pandanus*
SEA URCHIN CACTUS – see *Astrophytum* and *Echinopsis*

Sedum

sedum

Sedum morganianum

- ☐ Height 7.5-30m (3-12in)
- ☐ Temperature minimum 4°C (40°F)
- ☐ Bright light
- ☐ Cactus compost
- ☐ Succulent

The large genus of *Sedum* includes many tender species suitable for growing as indoor pot plants. They are chiefly valued for their foliage of fleshy stalkless leaves; some also produce flower clusters of star-like blooms in spring. They are good subjects for sunny window-sills, planted in half pots or hanging baskets.

Popular species
Sedum adolphi (golden sedum) grows only 15cm (6in) high. The upright stems are covered with elliptic 2.5cm (1in) long waxy leaves that are yellow-green edged with red. White flowers may appear.
Sedum morganianum (donkey's tail) has trailing stems up to 90cm (3ft) long, densely covered with 2cm (¾in) long, overlapping grey-green leaves that are cylindrical and taper to a point. Rose-pink flowers occasionally appear.
Sedum pachyphyllum has upright branching stems up to 30cm (1ft) tall. The tightly packed, cylindrical, 2.5cm (1in) long green leaves are tipped with red. The flowers are bright yellow.
Sedum rubrotinctum (Christmas cheer) grows upright to 10-15cm

Selaginella
moss fern, selaginella

Sedum sieboldii 'Medio-variegatum'

Selaginella martensii

Sedum rubrotinctum

(4-6in), with thin branching stems bearing tight clusters of fleshy, egg-shaped 2cm (¾in) long leaves. They are green, turning red in full sun.

Sedum sieboldii grows only 10cm (4in) high, with thin trailing stems 23cm (9in) or more long. The 2cm (¾in) round, grey-green leaves are borne in groups of three. Pink flowers appear in autumn. 'Medio-variegatum' has creamy blotches on the leaves.

Cultivation
Sedum needs bright light in normal room temperatures. Water moderately during active growth; feeding is unnecessary. Water sparingly during the winter rest period, at around 10°C (50°F).
Propagation Take stem cuttings in spring or summer.
Pests and diseases Mealy bugs show as white waxy wool.

☐ Height 5-30cm (2-12in)
☐ Temperature minimum 16°C (61°F)
☐ Shade or medium light
☐ Peat-based compost
☐ Foliage plant

Selaginellas, also known as moss ferns, have attractive ferny leaves borne in moss-like hummocks or on upright or creeping stems. Coming from tropical rainforests, they need constantly humid conditions and are best grown in bottle gardens or terrariums.

Popular species
Selaginella apoda, syn. *S. apus*, has creeping stems up to 10cm (4in) long and tiny pale green leaves forming a dense moss-like mat.
Selaginella kraussiana, syn. *S. denticulata* (spreading club moss), is a quick-growing creeping species. The stems, up to 30cm (1ft) long, branch freely and root as they grow to form a dense bright green mat.
Selaginella martensii has branching stems, up to 30cm (1ft) long, which are upright for half their length, then arch. The mid green leaves are fleshy.

Selaginella martensii 'Albovariegata'

All moss ferns have variegated forms with leaves tipped with golden green or silvery white – 'Albovariegata' is white-tipped.

Cultivation
Moss ferns need shade and temperatures of 16-24°C (61-75°F). A humid atmosphere is essential – grow in a bottle garden or terrarium, or mist-spray daily with tepid water. Water plentifully and liquid feed every fortnight.
Propagation Take stem cuttings in spring.
Pests and diseases Trouble free.

Senecio

senecio

Senecio rowleyanus

- ☐ Height 2.5-90cm (1-36in)
- ☐ Temperature minimum 7°C (45°F)
- ☐ Bright light
- ☐ Soil-based compost
- ☐ Foliage and flowering plants

Senecio x hybridus (cineraria)

The vast *Senecio* genus includes hardy, half-hardy and tender plants of shrubby, prostrate, climbing or trailing habit. Some are prized for their attractive, often succulent, foliage, others for their flowers.

Popular species

Senecio articulatus, syn. *Kleinia articulata* (candle plant), is a branching succulent with grey-green cylindrical stems 30-60cm (1-2ft) tall. They consist of jointed segments covered in a waxy white patina. In late summer tufts of ivy-like leaves appear from the stem tips. They shrivel and drop off by the following spring.

Senecio x hybridus, syn. *S. cruentus* (*cineraria*), is a popular group of short-term pot plants grown for the brilliantly coloured flowers produced for several weeks in late winter and early spring. They are borne in dense clusters, 15-23cm (6-9in) across, and may be single, double or semi-double, in a large colour range – red, pink, blue, purple, white and combinations of these – usually with prominent white eyes. The heart-shaped leaves have toothed edges and usually purple undersides. The plants grow 23-60cm (9-24in) high

and are discarded after flowering. *Senecio macroglossus* (Cape/Natal ivy, wax vine) is usually seen in the variegated form, *S. m.* 'Variegatus'. This has ivy-like, 6cm (2½in) long, almost triangular, waxy green leaves, randomly marked with cream and borne on purple stalks. The twining purple stems can be trained up canes or cascade from hanging baskets.

Senecio mikanioides, syn. *S. scandens* (German or parlour ivy), is a climber with semi-succulent, dark green ivy-like leaves, 5-10cm (2-4in) long with five to seven pointed lobes and deeply indented veins.

Senecio rowleyanus (string-of-beads) is a prostrate succulent with stems trailing for 60-90cm (2-3ft). The tiny grey-green bead-like leaves appear at regular intervals along the slender stems; each has a vertical translucent band and a minute pointed tip. The fragrant flowers are borne on upright stalks in autumn.

Cultivation

Candle plant and string-of-beads are desert plants and need bright light and normal room temperatures. Water moderately through-

out the year; feeding is unnecessary. They benefit from a winter rest around 18°C (64°F); they tolerate lower temperatures when watering should be curtailed or withheld.

Cinerarias enjoy bright filtered light and cool room temperatures, no more than 16°C (61°F). Stand the pots on moist pebbles. Water plentifully, never allowing the compost to dry out. No feeding is required.

Ivy-leaved senecios thrive in bright light, including direct sun, and ordinary room temperatures. Water moderately during active growth and feed fortnightly. Water sparingly during the winter rest, at 10-13°C (50-55°F).

Propagation Take tip cuttings from ivy-leaved senecios; grow cinerarias from seed and increase succulent species from stem cuttings in spring.

Pests and diseases Aphids may infest cinerarias and ivy-leaved senecios.

SENSITIVE PLANT – see *Mimosa*
SENTRY PALM – see *Howeia*

Setcreasea

purple heart

Setcreasea purpurea

☐ Trails 30-45cm (12-18in)
☐ Temperature minimum 7°C (45°F)
☐ Bright light
☐ Soil-based compost
☐ Foliage plant

Purple heart (*Setcreasea purpurea*) is popular for its rich violet-purple trailing stems and leaves. It is ideal in a sunny window, as it needs plenty of sun to maintain its colour. The leaves are lance-shaped and 10-15cm (4-6in) long. In spring the plant throws up branching stems about 30cm (1ft) high, crowned with pairs of boat-shaped purple bracts. These shelter clusters of small rose-purple flowers which open in succession right through to early winter.

Cultivation
Purple heart flourishes in bright light, including three to four hours direct sun every day, at normal room temperatures. Water moderately throughout the year, and feed monthly from spring to autumn. Remove old flower stems at the end of the season. Repot every six months and discard when plants become straggly.
Propagation Take tip cuttings in spring or summer.
Pests and diseases Trouble free.

SHRIMP PLANT – see
Beloperone
SILVER RUFFLES – see
Cotyledon
SILVER TORCH CACTUS – see
Cleistocactus

Sinningia

sinningia

Sinningia cardinalis

☐ Height 7.5-25cm (3-10in)
☐ Temperature minimum 7°C (45°F)
☐ Bright filtered light
☐ Peat-based compost
☐ Flowering plant

Most sinningias need greenhouse cultivation but can be brought indoors for their flowering period in summer and autumn. The most familiar types are the hybrids known to florists as gloxinias. All are tuberous-rooted plants bearing large handsome leaves and bell-shaped flowers.

Popular species and hybrids
Sinningia cardinalis, syn. *Rechsteineria cardinalis* (cardinal flower), grows 25cm (10in) or more high. The tubular 5cm (2in) long flowers are blood-red and carried in loose clusters.
Sinningia regina (Cinderella slip-

Sinningia regina

Smithiantha

temple bells

Sinningia speciosa 'Gregor Mendel'

Smithiantha 'Discolor'

pers) grows up to 20cm (8in) high. The violet-purple bell-shaped flowers are 5cm (2in) long and pendent. The oval, 15cm (6in) long leaves are velvety deep green. *Sinningia speciosa* (gloxinia) is the parent of numerous hybrids. It grows 23-25cm (9-10in) high with large ovate, dark green, velvety and fleshy leaves. The single or double flowers, up to 7.5cm (3in) across, resemble upturned bells, and come in combinations of white, pink, red or purple.

Popular hybrids include: 'Emperor William' (white-edged blue-purple); 'Gregor Mendel' (double white-edged scarlet); and 'Mont Blanc' (pure white).

Cultivation

Sinningias need bright filtered light, temperatures between 18-24°C (64-75°F) and high humidity – stand the pots on moist pebbles or mist-spray the air; do not spray the plants as water droplets will mark the flowers. Water plentifully when in active growth; feed fortnightly.

Once the flowers are finished, gradually reduce watering until the stems die down. Store the tubers in a frost-free place.

Propagation Buy dormant tubers or new plants in spring. Grow from seed or root leaf cuttings in a heated propagator.

Pests and diseases Trouble free.

SLIPPER FLOWER – see *Calceolaria*
SLIPPER ORCHID – see *Paphiopedilum*
SMILAX – see *Asparagus*

☐ Height 20-75cm (8-30in)
☐ Temperature minimum 18°C (64°F)
☐ Medium light
☐ Peat-based compost
☐ Flowering plant

Temple bells (*Smithiantha*) is grown for its showy pendent flowers, usually streaked with red and spotted with yellow. The plants belong to the Gesneriad family and go into prolonged dormancy after flowering, in mid winter. Most smithianthas are hybrids growing 20-30cm (8-12in) tall as pot plants.

Popular species

Smithiantha cinnabarina, 45-60cm (1½-2ft) tall, has heart-shaped leaves up to 15cm (6in) long, covered with red hairs that give a velvety look. The 5cm (2in) pendent tubular flowers are brick-red with pale yellow or white bands and spotted in the throat with light red.

Smithiantha zebrina can grow 75cm (2½ft) tall and has 18cm (7in) long leaves mottled with brown-purple around the veins. The flowers are red, streaked and spotted with yellow.

Hybrids produced from these and other species have red, orange or yellow flowers, in different patterns of streaks and spots; leaves may be plain or mottled. Popular varieties include 'Discolor' (red and yellow flowers, strongly marked leaves) and 'San Gabriel' (pale yellow flowers, plain green leaves).

Smithiantha 'San Gabriel'

Cultivation

Temple bells need medium light and, ideally, greenhouse temperatures between 18-27°C (64-81°F). Increase humidity by standing the pots on moist pebbles. Water moderately when the top of the compost is dry and feed with quarter-strength fertilizer each time. After flowering let the top growth die down, then dry off the rhizomes and store frost-free in coir until ready for repotting, between early and late spring.

Propagation Divide the rhizomes at potting time.

Pests and diseases Trouble free.

Solanum

solanum

Solanum capsicastrum 'Snowfire'

☐ Height 30-75cm (1-2½ft)
☐ Temperature minimum 10°C (50°F)
☐ Bright light
☐ Soil-based compost
☐ Berrying foliage plants

Two species of solanum are commonly seen, popular for their red cherry-like berries in early winter. Usually discarded when the berries shrivel, the plants can be kept for another year if stood outdoors for the summer.

Popular species
Solanum capsicastrum (winter cherry, false Jerusalem cherry) grows about 45cm (1½ft) tall. Its softly hairy, lance-shaped leaves, up to 7.5cm (3in) long, thickly cover the branching stems. The shiny, red or orange berries are up to 2.5cm (1in) across. 'Snowfire' bears red and white berries. *Solanum pseudocapsicum* (Jerusalem cherry) is more robust, growing up to 75cm (2½ft) tall. It produces larger, almost pure scarlet berries. Dwarf hybrid forms reach only 30cm (1ft), but retain the large berries. Popular varieties are 'Pattersonii' and 'Tom Thumb'.

Cultivation
Solanums need constant bright light and full sun, in temperatures around 16°C (61°F). Stand the pots on moist pebbles and mist-spray daily. Water plentifully, keeping the compost moist, and feed fortnightly.

To keep the plants for a second year, cut back the top growth by two-thirds and put in a shady spot outdoors in late spring. Mist-spray in dry weather and when flowering to encourage fruiting.
Propagation Buy new plants or raise from seed.
Pests and diseases Aphids may infest the leaves.

Soleirolia

mind-your-own-business

Soleirolia soleirolii 'Argentea'

☐ Height 7.5-10m (3-4in)
☐ Temperature minimum 4-7°C (40-45°F)
☐ Bright filtered light
☐ Soil-based compost
☐ Foliage plant

Mind-your-own-business or baby's tears (*Soleirolia soleirolii*, syn. *Helxine soleirolii*) is a near-hardy carpeting plant with miniature leaves. It is useful for underplanting in large pots, where it quickly covers the compost and tumbles prettily over the edges.

The tiny mid green round leaves are born on thread-like 10cm (4in) long pinkish stems. The variety 'Aurea' has golden yellow leaves; 'Argentea' has variegated silvery leaves with white edges. Plant all three together for attractive effects.

Cultivation
Mind-your-own-business thrives in bright filtered or medium light and normal room temperatures. Providing humidity by standing the pots on moist pebbles or mist-spraying daily helps to produce plenty of fresh growth. Water plentifully in spring and summer and feed fortnightly. Reduce watering in winter but keep the compost just moist.
Propagation Remove and pot up rooted stem pieces during the growing season.
Pests and diseases Trouble free.

SPANISH MOSS – see *Tillandsia*

Sparmannia
African hemp

Sparmannia africana

- ☐ Height 1.8-3m (6-10ft)
- ☐ Temperature minimum 16°C (61°F)
- ☐ Bright filtered light
- ☐ Soil-based compost
- ☐ Flowering shrub

African hemp (*Sparmannia africana*) is a tree-like shrub with handsome heart-shaped leaves and golden-centred white flowers. Pot-grown plants are usually the dwarf varieties 'Flore Pleno' or 'Nana'. They make good specimen plants for cool rooms, where flowers may continue to appear almost all year.

The pale green, slightly hairy, 23cm (9in) long leaves are borne on long stalks. Clusters of long-stalked white flowers, 4cm (1½in) across, appear in late winter. They are pendent at first, becoming erect to display prominent yellow stamens.

Cultivation
Sparmannia flourishes in bright filtered light at a steady temperature of 16°C (61°F). In warmer conditions, increase humidity by standing the pot on moist pebbles. Water moderately when the top of the compost is dry and feed fortnightly once buds begin to appear.

Pinch out the main shoot to encourage bushiness; over-large plants can be cut hard back after flowering.
Propagation Take tip cuttings in spring.
Pests and diseases Trouble free.

Spathiphyllum
peace lily

Spathiphyllum wallisii

- ☐ Height 30-60cm (1-2ft)
- ☐ Temperature minimum 13°C (55°F)
- ☐ Medium light
- ☐ Peat-based compost
- ☐ Flowering plants

Peace lilies have striking glossy leaves and arum lily-like fragrant white flower heads in spring and summer.

Popular species and hybrids
Spathiphyllum 'Mauna Loa' is a popular hybrid, up to 60cm (2ft), with long lance-shaped leaves. The flower heads are 10-15cm (4-6in) long.
Spathiphyllum wallisii is about 30cm (1ft) high, with glossy, lance-shaped leaves. The 7.5-10cm (3-4in) long spathes, held above the foliage on stiff dark stems, age from white to pale green.

Cultivation
Spathiphyllums thrive in medium light at normal room temperatures and in high humidity. Water moderately whenever the compost is dry and feed fortnightly.
Propagation Divide the rhizomes.
Pests and diseases Red spider mites may infest the leaves.

SPIDER CACTUS – see *Gymnocalycium*
SPIDER LILY – see *Hymenocallis*
SPIDER ORCHID – see *Brassia*
SPIDER PLANT – see *Chlorophytum*
SPIDERWORT – see *Tradescantia*
SPLEENWORT – see *Asplenium*

Sprekelia
Jacobean lily

Sprekelia formosissima

- ☐ Height 30-45cm (1-1½ft)
- ☐ Temperature 7-10°C (45-50°F)
- ☐ Bright light
- ☐ Soil-based compost
- ☐ Flowering bulb

Jacobean lily (*Sprekelia formosissima*, syn. *Amaryllis formosissima*) bears attractive funnel-shaped crimson flowers in summer. It needs cool-greenhouse treatment, but can be brought indoors to display the flowers. They appear singly on 30-45cm (1-1½ft) tall stems and are 10cm (4in) across, with one broad upper petal flanked by two narrow recurved ones, and three lower ones. A few strap-like leaves appear as the flowers die away.

The Jacobean lily is closely related to *Hippeastrum*.

Cultivation
Jacobean lily requires bright light and winter temperatures of 7-10°C (45-50°F). Pot the bulbs in early autumn and withhold water until spring, then keep moist until the leaves begin to die down. Feed fortnightly once the flowers appear.
Propagation Pot up offsets.
Pests and diseases Trouble free.

SQUIRREL'S FOOT FERN – see *Davallia*
STAG'S HORN FERN – see *Platycerium*

Stapelia

stapelia, carrion flower

Stapelia variegata

☐ Height 15-20cm (6-8in)
☐ Temperature minimum 16°C (61°F)
☐ Bright light
☐ Cactus compost
☐ Succulent

Stapelias take their common name from the unpleasant smell of their huge, bizarre flowers. Succulent plants, they usually do better under greenhouse conditions than as house plants. They flower from spring to autumn.

Popular species
Stapelia gigantea (giant toad plant or Zulu giant) has the largest flowers of any known plant, sometimes exceeding 30cm (1ft) across. They are yellow, red-lined and hairy.
Stapelia variegata (toad plant, star-flower or starfish plant) has 15cm (6in) high stems with tooth-like leaf projections. The 5-7.5cm (2-3in) wide flowers are yellow with purple-brown spots.

Cultivation
Stapelias need bright light and direct sun in temperatures of 16-24°C (61-75°F). Water when the top of the compost has dried out by standing the pot in water until the compost is moist through. Feed once a month during active growth. During the winter rest, water once a month.
Propagation Take cuttings or pot up rooted stems.
Pests and diseases Stem rot and fungus may occur.

STARFISH PLANT – see
Cryptanthus and *Stapelia*
STAR WINDOW PLANT – see
Haworthia

Stephanotis

wax flower

Stephanotis floribunda

☐ Height 30cm-3.6m (1-12ft)
☐ Temperature 18-21°C (64-70°F)
☐ Bright filtered light
☐ Soil-based compost
☐ Flowering climber

Wax flower (*Stephanotis floribunda*) is prized for the beauty and fragrance of its waxy white flowers. It is difficult to bring regularly into flower in a domestic setting and is often treated as a short-stay house plant. However, in a conservatory or closed plant window where temperatures and humidity do not fluctuate, it is long-lived and free-flowering.

A vigorous grower, stephanotis can climb to 3.6m (12ft) or more if trained on a trellis. As a house plant it is usually grown on a hoop of wire and kept to no more than 60cm (2ft) tall.

Stephanotis is also known as floradora because of its free-blooming habit; as Madagascar jasmine because it came originally from Madagascar; and as wax flower from the texture of its blooms.

The fragrant flowers start to appear in late spring and may continue until the summer or even mid autumn, forming in loose clusters of six to ten from the leaf axils. They are 4cm (1½in) long, tubular in shape, opening out at the tip into five waxy white petals. The leaves are glossy dark green, leathery ovals up to 10cm (4in) long.

Cultivation
Wax flower flourishes in bright light but out of direct sun, at even temperatures of 18-21°C (64-70°F) – temperature fluctuations or draughts must be avoided as they cause the buds to drop off. At higher temperatures, increase humidity by standing the pot on moist pebbles and mist-spray daily.

Water plentifully during active growth, keeping the compost constantly and thoroughly moist. Feed every two weeks. During the winter rest, water sparingly when the top half of the compost has dried out, but do not allow it to dry out completely.

Train the stems round cane or wire supports as they grow. Remove any short straggly growth in early spring and cut the stems back hard if the plant outgrows its space. When grown on a trellis, train shoots horizontally rather than vertically to encourage flower buds to break.
Propagation Take tip cuttings of non-flowering side-shoots in the summer.
Pests and diseases Scale insects and mealy bugs may infest the undersides of leaves.

Strelitzia

bird of paradise flower

Strelitzia reginae

- ☐ Height 90cm-1.2m (3-4ft)
- ☐ Temperature minimum 13°C (55°F)
- ☐ Bright light
- ☐ Soil-based compost
- ☐ Flowering perennial

Bird of paradise flower (*Strelitzia reginae*), from South Africa, is the most striking of all house plants, with bracts and flowers resembling the head of some exotic bird. It flowers readily provided the plant gets ample light. Growing 90cm-1.2m (3-4ft) tall and wide, it is perhaps best suited as a tub plant in a sunny conservatory. The grey-green leathery leaves, shaped like paddles, are 30-38cm (12-15in) long, carried singly at the top of strong rounded stalks up to 75cm (2½ft) long.

In spring and summer mature plants produce 20cm (8in) long, boat-shaped, almost horizontal bracts, from which the erect, orange flowers, up to 15cm (6in) long, appear in succession. Each flower has a purple or blue tongue-like projection in the centre.

Cultivation

Bird of paradise flower needs bright light, including at least three to four hours of direct sun daily, in normal room temperatures. During active growth, water moderately when the top of the compost is dry and feed fortnightly. Give a long rest during autumn and winter at 13°C (55°F), watering sparingly.

Propagation Detach small rooted sections and pot up.

Pests and diseases Scale insects may infest the leaves.

Streptocarpus

Cape primrose

Streptocarpus 'Concord'

- ☐ Height 15-25cm (6-10in)
- ☐ Temperature minimum 13°C (55°F)
- ☐ Bright filtered light
- ☐ Peat-based compost
- ☐ Flowering perennial

Cape primroses, with their showy, freely produced, trumpet-shaped flowers, are almost all hybrids of *Streptocarpus rexii* and a dozen or so other species. The flowers are produced in shades of purple, blue, red, pink and white for a period of six months or even longer given ideal conditions. They rival gloxinias in beauty, without the disadvantage of a dormant period. Although sometimes considered greenhouse plants, they make excellent house plants, being much less sensitive to dry air and draughts than many foliage plants.

Cape primrose, from South Africa, has leaves similar to those of the common primrose although they are not related.

Popular species and hybrids

Streptocarpus x *hybridus* includes all the Cape primroses developed from *S. rexii* and other species. The first of these was the popular 'Constant Nymph', which bears loose clusters of 5cm (2in) wide violet-blue flowers with yellow and white throats and pronounced violet veining on the

Streptocarpus hybrid

lower three petals. They are carried on upright stems 20-25cm (8-10in) high. The strap-shaped wrinkled leaves are up to 30cm (1ft) long and borne in a loose rosette beneath the flowers.

'John Innes' hybrids are similar to 'Constant Nymph' but can flower almost all year round given the right conditions. They come in a wide range of colours, from pale pink to blue and purple. The pale shades feature strongly contrasting coloured veins on the lower petals; deep shades often have a white or yellow throat.

Streptocarpus 'Marie'

Varieties are rarely labelled in garden centres, and new ones are constantly being introduced. Popular types are likely to include the following: 'Albatross' (white, yellow throat); 'Marie' (dusky purple, white throat); 'Neptune' (deep blue); 'Paula' (red purple, darker veins, yellow throat); 'Sandra' (blue, purple veins); and 'Tina' (pink, magenta veins). F1 seed mixtures, producing purple, pink, lilac and white flowers with contrasting veins or darker throats, include 'Concord', 'Lipstick', 'Royal Mixed' and 'Windowsill Magic Mixed'.

Streptocarpus rexii has funnel-shaped mauve to purple-blue flowers, 4-7cm (1½-2¾in) long; they are borne in clusters of one to six on 10-15cm (4-6in) high stalks. The strap-shaped and wrinkled, hairy leaves are up to 25cm (10in) long.

Cultivation
Cape primroses flourish in bright light out of direct sun, in normal room temperatures. Water moderately when the top of the compost is dry and feed fortnightly. If the temperature exceeds 24°C (75°F), increase humidity by standing the pots on moist pebbles. Keep roots cool by covering the surface of the compost with moist sphagnum moss.

During the winter rest reduce the temperature to around 13°C (55°F) and water sparingly.
Propagation Divide and repot clumps; take leaf cuttings or sow seeds in spring.
Pests and diseases Mealy bugs may attack the leaves. Mildew can occur where ventilation is poor.

Streptosolen
marmalade bush

Streptosolen jamesonii

☐ Height up to 1.8m (6ft)
☐ Temperature minimum 7°C (45°F)
☐ Bright filtered light
☐ Soil-based compost
☐ Flowering shrub

The marmalade bush (*Streptosolen jamesonii*) bears a profusion of orange flowers at the tip of every wrinkle-leaved branch. An evergreen shrub, it does best in a cool conservatory.

The shrub can reach 1.8m (6ft) in height, but can be kept smaller by pruning. The tubular flowers, 2.5cm (1in) across at the mouth, are borne in large clusters from late spring to late summer. Buds and young flowers mature from yellow to orange.

Cultivation
Marmalade bush needs bright filtered light and cool temperatures – 10-16°C (50-61°F). Water moderately when the top of the compost is dry and feed fortnightly when in active growth. Support on canes and cut the stems back by one-third in late winter to keep the plant bushy.
Propagation Take cuttings of non-flowering shoots in spring.
Pests and diseases Trouble free.

STRING-OF-BEADS – see *Senecio*
SUN CACTUS – see *Heliocereus*
SWEDISH IVY – see *Plectranthus*
SWEET FLAG – see *Acorus*
SWEETHEART PLANT – see *Philodendron*
SWISS CHEESE PLANT – see *Monstera*
SWORD FERN – see *Nephrolepis*

Syngonium
arrowhead vine

Syngonium podophyllum

☐ Height up to 1.8m (6ft)
☐ Temperature minimum 13°C (55°F)
☐ Bright filtered light
☐ Soil- or peat-based compost
☐ Foliage climber

Arrowhead vine (*Syngonium podophyllum*) is also called goosefoot plant from the shape of its attractive, often variegated leaves which change shape, and sometimes colour, as they mature. Upright-growing at first, the plant later climbs or trails, and can be trained up a moss-covered pole, or allowed to tumble from a hanging basket.

The glossy, 20cm (8in) long leaves, borne on slender stalks up to 60cm (2ft) long, develop from a central growing point. At first they are arrowhead-shaped, but as they mature they divide into three, five or more leaflets. Juvenile leaves may have silvery white veins or mottling; the mature leaves are bright green. Most plants bear both types of foliage.

Variegated forms of arrowhead vine are popular. They include: 'Albolineatum' (dark green leaves with silver markings); 'Albovirens' (silver-cream bands along the veins); 'Emerald Gem' (compact plant with short leaf stalks, mid green leaves with lighter zones along the veins and around the leaf margin); and 'Imperial White' (silver-white with dark green edges).

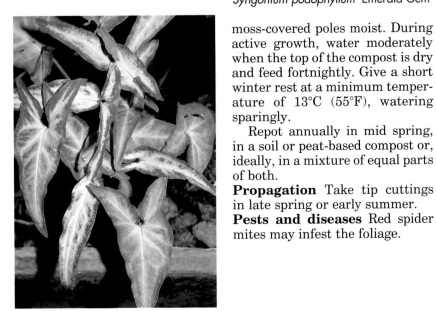

Syngonium podophyllum 'Emerald Gem'

Thunbergia

thunbergia

Thunbergia alata

- ☐ Height up to 3m (10ft)
- ☐ Temperature minimum 7-10°C (45-50°F)
- ☐ Bright light
- ☐ Soil-based compost
- ☐ Flowering climber

The most commonly grown thunbergia is black-eyed Susan (*Thunbergia alata*), a quick-growing twining plant which produces masses of shiny trumpet-shaped flowers, usually light orange or golden yellow, with deep brown centres. It is an annual and discarded after flowering, which can last from late spring to late autumn. In sheltered regions, it can be grown outdoors.

Popular species

Thunbergia alata (black-eyed Susan) can reach a height and spread of 1.2m (4ft) or more. The long tubular flowers flare out into five lobed petals. In the most common form, 'Aurantiaca', the lobes are golden yellow, but 'Lutea' has paler yellow lobes, and 'Alba' is white. The characteristic dark brown eye lures insects into the tube in search of nectar. Each flower has a pair of 2cm (¾in) long green bracts behind it. The roughly triangular, tooth-edged leaves are carried on slender stalks along the twining stems. Seed mixtures are available in shades of orange, yellow and white, with or without dark centres.

Thunbergia grandiflora is a larger evergreen climber, up to 6m (20ft). It is suitable for the

moss-covered poles moist. During active growth, water moderately when the top of the compost is dry and feed fortnightly. Give a short winter rest at a minimum temperature of 13°C (55°F), watering sparingly.

Repot annually in mid spring, in a soil or peat-based compost or, ideally, in a mixture of equal parts of both.

Propagation Take tip cuttings in late spring or early summer.

Pests and diseases Red spider mites may infest the foliage.

Syngonium podophyllum 'Albovirens'

Cultivation

Arrowhead vines flourish in bright filtered light at normal room temperatures. If temperatures exceed 24°C (75°F), increase humidity by standing the pots on moist pebbles and mist-spraying frequently with tepid water. Keep

TABLE FERN – see *Pteris*
TEDDY-BEAR PLANT/VINE – see *Cyanotis*
TEMPLE BELLS – see *Smithiantha*
THISTLE GLOBE – see *Echinopsis*

Tibouchina

glory bush

Tibouchina urvilleana

Thunbergia grandiflora

conservatory or greenhouse. The flowers, 5-6cm (2-2½in) across, are pale purple-blue, with a pale yellow centre; they are borne from early summer to early autumn.

Cultivation

Thunbergias thrive in bright light, including three to four hours of direct sun daily, at normal room temperatures. Water young plants moderately when the top of the compost is dry, then plentifully when in flower, keeping the compost thoroughly moist. Feed fortnightly throughout the flowering period. In the greenhouse or conservatory, evergreen species tolerate winter temperatures of 7°C (45°F).

Annuals grow rapidly and should be potted on as necessary; they will climb up canes or string and can be allowed to trail from hanging baskets. Dead-head to ensure a long flowering period.

Propagation Sow seed of annual types in early spring; evergreen climbers can be increased from cuttings of stem sections taken in mid and late spring.

Pests and diseases Generally trouble free.

☐ Height 1.2m (4ft) or more
☐ Temperature minimum 10°C (50°F)
☐ Bright filtered light
☐ Soil-based compost
☐ Flowering shrub

Glory bush (*Tibouchina urvilleana*, syn. *Tibouchina semidecandra*) is the only species of this large genus in general cultivation. It is also known as princess flower, or purple glory tree, to describe the magnificent silky purple flowers. It can be grown as a pot plant, supported by canes or a moss pole, and kept bushy – up to 1.2m (4ft) – by annual pruning. Alternatively it can be planted in a greenhouse border or a large tub and trained up the back wall and along the roof of a large greenhouse or conservatory.

Glory bush, from Central and South America, is a comparative newcomer and absent from most garden centres. Many seedsmen offer seed for sowing in spring.

The flowers, borne in clusters at the tips of branches, appear between mid summer and early winter, opening from rose-red buds. They are saucer-shaped and 5cm (2in) across, with a prominent centre of long, purple, hook-shaped stamens. The stems are four-angled, soft and green with reddish hairs when young, woody and brown when mature. The 5-10cm (2-4in) long, pointed-oval leaves are velvety, with pronounced pale green lengthways veins and finely toothed edges.

Cultivation

Glory bush enjoys bright filtered light and temperatures of 16-24°C (61-75°F). Water freely during active growth, keeping the compost permanently moist, and feed fortnightly. Increase humidity by standing the pot on moist pebbles. During the winter rest, keep the plant in the brightest light possible, at temperatures of around 10°C (50°F), and water sparingly.

For a compact and bushy plant, cut it back hard in late winter: prune main shoots by up to half each spring, and reduce sideshoots to two pairs of leaves. At the same time move into a larger pot. On free-growing specimens, cut back lateral stems to two pairs of buds in spring to stop the plant becoming leggy.

Propagation Take stem or tip cuttings in spring; alternatively, raise from seed.

Pests and diseases A physiological disorder may lead to discoloration of the foliage; the leaves may fall prematurely.

Tillandsia

air plant

Tillandsia caput-medusae

Tillandsia cyanea

Tillandsia ionantha

□ Height mainly 5-15cm (2-6in)
□ Temperature 16-24°C (61-75°F)
□ Bright filtered light
□ Bromeliad compost
□ Bromeliad

Air plants are members of the *Tillandsia* genus, a specialized group of bromeliads, largely epiphytic, which absorb water from the air and nutrients from airborne dust through minute furry scales on the foliage. Their native habitats range from steamy rainforests to dust-dry deserts. They need no compost, and small types are sold fixed to pieces of coral, shells, rock, driftwood, bark or cork. Larger, rosette-forming types are usually grown in pots of bromeliad compost to give them a stable base.

Tillandsias are grown for their foliage and curious habit; some produce flowers, which only last for a few days, but the attractive bracts are long-lasting. Air plants vary greatly in shape and size; most of those grown as house plants form small grass-like tufts or rosettes.

Popular species

Tillandsia argentea is a silvery coloured species which produces rather straggly, thread-like leaves up to 15cm (6in) long. Twisted, bending flower stalks bear blue or red flowers.

Tillandsia caput-medusae is possibly the most popular of the air plants, with thick, strap-like green leaves curling out of a bulbous base. It grows up to 15cm (6in) high and produces showy red bracts and blue flowers.

Tillandsia cyanea, syn. *T. morreniana*, *T. coerulea*, has many arching strap-like leaves, 30-45cm (1-1½ft) long and 12mm-2.5cm (½-1in) wide, arranged in a loose rosette. They are grey-green, with red brown stripes on the undersides. It is a terrestrial bromeliad and should be grown in a pot. When mature the plant produces a striking flower head from the centre of the rosette. This is a hard fan-shaped structure composed of numerous overlapping rose-coloured bracts. The violet-blue flowers appear singly between the bracts. Although the flowers are short-lived the bracts can last up to ten weeks. After flowering the plant gradually dies back; offshoots are produced from the leaf axils, which can be left to grow where they are or potted on.

Tillandsia ionantha grows no more than 5cm (2in) high, with a compact rosette of silvery leaves arching from a bulbous base. When the stalkless violet-blue flowers appear the leaf rosettes turn red.

Tillandsia usneoides (Spanish moss) is common in warmer parts

Tolmiea menziesii 'Variegata'

Tolmiea menziesii

Tillandsia usneoides

of America, where it trails from trees and rock faces. As a house plant it can be attached to a small square of cork or bark and hung up high on a wall, where it will trail for about 1m (3ft). The thread-like stems are covered with minute silvery grey, scaly leaves, and grow in a tangled mass.

Cultivation
Air plants flourish in bright filtered light at normal room temperatures. They will not tolerate conditions below 13°C (55°F). As they have virtually no roots they need little water, which can be provided by mist-spraying regularly.

T. usneoides should be submerged in water, base and all, for 10 minutes every week; it needs no feeding. Feed other species once a month by adding a liquid feed to the water when mist-spraying.

Propagation Pot up offsets from rosette-forming species; divide Spanish moss. Otherwise buy new plants.

Pests and diseases Trouble free.

TI TREE – see *Cordyline*
TOAD PLANT – see *Stapelia*

Tolmiea
piggy-back plant

☐ Height up to 30cm (1ft)
☐ Temperature minimum 10°C (50°F)
☐ Bright or medium light
☐ Soil-based compost
☐ Foliage plant

Piggy-back plant (*Tolmiea menziesii*) is sometimes known as mother-of-thousands, both names coming from its charming habit of producing numerous plantlets on the tops of mature leaves where they join the stalks. The weight of the new plantlets causes the leaf stalks to droop so that the plants appear to be trailing, making them good subjects for hanging baskets.

Piggy-back plant grows about 30cm (1ft) high. The heart-shaped leaves, 5-7.5cm (2-3in) across, toothed and softly hairy, are borne on 10cm (4in) long leaf stalks from a scarcely noticeable stem. 'Variegata' has irregular cream-coloured marbling, with some leaves only faintly marked, others almost completely cream or green. Spikes of insignificant greenish white flowers may occasionally appear.

Cultivation
Piggy-back plant flourishes in bright or medium light, at ordinary room temperatures. In low light the leaves are pale green, on elongated stalks. During active growth, water moderately when the top of the compost feels dry;

feed fortnightly. Give the plants a brief winter rest, watering them sparingly; they will tolerate temperatures down to 10°C (50°F).

Repot the plants once or twice when the roots have filled the container; thereafter replace with fresh stock.

Propagation In late spring or summer, cut off leaves bearing well-developed plantlets, with about 2.5cm (1in) of stalk, and bury the stalks in moist compost with the plantlets resting on the surface.

Pests and diseases Red spider mites may infest the leaves.

Torenia
wishbone flower

Torenia fournieri

☐ Height 30cm (1ft)
☐ Temperature 16-21°C (61-70°F)
☐ Partial shade
☐ Soil- or peat-based compost
☐ Flowering annual

Wishbone flower (*Torenia fournieri*) is a short-term plant prized for its velvet-petalled tubular flowers which are borne from mid summer to early autumn in such profusion that they almost hide the pale green foliage. They are 4cm (1½in) long, with deep violet-purple lips and lilac-purple throats marked with a vivid blotch of yellow.

The serrated oval leaves are 5cm (2in) long and the plants grow about 30cm (1ft) high.

Seed selections are available. The 'Clown Mixture' produces compact, large-flowered plants in a range of colours. 'Pink Panda' grows 10-20cm (4-8in) high and does equally well in sun or shade.

Cultivation
Torenias enjoy partial shade in temperatures of 16-21°C (61-70°F). Water plentifully when in flower, keeping the compost permanently moist, and feed fortnightly. Pinch out the growing tips to encourage branching.
Propagation Buy new plants or grow from seed.

Pests and diseases Trouble free.

Trachycarpus
windmill palm

Trachycarpus fortunei

☐ Height up to 2.4m (8ft)
☐ Temperature minimum 7°C (45°F)
☐ Bright light
☐ Soil-based compost
☐ Palm

Windmill palm (*Trachycarpus fortunei*, syn. *Chamaerops excelsa* and *C. fortunei*) is named after its large fan-shaped leaves, divided into many segments up to 30cm (1ft) long and 2.5-4cm (1-1½in) wide. It is a slow-growing palm, eventually reaching a height of 2.4m (8ft); it looks striking in a conservatory or sun room.

Cultivation
Windmill palm needs bright light, including three to four hours a day of direct sun to encourage new growth. It thrives in normal room temperatures and is unharmed by temperatures as low as 7°C (45°F). Water moderately

Trachycarpus fortunei, leaf

during active growth, when the top of the compost is dry. Feed fortnightly. Stand the plant outdoors in a sunny but sheltered spot from late spring to autumn.
Propagation Buy new plants.
Pests and diseases Trouble free.

Tradescantia

tradescantia

Tradescantia albiflora 'Aurea'

☐ Trails to 60cm (2ft) or more
☐ Temperature minimum 10°C (50°F)
☐ Bright light
☐ Soil-based compost
☐ Foliage plant

Tradescantias belong to a large group of trailing plants with variegated, pointed-oval leaves growing directly from prominent nodes on the stems. These grow 60cm (2ft) or more long and change direction slightly at each node, accounting for the plants' many common names: wandering Jew, wandering sailor, spiderwort and inch plant.

The terminal clusters of small, three-petalled flowers are insignificant and infrequently produced.

Popular species
Tradescantia albiflora (wandering Jew) has plain green leaves and white flowers, but is usually seen in various variegated forms. All have leaves 5-6cm (2-2½in) long. 'Albovittata' has white-striped leaves; 'Aurea' has almost entirely yellow leaves; and 'Tricolor' has striped white and pale purple leaves.
Tradescantia blossfeldiana (flowering inch plant) has dark olive-green fleshy leaves up to 10cm (4in) long, with purple undersides. The flowers are pink and white. All parts of the plant are covered with fine white hairs. 'Variegata' has green, cream or green and cream striped leaves flushed pink in bright light.
Tradescantia fluminensis (wandering Jew) is similar to *T. albiflora* but the leaves are deep purple beneath and more pointed. There are white- and cream-striped forms, notably 'Variegata'. 'Quicksilver' is particularly fast-growing, evenly striped green and white, with 7.5cm (3in) long leaves and star-like white flowers.

Cultivation
Tradescantias thrive in bright light and need some direct sun every day to maintain the leaf colouring. The ideal temperature is 21-24°C (70-75°F). Water plentifully during active growth, keeping the compost thoroughly moist. In hot dry rooms, increase humidity by standing the pots on moist pebbles. Feed all plants fortnightly.

Pinch out growing tips to keep plants bushy; remove old dry leaves from the bases of the trailing stems and any green shoots on variegated plants. Repot as necessary, but replace ageing plants with fresh stock.
Propagation Take tip cuttings at almost any time.
Pests and diseases Trouble free.

Tradescantia fluminensis 'Quicksilver'

TREE IVY – see x *Fatshedera*
TUBEROSE – see *Polianthes*

Tulipa

tulip

Tulipa greigii 'Red Riding Hood'

Tulipa tarda

☐ Height 15-35cm (6-14in)
☐ Temperature 13-16°C (55-61°F)
☐ Bright light
☐ Peat-based compost or bulb fibre
☐ Flowering bulb

Although tulips are mainly grown outdoors, several compact species and hybrids make good short-term house plants. The most suitable are those that flower early, brightening the dark winter days with their jewel-like goblets in rich red and yellow colours. Early flowering singles and early flowering doubles grow no more than 35cm (14in) high and have flowers up to 13cm (5in) across.

Some tulips are especially suitable for forcing and produce sturdy short-stemmed plants, about 12.5cm (5in) tall. 'Brilliant Star' (bright red) and 'Marechal Joffre' (deep yellow) are recommended; 'Christmas Marvel' (carmine-rose) is slightly taller.

Popular species and hybrids

Tulipa greigii grows 20-30cm (8-12in) high with 7.5cm (3in) long blunt-pointed scarlet flowers. The leaves are streaked or marbled with purple-brown. Popular hybrids include 'Plaisir' (red-and-cream); and 'Red Riding Hood' (all red).

Tulipa kaufmanniana is known as the water-lily tulip because the 9cm (3½in) long flowers open out flat in sunlight. It grows 15-25cm (6-10in) high. Popular hybrids include 'Shakespeare' (salmon, apricot and orange); 'Stresa' (red and yellow); and 'The First' (red and white).

Tulipa tarda, syn. *T. dasystemon*, grows only 15cm (6in) high, with strap-shaped green leaves carried in a rosette below the flowers. These, 6cm (2½in) long and borne in clusters of up to five on each stem, are soft yellow on the inside, tinged with white and green on the outside.

Cultivation

Plant tulip bulbs in early autumn, five or six to a pot, not quite touching and with the tips showing just above the compost. Moisten the compost well, wrap the container in black plastic and stand it outdoors on a shaded balcony or window ledge, at a temperature no higher than 10°C (50°F).

Water just enough to keep the compost barely moist. When 5-7.5cm (2-3in) of leaf is showing (after 8-10 weeks), move the containers into medium light and a temperature of 16°C (61°F). As the plants grow they will tolerate higher temperatures, but if they can be kept at 13-16°C (55-61°F) the flowers will last for three to four weeks.

Propagation Buy new bulbs – the original ones can be planted outside, but they cannot be forced again.

Pests and diseases Trouble free.

Vriesea

vriesea

Vriesea splendens

Vriesea hieroglyphica

☐ Height 60-90cm (2-3ft)
☐ Temperature minimum 18°C (64°F)
☐ Bright light
☐ Bromeliad compost
☐ Bromeliad

The genus *Vriesea* includes a number of handsome house plants, grown as much for their broad strap-shaped leaves as for their showy flower spikes. The stiff but arching leaves grow in rosettes around a cup-shaped centre, which in the wild is a vital water reservoir, enabling the plants to withstand drought.

Like most bromeliads, vrieseas do not flower for several years, then produce one magnificent flower, after which they die, leaving offsets to take their place. The flowers are short-lived, but the colourful bracts persist for a long time. There are numerous hybrids in addition to the species described.

Popular species

Vriesea carinata has plain pale green leaves up to 20cm (8in) long. The flower spikes, up to 30cm (1ft) high, bear broad, flattened bracts which are scarlet at the base and yellow above. The 5cm (2in) long yellow flowers appear between the bracts.

Vriesea fenestralis is grown mainly for its yellow-green leaves conspicuously marked with dark green veins. It forms a low rosette, the leaves reaching 40cm (16in) long and curving downwards at the tips. The 45cm (1½ft) tall flower spike consists of green purple spotted bracts surrounding yellow fragrant flowers which open in summer.

Vriesea hieroglyphica (king of the bromeliads) is prized for its leaves. They are up to 60cm (2ft) long and 10cm (4in) wide, yellow green with irregular purple markings. The flower spikes, which appear in spring, are up to 75cm (2½ft) tall, and consist of pale green bracts and tubular yellow flowers.

Vriesea fenestralis

x *Vuylstekeara*

vuylstekeara

x *Vuylstekeara* 'Edna Stamperland'

☐ Height up to 45cm (1½ft)
☐ Temperature minimum 13°C (55°F)
☐ Bright filtered light
☐ Orchid compost
☐ Orchid

Vuylstekeara orchids are hybrids produced by crossing *Odontoglossum* with *Cochlioda* and *Miltonia* (pansy orchid). They combine the large lobes and glowing colours of *Miltonia* with the ease of cultivation associated with *Odontoglossum,* and are some of the best orchids for beginners.

'Cambria Plush' grows up to 45cm (1½ft) tall, with arching strap-shaped leaves. The flowers, in winter and spring, are 7.5cm (3in) across and deep red, with large red and white lips. 'Edna Stamperland' has carmine-red flowers with paler lips.

Cultivation

Vuylstekearas need bright filtered light in day temperatures of 18-24°C (64-75°F). Maintain humidity by standing the pots on moist pebbles and mist-spraying daily. Ensure ample ventilation. When in active growth, water freely, keeping the compost permanently moist. Foliar feed fortnightly during active growth.

Propagation Divide and repot every two to three years.

Pests and diseases Scale insects, aphids and thrips may occur.

WANDERING JEW – see *Tradescantia* and *Zebrina*
WART PLANT – see *Haworthia*

Vriesea carinata

Vriesea splendens (flaming sword) forms a loose rosette of about twenty leaves. They are up to 45cm (1½ft) long, 5cm (2in) wide, and dark green, striped crossways with broad deep purple bands. The flower stem, in late summer, is up to 60cm (2ft) tall, crowned by a 30cm (1ft) long sword-shaped blade of bright red bracts and yellow flowers.

Cultivation

Vrieseas need bright light, including three to four hours direct sun daily, but away from scorching midday sun, in normal room temperatures.

Maintain high humidity by standing the pots on moist gravel. During active growth, water plentifully by filling the cup in the centre of the leaf rosettes with tepid water. Keep the cup permanently filled. Liquid-feed monthly, using a half-strength solution, pouring it into the central cup and on to the compost.

Give a winter rest at a temperature of 18°C (64°F) and reduce watering so that the compost is barely moist – leave the cups filled with water.

Propagation Detach and pot up offsets produced at the base of rosettes around flowering time.

Pests and diseases Trouble free.

Washingtonia
Washington palm

Washingtonia filifera

Washingtonia filifera, leaf filaments

Cultivation
Washington palms thrive in bright light, including several hours of direct sun daily, in temperatures up to 27°C (81°F). They tolerate dry air, but if increased humidity is provided by standing the pots on moist pebbles, the palms produce larger and brighter leaves. During active growth, water plentifully, keeping the compost thoroughly moist, and feed fortnightly. If possible move to a sheltered position outdoors from early summer to mid autumn.

Do not repot until roots appear on the surface of the compost. Use a proprietary soil-based compost with added peat substitute to improve the water-holding capacity of the compost.

Propagation Seed propagation is the only means of increase, and impractical for amateur growers. Buy new plants.

Pests and diseases Trouble free.

☐ Height 90cm-1.8m (3-6ft)
☐ Temperature minimum 10°C (50°F)
☐ Bright light
☐ Soil-based compost
☐ Palm

The two species of Washington palm are used for street planting in their native California and Arizona, where they can grow 24-30m (80-100ft) high. Both also make easily grown house plants, although they need plenty of space.

They have short, tapering, mahogany-coloured trunks, from which grow long spiny leaf stalks. These carry large fan-shaped leaves divided into segments for half their length. Decorative thread-like filaments curl from the margins of the leaves.

Popular species
Washingtonia filifera (desert fan or petticoat palm) has grey-green leaves spanning 60cm (2ft) or more. The 45cm (1½ft) long stalks, covered in spines, are green.
Washingtonia robusta (thread palm) grows taller than desert fan palm, and quicker. The leaves are bright green with a brown patch at the base, and the segments are stiffer and less deeply cut. Few if any filaments are produced on the leaf margins.

Yucca

spineless yucca

Yucca elephantipes

☐ Height 90cm-1.8m (3-6ft)
☐ Temperature minimum 10°C (50°F)
☐ Bright light
☐ Soil-based compost
☐ Foliage shrub

Although yucca can reach up to 12m (40ft) high in the wild, it grows slowly indoors, and is prized for it spiky leaves growing from a trunk-like stem. The species commonly grown is the spineless yucca (*Yucca elephantipes*).

Spineless yucca has a single 4cm (1½in) thick trunk. Commercially, plants are raised by rooting stem sections, and the height of the trunk depends on the length of the original piece. A tall yucca is more expensive than a short one. Rosettes of soft, downward-arching, glossy dark green leaves, with roughly toothed edges but soft tips, grow from the top of the trunk. The leaves can reach 1.2m (4ft) long and 7.5cm (3in) wide. 'Variegata' has creamy leaf margins.

Cultivation

Spineless yucca must have bright light, including at least three hours direct sun daily, in normal room temperatures. During active growth, water plentifully and feed fortnightly. During the winter, water sufficiently to prevent the compost from drying out.
Propagation Buy new plants.
Pests and diseases Trouble free.

ZEBRA PLANT – see *Aphelandra* and *Calathea*

Zebrina

wandering Jew

Zebrina pendula 'Quadricolor'

☐ Trails 30-90cm (1-3ft)
☐ Temperature minimum 13°C (55°F)
☐ Bright light
☐ Soil-based compost
☐ Foliage plant

Wandering Jew (*Zebrina pendula*), sometimes called silvery inch plant, is one of the most popular foliage plants. It is quick-growing and easy to care for and propagate. The colourful, attractively variegated foliage is usually displayed trailing from hanging baskets, but can also be trained up a trellis. The 5cm (2in) long, pointed oval leaves have iridescent upper surfaces, variously variegated, and are rich purple underneath.

The clusters of small three-petalled flowers produced in spring are fairly insignificant, but add to the colourful effect.

Zebrina is very similar to the related *Tradescantia*; botanists distinguish the two by slight differences in the flowers.

Popular species and varieties

Zebrina pendula has two broad silver stripes running the length of the leaves on either side of a mid green centre. The flowers are purple-pink.

It is the parent of a number of varieties. 'Discolor' has more slender leaves with narrower silver stripes enclosing a bronze-tinged centre. 'Purpusii' has large leaves which are deep purple bronze on the upper surfaces; the flowers are lavender-pink. 'Quadricolor' has leaves irregularly striped with pink, cream, green and silver; the colours may fade during the winter but reappear with better light in spring.

Cultivation

Zebrinas need bright light at all times in order to maintain the variegated leaf colours; this is especially important with 'Quadricolor'. Warm temperatures, up to 24°C (75°F), encourage fast growth, but the plants can tolerate temperatures down to 13°C (55°F). During active growth, water moderately when the top of the compost has dried out. Feed fortnightly. During the winter rest, give just enough water to moisten the compost when the top half has dried out.

Pinch out growing tips regularly to encourage the plant to develop side shoots and remain bushy. Remove poorly coloured and all-green stems.
Propagation Take tip cuttings in spring and root in water; pot up when the roots are 2.5-5cm (1-2in) long. Plant several cuttings to a pot to create a bushy effect.
Pests and diseases Trouble free.

ACKNOWLEDGEMENTS

Photographer's Credits
Agence Bamboo (A.Descat) 20(tl,c), 28(tl), 45(tr), 46(tl), 51(tl), 59(tr), 61(tr), 63(tl), 71(b), 74(tr), 76(tr), 77(tl), 79(tr), 81(tl), 83(b), 95(tr), 113(tr), 129(r), 134(tr), 142(tr,b), 152(tl), 166(tl); Gillian Beckett 27(tc), 30(tr), 32(tr,b), 34(tl), 35(tl), 37(tl), 38(tr), 39(tl), 44(tl), 45(tl), 49(tl), 52(tr), 56(tl), 59(tl), 60(tr), 61(b), 64(tr), 72(tr), 73(tr), 74(tl), 83(tl), 85(tl), 92(tl), 94(tl), 100(tr), 110(tl), 119(tr), 120(tl), 126, 131(tl,b), 133(tl), 134(tl), 137(tl), 140, 146(tl), 148(tl), 149(tl), 155(tc,tr), 156(b), 157(tl), 158(tl), 164(tl), 165(b), 166(tr), 168(b); P Brindley 66(tl); Eric Crichton 16(tr), 25(tl), 27(tl), 31(tl), 36(tr), 38(tc), 39(tr), 46(tr), 47(tr), 48(c), 51(tr), 54(tc), 55(tr,b), 57, 65, 66(tr), 67, 70(tl), 71(tr), 79(tl), 84(b), 90(tl), 91(tl), 96(tl), 98(tl), 101(tr,b), 103(tl), 104(b), 106(tr,b), 107, 110(tc,tr), 113(tl,tc), 114(tr), 120(tr), 121(tl), 122, 125(tl), 128(tr), 129(l), 130(tc), 135(b), 138(tl), 141(b), 144(tl), 147(tl), 149(b), 152(b), 159(b), 161(tl), 162(tr), 164(tr), 170(r), 172(tr); EWA (M Nicholson) 8, (S Powell) 10, (T Street-Porter) 10-11; P Ferret 96(b); Garden Picture Library (J Baker) 151(tr), (L Brotchie) 4-5, 12, (B Carter) 102(b), 104(tr), (H Dijkan) 156(tr), (V Flemming) 146(tr); (Lamontagne) 2-3, (Perd/Thomas) 27(tr), 50(tr), 56(tr), 99(tl), (M Read) 69(tr), (D Russel) 34(c), 153(tc), 154(bl), (J S Sira) 108(tl), 118(b); Patrick Johns 103(tr), 139(tl), 148(tr), 161(tc), 165(tr), 168(tr), 175(tl); Lamontagne 11, 15(b), 17(tl), 19(tr), 21(b), 29(tl), 34(tr), 35(c), 38(tl), 44(tc,tr), 49(tr), 53(tl,tc), 56(tc), 69(tl), 86(tl), 88(tr), 93(tc), 95(tl), 99(tr), 105(b), 115(tl), 118(tr), 119(tl), 124(bl), 133(b), 153(tl), 157(tr), 161(tr), 163(b), 167(tr), 168(tl), 169(tl,b); Andrew Lawson front cover (tl,tc,cr,bc,br,), back cover, 18(c), 23, 24(tr), 25(tr), 26(b), 28(tr), 48(tl,tr), 53(tr), 68(tr), 72(tl), 75(tl), 80(tl), 90(tr), 104(tl), 109(tr), 112(b), 120(tc), 124(tl), 145(b), 149(tr), 150, 154(cr), 159(tr), 163(tl), 167(tl), 170(l), 173(tl); MAP/A Schreiner 80(b), 93(tl), 123(tl), 124(br), 127(tl); S & O Mathews 9(b); Tania Midgley 9(t), 97(tr); Natural Image (R Fletcher) 17(c), (L Gibbons) 101(tl); OSF (D Brown) 73(tr); Photos Horticultural front cover (cl,cc), 6-7, 14(t), 15(tr), 18(tl), 19(tl), 21(tl), 22(tl), 26(tl), 31(c), 32(tl), 33, 35(tr), 36(tl), 41, 42(tr), 43(tl,c), 47(tl), 54(tl,tr), 58, 61(tl), 68(tc), 71(tl), 73(tc), 75(tr), 76(tl), 77(tr), 78, 80(tr), 82(tl,tr), 83(tr), 84(t), 85(tr,b), 86(tr,b), 89(tl), 94(tr), 96(tr), 98(tr,b), 100(tl,tc), 102(t), 105(tl), 108(tc), 109(tl), 111(tl), 112(t), 114(tl), 116, 117(b), 118(tl), 127(tr), 128(tl,tc), 131(tr), 132(tr), 133(tr), 135(tl), 136, 137(tr), 138(tr), 139(tr,b), 143(tl), 144(tr), 145(tr), 151(b), 154(tl), 155(b), 156(tl), 159(tl), 162(tl), 165(tl), 167(b), 169(tr), 171, 173(tr), 175(tr); Harry Smith Collection front cover (tr, br), 1, 14(b), 15(tl), 16(tl), 17(tr), 18(tr), 20(tr), 21(tr), 22(tr), 24(tl), 29(tr), 30(tl), 31(tr), 37(tr), 40, 42(tl), 43(tr), 47(b), 50(tl), 52(tl,tc), 55(tl), 60(tl), 62, 63(tr), 64(tl), 68(tl), 70(tr), 74(b), 81(tr), 82(tc), 87, 88(tl), 89(tr), 91(tr), 92(tr), 93(tr), 94(tc), 97(tl), 103(b), 105(tr), 106(tl), 108(tr), 111(tr), 115(tr,b), 117(t), 121(tr), 123(tr), 125(tr), 130(tl,tr), 132(tl), 135(tr), 141(t), 142(tl), 143(tr,b), 145(tl), 146(b), 147(tr), 151(tl), 152(tr), 153(tr), 154(tr), 155(tl), 158(tr,b), 160, 163(tr), 164(tc), 172(tl,b), 174.

Printing & Binding PRINTER INDUSTRIA, GRÁFICA S.A. BARCELONA
Separations COLOURSCAN OVERSEAS CO PTE LTD, SINGAPORE; Paper PERIGORD-CONDAT, FRANCE
53-018-1